To Papa —
This is my teachers book
enjoy, Happy Hanukah!

— Julien

D1369487

HOME AWAY

A Year of Misapprehensions, Transformations,
and *Rosé* at Lunch

by Launa Schweizer

Enjoy the Journey!

Launa S

I have tried to recreate events, places, and conversations from my memories, although I will admit to the usual blurring of chronology for the sake of improving the story. Some names and identifying details have been changed to protect other people's privacy.

HOME AWAY: A Year of Misapprehensions, Transformations, and *Rosé* at Lunch
by Launa Schweizer

ISBN-13: 978-1484113752
ISBN-10: 1484113756

First printing: April, 2013

Printed in the United States of America
Set in Garamond
Book design by Greg Simpson, Ephemera.
Copyediting by Scott Sullivan and Stephanie Kaye Turner
Author photograph by Jacqueline Sherman

Ne pleure pas
la bouche pleine...

Blues-154

Moustiers Ste Marie Star 2 6

TABLE OF CONTENTS

for my family

PART ONE:
SHIPS AT A DISTANCE

An *Amuse-Bouche,* In Which I Fail At Shopping

WE ARRIVED IN FRANCE ON A national holiday of some sort. We were too new to know what we were to be celebrating or mourning, but while I was in the middle of doing my shopping at 1:00 in the afternoon, the staff started folding the big metal doors at the front of the shop. A voice announced that the store would close in 15 (or 5, or perhaps 2) minutes. I understood about 30 percent of the French that I heard then, but drastically less when the French was piped through the speakers at the *supermarché.* To this day, the failing-grade percentage of French words I comprehend never includes any of the words for numbers.

I fell back on other methods. Alert and anxious, I had already noticed the store emptying of customers, even before the doors started clanging shut. The actual French people disappeared, leaving me behind with a few English characters leisurely deciding which of several lettuces to purchase.

I faux-ignored the worrisome signs, taking courage from the casually blank English faces until I heard a second unintelligible announcement, panicked, and shoved my uncooperative cart faster than it wished to go to the checkout counter. Without garlic. Without onions. Without sunscreen. Even without baguettes — but that was because the bread, I would soon learn, was always gone by noon.

Safely in line, I focused on the successes of my hunt: recognizably fruited yogurt, several different kinds of meat, and cheeses that would make any American foodie drool. While there wasn't any pie, I did find a strawberry tart for Bill and the girls. The simple white box listed five completely identifiable ingredients: *fraises, farine, sucre, beurre, sel.* This was nothing like the desserts back home made with 28 unpronounceable processed things one would never mistake for "food."

So what if I hadn't found garlic, onions, or sunscreen? I had driven to a strange town in a foreign land and found the supermarket. (Enormous signs all over town had been helpful in directing me there.) I had managed to use a weird shopping cart that required me to insert a euro to win its release. True, I hadn't shopped the French way (in the morning, in tiny little amounts, at an outdoor market) but I had done my American best to provide for my hungry and culturally displaced little family. Yay, me.

The glow of success faded when the *femme* at the register said something about my vegetables. I could tell that she was not congratulating me for my achievements, but beyond that, I had no idea what she was saying. I understood only that she disapproved. She brandished a zucchini and started in on it with a bizarre collection of syllables, 30 percent of which were clearly hostile. I raised my arms up to shoulder height, smiled foolishly, and shrugged as endearingly as I could. She immediately understood me to be an idiot, but repeated the same unintelligibly disapproving phrases about the lemon. And then the lettuce. The British tourists in the next aisle looked blankly away.

At first I thought the issue was my failure to bag things. Trying to be environmentally-friendly, I had left them *au naturel.* "*Un sac?*" I asked, attempting again to endear, but received only a strange look in return. Maybe I had used the masculine instead of the feminine, and said something like "I should putting them in Mr. Bagglesworth?" rather than "I no have them held by Ms. Bagley?" Maybe "*sac*" was a dirty word. To my dismay, she called over another woman, who gathered the vegetables and took them away.

I quietly accepted my fate, as I had no words with which to protest and no leg on which to stand. I had already squandered however many minutes the announcement said I had. It was long past the hour of baguettes, and I was on borrowed time in a borrowed land. I would graciously endure the removal of my unbagged vegetables, my head lowered in what I hoped translated as remorse.

Judgmental Checkout Lady further punished me by quietly neglecting to provide me with shopping bags, clearly due to my fatal error with the vegetables. I had brought along two empty backpacks in which to pack my groceries, but when they were full and I started throwing individual items back into the cart, the cashier took no pity. My condemnation was made final when I saw a tall thin brunette in the next aisle receiving not one, but two shopping bags from her checkout ladies, and she had hardly any groceries whatsoever.

It all seemed very unfair.

But then I looked up to see my vegetables being returned to me by the woman who had taken them away moments before. She now appeared to be expressing the genuine pleasure of someone who has done a good deed for someone pathetic. This nice lady had not stolen the vegetables, but instead had weighed and labeled them for me. It was not "*le sac*," but "*le* scale," that I had missed. I said "Ah, *le* scale," in a grateful way and mimed weighing with my hands, knowing full well that adding "*le*" to an English word and doing lame charade gestures rarely works the way it should.

This suddenly very nice lady presented my zucchinis, now "*courgettes*," with the proper weight affixed. Same with the lettuce and the cabbage. Before I could be flooded with gratitude, I was flushed with shame. Instead of a persecuted victim, I was the slothful shopper who had not done my prep work. I was duly and doubly sorry, having realized my mistake, but I had nothing but a shrug to offer.

"*Je suis desolée*," I tried, quoting the only phrase my older daughter Grace had learned back home in July during two weeks of French camp. I was in fact sorry, but not so much sorry that I had not weighed my vegetables. Instead I was sorry to be me with my very sorry skills.

Flash back three months to my former life of impeccable competence. There I had sat in the principal's chair, one hand holding up my office phone, the other hunt-and-peck typing out a grocery order online. Without even thinking, I scrolled through to one of my four standard grocery orders, each including adequate variety and nutrition to get us through a week of meals I could heat up in the 20 minutes between work and dinnertime. The whiteboard calendar above my desk showed five solid weeks of back-to-back meetings coded in four different colors of dry-erase marker, including a meeting happening five minutes later upstairs in the Kindergarten. But I had more pressing problems just then, because two tear-smeary boys were waiting in the hallway for me to gently rebuke and then generously absolve them after a tussle on the playground.

I hit the "order" button while speaking soothingly on the phone to one boy's mother, who was incensed that her child had been driven to such heights of depravity by *some awful* child. Five minutes before, I had said the same calming things to the equally furious mother of the other little boy.

The mothers were the hard ones, as they were each equally certain that the problem was the other child; the little boys themselves would be easy to calm and teach. In a few minutes, I would have both boys sitting with me to read *Where the Wild Things Are*, that magical book with which I could work through and absolve any second grade boy's worst moments. And the next morning, six boxes of groceries would arrive just after I served my own children breakfast. I could unpack them straight into the fridge before running back out the door to my meetings and my chair and my endless list of multitasked to-do items.

Not so that August afternoon on another nation's holiday. I was chagrined to realize that in France I lacked even the most remedial abilities, like the ability to know about holidays and buy food. I paid and left the cool store for the hot asphalt lake of parking. My cart had the wonkiest wheel ever, and was determined to take the groceries anywhere but the car. My feet slipped liquidly in my shoes. As I stood beside my car transferring unbagged groceries into the trunk, (carrots with their tops, a glass jar of *cornichons,* Dijon mustard, an avocado) the store closed for real and for good, and for who knows how many more days — glad to be done with the likes of me before 2:00 PM, which I think they called fourteen o'clock.

Happy Stupid French Holiday to you, too.

But just as I was about to give up hope on my failed self, the tall brunette who had been on the receiving end of all those free shopping bags came up quietly behind my rental Renault. "Excuse me," she said gently, in lovely accented English, "But I believe you forgot your lemon." The lemon, huge and sunshine yellow, had been affixed with a pink sticker naming it *"citron."* For a moment I could not believe my luck, or even believe that I had even paid for *le citron.* But someone had weighed it, someone kind decided I could have it, and this beautiful someone else delivered it to my car, even though I had not had the presence of mind to get it out of the store myself.

My family and I had learned a lesson months before we arrived, during protracted misadventures with the visa process: France is not free. It is not a gift granted you on the basis of your own desire to be there. There are rules upon regulations upon laws that are nothing like guidelines, and you really should know them already. In a homogeneous and rightfully self-satisfied society, everyone who is worth anything knows the rules, and there is no need to repeat them. Those who visit must endure the perils of not-knowing, and suffer the attendant shame, so like the hot-faced teary moments we suffer outside of metaphorical principals' offices the world over.

But there, in the palm of that woman's lovely hand, I saw the flip side of all that I had to earn, and everything I might somehow learn.

The famous French self-satisfaction is not a castle built on the sand, but a medieval fortification of well-placed and carefully carved stone upon stone upon stone. Although I had done nothing to deserve their beneficence and bounty, the French people grew me some peaches, bottled me white and red wine, made me a strawberry tart, weighed my vegetables despite my failure to do so myself, and handed me the sunshine of *un citron.*

There in the parking lot, I saw the weeks and months we would spend in France spool out before me, and knew I would find myself out of order, again and again. The lovely brunette drove away before I could promise her that, somehow, I would make her proud. I would impress her whole nation. I would be careful to watch the calendar and anticipate her holidays. I would weigh my own vegetables and bring all my own bags. I would never again sleep through the hour of baguettes.

CHAPTER ONE:

The Rule of We're Here

WHEN WE ARRIVED IN SOUTHERN FRANCE, the late-summer *provençal* Edenic fantasy was in full effect: everybody and their Parisian *cousins* were on vacation, light with a holiday mood. They were eating their juicy apples, they were wearing their figleaf Speedos, and they were taking utterly for granted the lush and orderly world they were feeling so pleased to deserve for the entire month of August.

Yet, since we had arrived planning to stay a year, we were not exactly on vacation, at least not in the way that they all were. A vacation, no matter how long it lasts, implies a break from work, and Bill and I had just quit our jobs, rented our Brooklyn house to another family, and flown ourselves and five pieces of luggage to France. We had signed a lease on a stone house in a tiny town and registered our children to attend the village school.

But since we couldn't even shop properly, we hardly felt like residents. Instead, we were a little adrift and a lot astonished. Although we had been promised 320 days of fair weather, we hadn't expected the sun to be quite so bright. There in the hills two hours northwest of Nice, we discovered a landscape much drier and hotter than we had expected. We were shocked to discover that the soil was orange. In the field in front of the house where we were staying, snails the size of my pinkie nail clung to every long blade of grass in the field. At the bottom of the field, below an olive grove, a blue-green waterfall spilled down into a bluer pool.

Our first day, we leapt in and swam around, not quite believing our luck. We scrambled out the mossy side and walked back up the hill, streaked with orange mud. The sky was impossibly blue, and the hills verdantly green. We knew we were in southern France, in Provence, temporary renters in the tiny town of Sillans-la-Cascade, near a somewhat larger town called Aups where we would spend the larger part of a year. But we didn't yet have the words to align with the intensity of the experience of actually being there.

At a party just before we left home, a friend's mother quizzed me on *where exactly* in France we were going. She was dumbfounded, clearly not in a good way, when I could not answer her question with adequately specific details. She had never heard of Aups, the town we had chosen, and wanted to know more.

I gave her my stock answer: Aups lies between Aix and Nice, in the hilly, rural *département* called *Le Var*. This reply had worked for a year or so on the rubes I had been speaking with, but it was wholly unsatisfying to this worldlier woman. She had traveled all over Provence, and kept throwing out the names of other, presumably more agreeable little towns, hoping that one might remind me of something I had forgotten — perhaps we chose our town because we so love truffles? Or we have friends in Nice? Or we spent time traveling there on a previous trip and couldn't wait to go back?

Of course, she wasn't the only one with pesky questions. Whenever we announced we were preparing to spend a year overseas, people produced one of these responses:

"So, do you have a fellowship to teach there?"
"Ah, so is your family French?"
"You must know people who have lived in Aups?"
"Do you and your daughters speak French fluently?"
"Will they attend a bilingual school?

Well, No. No. And No. Actually, no we don't. And no, that wasn't the plan.

When Bill and I decided to move overseas for a year, we chose our destination based on a tenuously linked series of optimistic notions. We had both studied French in high school. Provence wouldn't get as cold as Paris, we were sure, and people had said such lovely things about it. Although I had picked up a used copy of *A Year in Provence*, I hadn't actually gotten around to reading it.

We picked Aups once our Internet searches turned up a house advertised for rent there. The house looked comfortable, had extra bedrooms for visitors, and was inexpensive relative to its size. *Bastide de la Loge* wouldn't be ready until mid-September, so we picked a rental nearby in Sillans-la-Cascade, *Les Baumes*, for the first month and a half.

Plus, as legend has it, Julius Caesar once visited Aups during his conquest of the Gauls, and is reported to have bestowed on it this backhanded compliment: "I prefer to be first in Aups, rather than second in Rome."

That was all we knew. Other than the six days I spent behind the walls of a Club Med knockoff in St. Tropez with a French host family in 1985, I had never been to Southern France. Bill toured through the coast for about three days of a post-college European backpack trip.

The fact that we were moving to France sight unseen unnerved people, when it was not flooding them with barely-disguised envy. Polite folks would affect genuine excitement for us. But eventually they asked the most burning question: what was an urban American family doing leaving their perfectly nice jobs, school, and home for a year and moving somewhere they had never been? Not just *where* in rural southern France, but *why* were we going away at all?

I did have a ready answer to *that* question. It just happened to be a lie.

During the 18-month ramp-up to the trip, while we were busy quitting things and renting out our house and supplicating at the French consulate for a visa, I fibbed again and again. "It has always been Bill's dream for us to spend a year living overseas," I would say, as though I were the sort of wife who does things because my husband wants me to. As though I were capable of even following a single one of my dear husband's whims, instead of fighting and organizing them into submission. I am not that wife.

The real story was much less romantic. To tell it, I would have had to admit just how lost and confused we both had become.

The real story was that Bill and I had each achieved exactly what we had set out to do in terms of our careers and our family, and it was crushing us. This is not the sort of thing I could admit to my co-workers, friends, or parents without sounding like a whining ingrate. Hence, the partial truth. Otherwise known as a lie.

To tell the whole truth, I would also have had to admit that while Bill and I were heading to the same location, we were traveling for vastly different reasons, and were none too pleased with one another at that particular moment in time. He desperately needed adventure, while I just wanted calm. As we planned to leave, he was imagining all sorts of wild and outdoorsy plans to spice up an urban life that had begun to feel too routine for his tastes. I desperately wanted to slow down, and was imagining a tidy house in a quiet village where things would be simple and all hung in chintz. Bill and I only glancingly recognized this disconnect at the time. Of course, by then, I'm not sure we fully recognized one other.

In the case of explaining our year away, my half-truth about Bill's life dream just worked so much better than trying to explain that we were both running full-tilt from the life we had built together, and towards two entirely different goals.

It would be difficult to exaggerate how highly I value stability. I plan. I organize. I think as many steps ahead as I can, and then chart a sensible path. I come from people who build sturdy houses, sturdy marriages, and sturdy families, raising sturdy, responsible children, worrying and planning mightily as we go. In my family, people don't make mistakes — instead, we plan far enough ahead, and set our sights low enough so that things stay entirely on safe and solid ground.

I wasn't just living my life in Brooklyn — I was *administrating* it. It's hard to say whether my character led me to my career as an elementary school principal, or whether 37 years in school led me to think that I could — and should — spend all my days aggressively structuring my time and my environment (and the time and environment of anybody else who happened to cross my path).

And I didn't just meet my responsibilities — I worried them like a sheepdog, sounding an alarm whenever something seemed about to go awry. These qualities made me an effective person, I suppose, but perhaps not always the most *fun* gal to be with.

When I met Bill, back in college, I first fell in love with all the ways in which he felt like my opposite. Where I would plan, he would lunge. Where I would find some reason to worry about the perfectly mundane, he would find chaos, drama, and a great story. Or, if there were no story-worthy chaos to be found, he would invent some.

For example: I spent the summer before we began dating living in a stifling dorm room, heating up ramen noodles in a hotpot at night, and teaching an SAT prep course in an air-conditioned basement classroom by day. Bill spent part of that summer building backcountry trails for the forest service, where he learned to cut down trees with a two-man saw. He frequently got himself lost running in the mountains a dozen or so miles from the nearest logging trails. The rest of that summer Bill spent hiking and rock-climbing in Switzerland, and traveled to the USSR. There he once ate a thousand dollars' worth of caviar meant for a group of 20 fellow travelers without knowing what it was, drank vodka until 3:00 AM with two spies and several members of the cast of Up With People, and found himself out after curfew in Soviet Yaroslavl, having to feel his way home along the deserted streets on a night with no moon.

I idealized and idolized Bill's wanderlust and his relative freedom from the worry that so plagued and constrained me. That first year of our romance, Bill and I would lie on his futon mattress in his dorm room, listening to his cassette tape of the Velvet Underground, and he would tell me stories about his travels. The time he had been stopped by the KGB in a Soviet army jeep with Helga and Jens. The time he led a bike trip from Amsterdam to Paris, and pickpockets stole everyone's passports. The time the Aeroflot pilot was so drunk that everyone on the plane thought they were going to die.

The summer before that, when I had also taught SAT prep in an air-conditioned basement classroom, Bill had assisted obstetrician nuns performing a C-section at a hospital in Guatemala, and succumbed to food poisoning-induced hallucinations after eating a stray piece of lettuce. He had arrived late for his flight home, and had nearly been left on the tarmac for the next plane — scheduled to leave two weeks later. He ran out of the Guatemalan jungle, pots and pans clanging against his backpack, hollering for the plane to turn around and let him board. It did, because Wild Bill's adventures always ended happily.

Bill had had his palm read by a Gypsy fortuneteller in a campervan in Nova

Scotia. She took one look at the lines of his hand, all fused into one, blanched, and began shouting for him to take his "Devil Hand" and leave her forever. He and the teenagers on the summer bike trips he led had camped for weeks in the rain until their feet started to mold. Even when things went awfully awry, he emerged with enthusiasm intact. This boyfriend of mine was not so much charming, as charmed.

Bill had an artesian well of stories, and he would whisper them to me for hours. I was so thirsty for his tales, because I thought I had no stories worth telling. When he would ask me for a story from my childhood, it always sounded something like this:

"Um, first we planted the broccoli. Then it grew all summer because we diligently picked off all the bugs. When it was ready, we cut it and put it in the freezer to eat later. It was good, but sometimes Mom would overcook it a little."

But Bill's favorite stories — and mine — were about the year that his family had spent in England. He had been in second grade, and his sister in fifth, when his father earned a sabbatical in a Cambridge biochemistry lab. His family had spent a year in a quaint village, where Bill rode his bicycle everywhere, and his sister befriended the granddaughter of the famous anthropologist Louis Leakey. Our older daughter Grace, who has long planned a career digging up bones and writing poetry about them, was always very impressed by this story. Our younger daughter Abigail was most impressed with the bike, as she herself had still not learned to ride one.

Seven-year-old Bill had made an awful impression at his British school. Upon meeting him, the Headmaster remarked, "He seems a lovely boy, but we don't allow speaking to adults, bouncing balls, chewing gum, shorts, t-shirts, or sneakers." During that year, he was shot at by another boy's BB gun, forced to smoke a cigarette, and tricked into starting a fire in an open field. On another occasion, he filled a backpack with vomit in King's Cross Station. On his family's trip home on the QEII, the engine room had exploded in flames and he was separated from the rest of his family for two hours while everyone stood on the deck, preparing to die. He picked up a wee British accent there, learning to describe groovy things with words like "fab" and "won." As told by Bill, these were all exceptionally happy stories.

During grad school (me), law school (Bill), and all the ego-bursting experiences of our early twenties, Bill and I lived in separate states. We found every chance we could to be in the same place at the same time, but my homing instinct and his wanderlust often found us miles apart, heading in different directions. Bill got his first job in an underserved public school in Compton, California, thousands of miles away from friends and family. My first job was at a cushy prep school two hours from my childhood home. I signed the contract in part because I knew I could be certain of a roof over my head and three square meals a day in a dining hall.

He spent one summer wandering the capitals of Europe, sending me postcards every day. And there I was in tidy Connecticut, teaching SAT prep classes in yet another air-conditioned basement classroom.

Still, even with all the emotional upheaval born of our differences, the ongoing heartache of being young and apart, and the long-distance phone bills, Bill and I were more certain about one another than we could ever feel about anything else. Bill was mine, and I was his, despite and because of our differences.

So, on a sunny day in June nearly two decades ago, my stability-craving heart pledged itself to Bill's adventurous one. We made our promises in the firm grasp of a series of big ideas about one another, the most important of which was that we were opposites who belonged together.

We promised all the usual have-and-hold, sickness-and-health, forsaking-all-others business, of course, but we added a few pledges of our own. Knowing our proclivity to want to do different things at the same time, we promised to live our lives in the same place(s). We foresaw the tortured negotiations it would require for us to decide whose job or school or flight of fancy would take precedence, and naively decided to take turns. In our marriage, nobody would compromise any more than anybody else.

We also decided that we would inspire one another to bigger and better contributions to the world. In retrospect, I have come to understand just how insane that particular vow must have sounded to the older-and-wiser married people witnessing our ceremony: "I promise not to make your life easy, but to make it meaningful," we actually said aloud, beamingly pleased with ourselves and one another.

Another vow we wrote went something like this: "I promise to be married to you every day of our lives." Through this promise, we would recognize each day as a choice, not the default, and thus never feel trapped, and never take our marriage for granted. We would grow and change together, creating in each day of our marriage yet another opportunity to say, "I do." We chose a forever made of days.

And finally, we promised that someday, when we had children, we would live overseas, recapitulating the trip that launched a thousand stories. This last promise was entirely Bill's idea, and I only agreed because the promise had the word "children" in it. The whole living overseas part I would deal with later. Much, much later, and only if he forced the issue.

Sometimes with love, you hold a little something back without admitting it, even to yourself.

After the wedding, we lived in three more states in three more years before settling in to Brooklyn. We had each found a stable job, although mine had me teaching talented and well-behaved children, while his had him visiting city shelters to offer legal assistance to New York's homeless mentally ill. I would plan and grade papers at night, and he would figure out ways to keep his clients from being evicted from their tenuous grasp on the bottom rungs of society.

I was soon pregnant with our first child. When our little girl Grace arrived, Bill turned out to be a terrifically loving and fun dad. I idolized him and looked up to his relatively wilder side even as I sought to tether, organize, and ground his impulses. Yet, as parenthood added to our list of ways to make our lives meaningful, rather than easy, chores took over the time we had for one other.

I sought to teach him to do the dishes "the right way," and to live as planfully as my stability craving demanded. In service to our ideal of a feminist family, we counted out and divided up the household tasks, keeping close track of one another's failings. His disorganization and anti-domestic tendencies drove me crazy, and my control-freak ways threatened to do him in. We loved each other just the same.

Six years into our marriage we had another baby girl. Abigail was born a week after the towers fell. The weeks, months, and years after her birth we lived on a hair-trigger of anxiety, along with the rest of the city and the world.

Because Abigail never slept, and always wailed, Bill, Grace, and I also lived on the perpetually ragged edge of the sleep-deprived. It's a damn good thing we had so many big ideas to motivate us, because our early years as parents often got pretty squalid, hectic, and low. We joked then, mordantly, about the mental switch it required to take us from being busy, ambitious, childfree adults to 24/7 responsible for two kids. We felt like babysitters who had been abandoned by the "real" parents. Who would show up so that we could sneak off and go to the movies together? Or tell and listen to stories all night long? Or even just plain sleep?

Even our children puzzled us. Why did Abigail wriggle and shriek so constantly, and Grace shrink so persistently from the world, always seeking a deeper quiet and deeper solitude than we could provide?

We moved to a house in Park Slope, Brooklyn, a community full of families like ours dedicated to attachment parenting, idealistic careers, and their 19th century brownstones. Not only would we live under the same roof — now we had become the adults responsible for making sure that that roof would not leak. I became the head of a lower school, so deeply stable and responsible that hundreds of parents entrusted their children to me. Bill now managed his nonprofit, holding together the disparate interests and desperate hopes of thousands of socially marginal clients and a feisty group of idealistic advocates and lawyers.

We did some good things in those years, but my strongest memory was the feeling of always being late for the next thing I had crammed onto our schedule.

We would wake up every day, wrestle the girls into school clothes, and pull together their multiple belongings, schedules, and feelings. We were always late for school and work, sucking down a coffee on our trudge up the block, and rushing from subway to meeting to yet another phone call with a disappointed funder or an angry parent.

Rushing home after school, I'd throw my computer-ordered something or other into a pot on the stove, and heat it up at least to lukewarm before dishing it onto plates. The kids would fight for the shreds of attention we had left over after a long day of tending our gardens of other people's problems. Neither one of the girls had quite as easy a time with school as we had expected, and we always found ourselves flummoxed when they needed more support than we could provide.

For we had decided long ago that all four of us would be hardy and strong.

Sure, we'd be there to kiss their boo-boos when they fell, but we expected our girls to run bravely into the world, rather than to need quite as much reassurance and protection as they did. How exactly were these introverted and complicated children ever going to fit into the life that we had made for them? We clung stubbornly to our ideas about who we wanted to be — a feminist family with self-sufficient children. We thought that if we were tough-minded as their parents, they would become tough little achievers.

Instead, we had girls who resembled Andy Warhol and an orangutan. They were not friends. They were barely the same species.

Our own parents suggested in the gentle and wise way experienced parents learn to do that perhaps we had bitten off more than we could chew with our particular kids and those particular jobs. However, we were each so enamored with the virtuous sacrifices we were making for our careers that we couldn't quite imagine life any other way. Having been raised by exceptionally loving and dedicated parents, Bill and I on some level imagined them coming to rescue us, and couldn't quite get it through our heads that now *we were* the parents.

The reality of working parenthood was nothing like we'd imagined. For example, the house resolutely refused to take care of itself. We each spent our post-work hours tending to more work: dishes to do, toys to tidy, books to read, baths to draw, foreheads to kiss, lunches to make. We turned what should have been our most tender moments into thankless chores in a grungy commune.

Between Bill and me it became a race to the bottom. We both agreed to arrive home at 6:00 PM, but I sometimes found myself lingering at my office, hoping he would get there first to walk the dog and boil water for the spaghetti. This almost never happened. Sometimes at 6:15 PM I would see him walking towards me on our block. Instead of being overjoyed to see him, I was irrationally angry that he was late. After dinner, we would bicker over whose turn it was to put away the leftovers and make the next day's uninspiring lunches. At the very moment we should have been thoughtfully and carefully parenting our daughters, we both wanted nothing more than to take our rightful place flopped on the only sofa.

For Bill, his tendency to want to be on the sofa turned into a long intermittent battle with a funny little puzzler of a disease we learned to call Chronic Fatigue Syndrome. For me, it was just chronic fatigue, and picking up his share when he couldn't pick up his own head. We were living our lives full speed, and I am sure from the outside it looked like we were doing okay. Even well.

From the inside, though, I could only feel confused. Why did the successful achievement of the life we had pursued feel *so impossibly hard?* Although it sounds bizarre to me in retrospect, we often felt exhausted, bewildered, even cheated. *Nobody told us it would be like this,* I whined inside my own head, and sometimes aloud.

And what had happened to our touchstone: our marriage of opposites? Well, at dinner, in between the girls fighting for our attention, Bill still told great stories of his wild times in housing court. But now his stories, which had once so bewitched me, now seemed like something I was required to pretend to listen to.

I describe all this as though we were somehow the victims of our massive good fortune. Healthy children. Warm house. Good jobs. Beautiful city. Living out our vows to one another. What wretches we were not to see things that way, and instead to battle one another so that we could have an hour or so alone to do Sudoku puzzles or watch old sci-fi.

Somebody really should have smacked us both.

While the love we had for one another hadn't dissolved, we expressed it only in the most grudging of ways. Whole days, whole weeks went by when I would forget really to look into his eyes. When he called on the phone, it wasn't to murmur to me in his basso profondo, but rather to haggle with me over who would pick up the kids, the slack, the socks on the floor.

When I called out to him from underneath my laptop, I would rarely raise my eyes. "Hey honey, would you like to pick up the wet towels you left on the bathroom floor before you enjoy your four-mile run around the park, all alone? I'll just be here watching the girls, revising the entire preschool schedule around the yearbook photographer's whims, and making a pot of soup."

"I'll get the towels, but please don't make lentil."

"You know I love lentil."

"That's no reason to force it on the rest of us."

"I cook meals for you, and you call it force?"

"What about all those breakfasts and lunches I make?"

"Cold bagels set out on the counter do not count as a meal. Neither is a granola bar and a handful of grapes a lunch."

Bill was lacing up his shoes as I was just winding up my rant to its full volume. "Hmm. Point taken. Gotta go."

And then, presumably to punish me for making lentil, he would disappear and leave me to pick up the towels. For that moment, I loved the quiet reliability of lentil soup more than I loved my husband.

There were a lot of little moments like that, and a lot of bigger, badder moments that also took their toll. At work, somebody was always mad at one or both of us. At home, we were often mad at one another.

This constant state of somebody being mad led to a secret doubt that began to creep into the back of my mind, definitely against my will. It started back in the part of my brain that is supposed to process sound or touch or something, not in the rational part that orders groceries, plans meetings, and keeps track of time.

At first I could push it away, but over time the upsetting thought became more insistent: *Who are these people in my house? If I love them so much, why are we driving each other crazy?* I was not fond of this thought, and did all I could to pretend I wasn't thinking it. I certainly never said it aloud.

Instead, I took to looking for the evening star, and making wishes into deep space, a romantic and ultimately unhelpful way of dealing with such a fundamental disconnect. *Please,* I wished, to nobody but myself. *I would like to fall back in crazy love. With all of them.* Despite my wishing, my persistently messy wondering got bigger over time, not smaller.

This is why one day I woke up and knew, in no uncertain terms, that it had to end. Not the marriage, or the family, but the grind we had made of our lives. All of the tiny decisions we had made over the years were starting to look an awful lot like something somebody else had made for us. Although we were exceptionally lucky, we had started to feel like victims, which is just about the worst way to squander a pile of good luck.

The cure came to me out of the blue, in a flash. It was morning, and we were lying in bed. Our heads were sharing one pillow, like we used to do when we would lie on the futon in Bill's dorm room and his voice would rumble as he told me stories. Suddenly I saw it: if I found the right door to walk out of, maybe we could just pick up our kids and leave the place we had made. Maybe on the other side of just the right door would be a family life that didn't feel impossible. Maybe there, elsewhere, things would feel good for all four of us.

In a moment of early morning weakness and clarity, I took a breath and launched in. I was excited about this new thing I was going to tell him.

"Bill, I've had it with this stability I keep clinging so hard to."

"You and me both." We had talked hundreds of times on this point, always in circles. He had no way of knowing what I was about to say.

"It just keeps not working like I thought it all would."

"Yeah. Why is that?" He rolled towards me, and pulled me close.

"I don't know. But I wanted to ask you something. Remember how we promised that someday we would live overseas? And then I kept pretending I hadn't really promised that?"

"Yeah." His voice was quiet, but I had his attention.

"A year from now, Abigail will be finishing first grade. She will know how to read and write. Grace will be finishing fourth grade, and not yet in middle school. The girls aren't too young, and they're not yet too old. I will have finished five years at my job, and the school will be in solid shape so I can pass it on to the next head with a good conscience."

Even while busting out, I had to have a careful plan.

"Let's quit our jobs, rent out our house, and go. I think it's time."

He looked at me as though I had thrown him a winning lottery ticket. And a pony, and a beer.

His eyes widened, and then he pulled me close and squeezed me tight. "I knew if I waited long enough, someday you'd say that. I'll take care of everything. You can trust me."

I should have known just how fast and loose I was playing with the future by even whispering Bill's sacred word: travel. Once he had the green light, his idea of taking care of things meant that he would sprint ahead, dragging the rest of us behind him like noisy tin cans bumping on the highway. With a new adventure to motivate him, he was suddenly filled with an enthusiasm that had escaped him in his everyday life.

But here's the thing: while I had only wanted to leave where I was, he was dying to go somewhere else, and those two impulses had surprisingly little in common. I wanted to step out of my life, but he actually wanted to be in Rome. Or Bulgaria. Australia came up. Northern Africa. Iceland. Mars.

Soon enough, and for only the flimsiest of reasons, his somewhere became southern France.

We moved for the experience of spending a year away from our two-kid, two-job, too-chaotic New York life, but we were still utterly divided about what we were searching for there. Would we find the adventure Bill had lost? Or the stability I so craved? Did we even know that each of our searches imperiled the other's?

"Ships at a distance have every man's wish on board," Zora Neale Hurston began *Their Eyes Were Watching God*. Our marriage vows had focused our eyes on one distant ship. When it floated into port, we discovered that neither of us could find quite what we had expected packed into the hold.

When we started planning our year in France, we gazed together at another distant ship. Our wishes would be on board that one, we were sure.

Moving across an ocean did in fact upend all the usuals. The landscape we discovered was lush and gorgeous: orange, blue, and green beyond our ability to neatly understand or explain. But since we had only the barest understanding of the place we had landed, we were stunned by just how different everything was.

Overwork was replaced with an overwhelming natural landscape, and an incomprehensible cultural one. Our dismay started to fall into a pattern: in our first few weeks, things that should have been difficult were easy; things that should have been easy were hard.

Of course those newly easy things felt great. Leasing a new car at the airport in Nice was barely a blip. We paid some guy in Seattle a few thousand regular old American dollars online in May, and upon our arrival in mid-August, we got a free ride from the airport and drove away in a gray Renault after five minutes of instruction, provided in English.

Or when we wanted a bottle of wine? At home, it had always seemed remarkably difficult to find something both cheap and yummy. In France, any bottle I stumbled over contained something uniquely delicious, all for fewer than ten bucks. And if it was not delicious, French people instantly poured it down the sink.

Each pharmacy contained a phalanx of attractive and well-dressed women who doted on us (particularly on Bill) and sold us exactly what we needed, with each product subsidized by the French government. Talk about easy – buying medicine was downright pleasant. Finding fresh, delicious food? Easy. When we needed a beautiful vista, a cool body of water, fresh thyme, or free time? These things that had been impossible to find in our old life were suddenly abundant.

But then there were the pointless challenges. Things I had mastered years ago became *im-poss-SEE-bluh*, which is French for the same thing. For example: shopping and driving — the birthrights of Americans. They should have been easy, but the first time I tried to drive to the *boulangerie*, I stalled the rental car. Twice. I gave up, turned around, and drove home mortified, as I pride myself on my deep competence, on not being the kind of person who stalls any car, ever. How could driving suddenly be a challenge? Or shopping?

I have always kept track of even my most minor achievements in my mental Girl Scout Handbook, as you never know when somebody might be handing out merit badges. I was so pleased the next day, when I found my way in and out of town, and mustered the use of the plural personal pronoun to purchase bread. Given how tiny the town was, and the fact that I had been eliding the s in "*nous*," on and off since first grade, you might think this all was straightforward. But unless you're already French, it's really not.

When I drove to the bakery, the road into town coiled in on itself, like the shells of those tiny snails clinging to the grass. I found my way in, then wedged the car in a miniaturized space. As I walked to the bakery, Abigail clutching my hand, I rehearsed my phrasing.

"We have need of two baguettes," I believe I said, and, *voila*, there they were in a little (free) bag! I even got chocolate croissants, although I cannot with 100 percent certainty claim my pronunciation of *pain au chocolat* got them in the bag, and not Abigail's wide-eyed stare as she held up two hopeful fingers. I threw out my very first "*Bonne journée, Monsieur*," as Bill had told me that this phrase, "Good day, sir," was the only proper way to end a purchase in Provence. Monsieur looked perplexed by my attempted politesse, or my accent, or something else about me that was all wrong.

It's possible he just hated me because he thought I was English, and the

French hate the English more than they hate Americans. Southern France is crawling with English people for all of August. I soon realized that *Monsieur de la Boulangerie* was used to hopeless cases who offer strange phrases as they leave his store. At the Casino supermarket, where I first learned to weigh vegetables, the section right by the checkout counters was stocked with inedible English foods: Marmite and Lemon Curd and biscuits that looked like cardboard. This display depressed me — it was like I was standing at the bottom of the *Tour Eiffel* and looking up to see a cardboard cutout of Big Ben. I wanted then to become so much more French than I was. I also wanted my Frenchitude to be authentic, not some version tailor-made for Mr. and Mrs. Garnsworthy of Loftinside Place, Churchmouse Gardens, Heaventhshead.

Driving, parking, shopping: all hard. The other should-have-been-easy task I found impossibly difficult? Knowing how to hold my face. I had to learn never to smile in public. Never ever. While Americans smile reflexively — particularly female Americans when they are feeling uncertain about something — French people simply don't. Instead, they hold their faces in an impassive, blank stare into the middle distance. They mean no offense with their stony stares, and find it weird — an invasion of their privacy even — when strangers grin at them. Since my broad smile was making me stand out like a sore Yankee thumb, I implemented a no-smiling rule whenever I left the house.

So many things baffled me those first sunny weeks. Like, how could food taste *so good*? And, since the food tasted so good, how were the women so thin and gorgeous? For the first time in years, I felt just a tad bit plump and frump in comparison to the well-coiffed waifs all around. I made a mental note to purchase real lipstick. Maybe even do stomach crunches.

But with a whole year ahead of me, it felt that anything that strenuous could wait. Having been somewhat overemployed for what felt like forever, including all ten years of my children's lives, I found myself suddenly lolling around with no place to be but where I was. Given how essentially lost and pointless we had made ourselves, it's amazing we were being rewarded with such bounty.

How did we undeserving wretches escape New York and find ourselves in an earthly paradise? And yet there we were, in the dazzling sunshine, eating tomatoes in olive oil and drinking an entire bottle of pale *rosé*.

At lunch.

Yes, it was Eden. But another pesky problem complicated the driving, shopping, and smiling: speaking. For in all of our preparations to leave home, I had pretty much neglected to learn French. I assumed that just breathing French air would take care of this problem. This was a plan, just an exceptionally bad one.

But it wasn't based entirely in fantasy. The first time I visited France was the summer I was 15. I lived with a host family in the Loire Valley, and I was dreaming and thinking in French a few weeks into my stay. I listened to French music, pored over written lyrics, and dropped the needle of the record player over and over to one particularly beautiful love song, trying to learn all the words. I got my French sister to translate its poetry literally and then figuratively, and now Marc Lavoine's *"Elle a les Yeux Revolver"* is burned into my memory. I can still recall the meaning of every sad, lovely phrase about a woman so incredible that her very glance becomes a weapon, destroying the tortured singer: *"Elle a le regard qui tue…Elle a tiré la première…Elle m'a touché et c'est foutou…"*

I was way out of my depth with that song, but I am sure I learned whatever is most authentic in my accent by singing back to that poor eye-shot crooner.

Still, there were times that summer when I was frustrated and angry. I hated when my French father would correct my foolish, childish mistakes. I mixed up genders and botched verb tenses. I irritated shop owners and struggled to cover my errors when we played cards. During one particularly embarrassing exchange, my French sister was convinced I was cheating at *Tarot,* when I was convinced I was following the rules. She was sick of me, and I was sick of trying so hard. I fled back to my room in tears, wishing I could leave right then. I had no refuge, no private place away from the language I could not fully understand.

So for the five weeks, it was just my French family and me. They fed me so generously that I put on 15 pounds. They put up with my immaturity, painstakingly corrected my grammatical mistakes, took me to the many *châteaux* of the river valley, as well as to St. Tropez *and* the Alps, and wished sincerely for me to love their country as much as they did. Their patience, combined with my youthful inability to do anything but try my hardest, helped me make the shift into a new tongue.

That was then. This was now, and my family and my hardened perfectionist tendencies shielded me from even trying much French. The trip was all Bill's idea, I often lied to myself, conveniently forgetting the reasons I had set it in motion. He was the one who spent 100 hours in July in an intensive French language program while I was busy digging in my heels, pretending we'd never really leave. So when I felt unsure of myself, I pushed him ahead to speak for me. I put myself in a big English-only bubble for weeks, speaking precisely one successful French sentence outside of a commercial exchange. While I could understand people the third time they repeated something for me, as long as they did it slowly and without too much irritation, my spoken French was halting at best.

We visited a museum of prehistoric archaeology in Quinson, near the Gorge du Verdon, France's curt little answer to the Grand Canyon. Admission came with headphones in several languages. To hear things in English, I set the headphones on "2." I could understand the museum's ticket lady's directions about the headphones just fine, particularly when she held up fingers to indicate numbers. But when I fiddled with the dial on the headset to listen to the museum's narration in French, dissociated from text or from a human face, it sounded like this: "*Blah blah, le blah blah blah.*"

As a visual learner, I need to see something to get it, and have wisely arranged my adult life to be sure this is always the case. My trick has been choosing to do only things I can be good at fairly quickly. Like the woman in the song about the revolver, I eventually learned to kill with my eyes, and can still do so when I wish; I just choose not to. Instead I use them to conquer things I want to learn. Thus, I have been unaccustomed to playing in the spheres of my weakness, and would no more listen to language tapes than I would practice my godawful swing at a batting cage before my yearly humiliation at Bill's family's Fourth of July softball game. When I was a younger woman, still believing I should impress my potential in-laws, I bravely soldiered on through the whole game; now, I put in a few innings before slinking off to lie in the hammock. My team is always grateful, and it is only the opposing team members who miss my errors and easy outs.

But I realized after a few weeks that if I let myself off the hook with French, I was looking at an entire year of hammock time. To get better, I had actually to speak, and be spoken to. It was courage, rather than the past imperfect, that I had lost and needed to regain.

Grace was much less worried about French. To listen to her, two weeks of French camp gave her all the confidence and skill she would need to attend a rural public school where she would know nobody at all. When I stumbled with my words, Grace laughed at me. "You're going to be in trouble once Abigail and I get to school, Mom," she said. "Soon you're going to be the only one not speaking French."

Her comment got under my skin. So eventually, I climbed out of the comfy hammock, and off to the market. Not the *supermarché*, but the real outdoor one in the town square. On my own. I took my killer eyes and my own shopping bag, and refused to return until I managed to purchase several kilos of over-ripe red peppers, and entirely too much of the wrong kind of cheese.

Early on in my learning process, I frequently boxed my car into the wrong parking space. Merchants lost patience with me, and did that irritating thing of picking the money out of my hand rather than waiting for me to get the math right or learn their words for numbers. But then I crawled out of my bubble and spoke the words for green beans: *les haricots verts*. I listened to romantic French pop songs on the radio. I told Bill to stay home and sweep and fold the laundry while I got out there and foraged for food. A little necessity, even self-imposed necessity, became the mother of courage, and gave this mother the courage I needed to grow young and unfinished once again.

With just a few weeks under my belt, I may not have known what lay ahead, but at least I grew to understand where we were.

We were in the Var, the *département* just south of the *Alpes-De-Haute-Provence*, and west of the *Alpes Maritimes*. Since the *bastide* we planned to live in during the year wouldn't be available until the middle of September, we had found temporary digs for our first month or so, renting part of a renovated olive mill called *Les Baumes*, less than a kilometer from Sillans-la-Cascade, the cute town where we bought the baguettes. It was seven kilometers to Salernes, where there was a big market twice a week. We were 10 kilometers from Aups, the tiny village where the girls would be starting school in early September.

Gradually, we started to travel farther afield. Just north of Aups we discovered the Gorge du Verdon, the Lac St. Croix, and Moustiers-Sainte-Marie, a magical little place correctly labeled one of the most beautiful villages in France. Moustiers is home to a metal star hung between sharp peaked mountains by a knight returning from the Crusades, and also to some amazing rhubarb sorbet. In Sillans-la-Cascade, we were 45 minutes from Draguignan, the dreary provincial capital where we were able to purchase a French iPhone, but missed lunch because all the restaurants close firmly — signs all reading *fermé* — between 3:00 PM and 7:00 PM. Except in France they call that 15:00 to 19:00, numbers I can't understand when they are said aloud.

I slowly learned my way around, realizing that all the road signs thought the way I did. When you get to an intersection in France, there is no indication of north, or west, and often no route numbers. (You can however find the route numbers and kilometer markings on the *mille bornes*, stumpy little markers along even the tiniest of roads.) Signs at French intersections list the next towns over on arrows pointing in the proper direction, so I drove from point to point to point. French roads spill outward on a human scale rather than following a rational grid.

By driving from place to place, I started to build a web of understanding. It became the map in my head, and therefore was incomplete, as it only included the places I'd been, and the distances we traveled, in hours rather than kilometers, which kept confusing me by being so much shorter than miles.

The trip to Aix-en-Provence took about an hour and a half. We drove along a windingly beautiful road past the sweet little town of Barjols, and then through St-Maximin, with its enormous medieval basilica, then onto the A8 past Cezanne's *Montagne Ste-Victoire.*

Yes! That one! The one in all the paintings!

Aix is the place that most Americans would be visiting if they found themselves in our part of the south of France, not Aups. It has tons of cafés, well-dressed tourists, and fountains that nobody but us ever stuck their feet into.

The parking garage in Aix was built on a half-size scale in comparison to the ones in New York, and the first time we drove there, I was terror-struck and claustrophobic trying to get the Renault into a space. It was dark, deep under the street, and cars boxed me in on every side, wanting the same parking space that I couldn't manage to get into. It was over ninety degrees, whatever that is in Celsius — dank, stuffy, and oppressive. I broke rules without knowing them. There was honking. It got ugly, and I did not behave well.

Each time we stretched the boundary of the known, there was inevitably a moment when one of us had some sort of unattractive freak out — over a toll booth, a confusing sign at a roundabout, or maybe just our inability to procure the right sort of food as immediately as one or more members of our team would have liked. I would like to state for the record that the one freaking out was not always me.

But once we got past that freak out, the new place became familiar territory. Ours in a way. We added to our mental map that museum of prehistory in Quinson, as well as a beautiful road on a high plain between there and Riez. The road was planted with rows of lavender that had just been harvested. Some fields had been plowed under, revealing naked mounds of deep orange earth. In one field, a goatherd and his three big shaggy dogs were, as the man's job title would imply, herding goats. He also had some sheep with him, so he and the dogs were shepherding as well. He led his huge mixed herd/flock across the plain: no fence, just dogs. The goats had antlers like African deer, and one of his dogs looked like a polar bear. I had never seen anything like it, and suddenly, it was unfolding: France's gift, all for me.

Another day, we went to Antibes for a swim in the Mediterranean. The daily freak out again had to do with parking, because parking in Antibes on a Sunday in late August is a lot like showing up in Manhattan and expecting someone to have reserved you a spot right in front of the Empire State Building. Bill did the navigating while I tried not to hit anything, and he brought us straight to a lot that beamed, in promising flashing letters and several languages, "*Ouvert. Aperto.* Open." I was cheered, and we took a ticket and drove in.

Despite the sign, there were no spaces in any language, and plenty of cars rolling around looking for them. When one would open up, all the nearby cars would muscle towards it, although nobody had any real room to move.

After twenty minutes of this non-driving, non-parking activity, a Euro-little Toyotamobile pulled out of a space directly next to our car. I was halfway into the space when a tall blonde girl came and stood in it. She raised a perfectly straight index finger a foot in front of her face, just about at the height of her nose, and moved the whole hand sharply back and forth just once.

I was unfamiliar with the meaning of this gesture, and I wanted her out of my space. I shouted, "*NON! C'est la mien*! That space is mine!" which caused her to cross her arms in front of her chest, looking hateful and resolute.

I learned much later that the French use these two gestures — the finger swipe and then the crossed arms — to draw a line in the sand, or the air, as it were. The finger swish indicates total dominance and certainty of a situation, and the arm weave promises trouble if one dares persist. At the time, I was not aware that I was being threatened. I was only aware that she had taken my space.

Apparently, she felt differently. For when I shouted again, inching the car forward towards her, she gave me the finger. This I understood. In New York, I never push situations to the point of imminent conflict, but in that lot in Antibes I had waded in over my head right quick. Ten feet and a windshield separated our angry little faces. Bill did not (to his credit) use an insult that he called "The Nuclear Option" which involves a French phrase I desperately hoped he would never repeat in public, and which uses seven words to insult the recipient in matters of ethnicity, parentage, and choice of sexual practices.

Blonde girl was simply too mean to be moved, so I gave up. But I started to shake as I continued unsuccessfully to circle the lot. She and Bill shouted at each other each time I passed her and her folded arms. As she sauntered out of the lot with her weasel boyfriend, pointing threateningly at our car, I realized that she had an ugly back tattoo and two rotten-looking dogs, one of which wore a muzzle. Bill kept muttering, "I could take that guy," as though he ever would.

Eventually we decided to give up on the "*Ouvert*" lot entirely. But in a French parking situation, you don't pay at the exit. You pay at a machine elsewhere, then stick your validated ticket into a machine at the gate to be released. So once Bill gave up, and left to get the ticket punched, of course I found a space. I pulled in, proud and pleased. But we quickly realized that there would be no way to get another ticket without driving out, and ours had already been paid and cancelled *without our ever having parked at all*. We drove out, defeated, and then managed to route ourselves once again into some impossibly narrow and overcrowded streets. The snail shell of the old town sucked us in, then got sick of us and wisely spit us out up on the ramparts overlooking the sea, where we rolled down towards another set of beaches.

Little by little, freak out by freak out, we learned each new place. I learned how to park in Antibes, and how to slaughter the millipedes that covered the walls of our stone house in Sillans-la-Cascade after rainstorms. I knew that the *chèvre* on the road to Riez comes from real goats. I knew not to mess with badass girls with back tattoos. I deftly used *une toilette* in Antibes that was just two places to put my feet and a little hole in the floor. Afterwards Bill taught me that when asking for a bathroom in France, you refer to "*les toilettes*," as though there is always more than one toilet. It seemed strange to ask for something in the plural that turned out to be almost nothing at all. Even worse when that plural nothing cost a euro to enter.

As I fell asleep those summer nights, I was thousands of kilometers from my old job and its endless supply of problems. Instead, my mind filled with new questions. How many strangely-antlered goats to make a tiny ball of *chèvre*? How many legs on all of those floating millipedes floating in how many thousands of liters of water in the pool? How many snails per olive in the field? How many tens of thousands of years did it take for Provence's cavemen to evolve alongside that complex and beautiful place where the natural world fits into the human world so beautifully, but the plumbing is still so dodgy?

When Bill and his friend Alain were 22, they spent nine weeks touring Europe, and the stories of their epic trip became a part of family lore. Their travels also inspired our little family's adventures, although most of what they did we would not attempt.

They mooched sofas from Berlin to London, ate the cheapest food they could find, and sang Jackson 5 songs *a cappella* for money on the streets. They drank wine on the beach until dawn, tried to scam their way into a visit with Prince Albert of Monaco, and rode on the backs of mopeds driven by beautiful sisters along the Appian Way. When Bill bought an entire kilo of feta by mistake, Alain forced him to eat it all. They earned noisy social disapproval when they opened cans of tuna in a crowded train car on the slow route from Eze to Florence in the full sun. None of these activities are recommended for parents traveling with young children.

But they also developed The Rule of We're Here. It's a simple rule for travelers, particularly young ones on a cheap Eurailpass: whenever faced with an option to do something there and then, or something away and later, they agreed to choose what was present and directly in front of them. There would be no waiting, no returning, no planning to come back at the most opportune time for the moped trip, the debauched beach party, the visit to the Royal Palace. I've seen the photos, and I know that they were rarely properly dressed. They often had disagreements over when, where, and how much to eat, and they made a lot of mistakes and pissed people off. But based on what Bill has told me, it seems that their biggest regrets had to do with the moments that they broke their cardinal rule and waited for all stars to align before saying yes.

Which brings me back to our first trip to Aix-en-Provence, that time I got so stuck in the parking garage. On the way there, I drove our Renault past a field of drying, drooping sunflowers, their mournful heads turned all in one direction. Bill's enthusiasm alarm went off, and he demanded that I stop the car and turn around so that he could take a photograph. But I was driving many, many kilometers per hour, with several cars just behind me, on a road with no shoulder. Plus, we were going to Aix that day, not photographing fields of sunflowers. "Later," I said. We would take the picture later. I had my eye on the merit badge for Pointlessly Timely Arrivals to Aix-en-Provence.

This sort of exchange was repeated perhaps hundreds of times a week in our house. Bill got enthusiastic about some New Something, and I got focused on The Thing That Is To Be Done. For this, you can give both of us names that are either flattering or damning.

Her name is Launa, High Priestess of That Which Is Organized and Efficient. She Who Darest Not Improvise Her Way Out of a Paper Bag. Self-Righteous Tier of Loose Ends. Our Lady of the Miracle of Perpetually Delayed Gratification.

And he is called Bill, the Fresh Prince of Spontaneity. Dude of the Diverting Detour. Master Fun Blaster with a Capital FB. His Highness of Great Enthusiasms. Or just plain Irresponsible.

Choose any moniker you like, nice or nasty; it's not who we *really* are, but just who we are relative to one another. Sometimes he's right, sometimes I am; either careful planning or serendipity has led us to paradise or created a fresh, fat disaster.

But back to our first visit to Aix. After speeding past the sunflowers and squeezing our car into that MRI tube of a parking garage, we came across a place at the end of the Cours Mirabeau that had been kitted out with enormous trampolines. Children were strapped to wires and could leap up and down on the trampolines and flip over, land on their feet or their little tender heads, then do it again and again. Instantly both girls wanted to try the AcroBungie. It is in fact one of Abigail's professional ambitions to be an acrobat, either before or after running a hotel, being an artist and a scientist, and spending two terms as President of the United States.

But we had just taken a ride on the world's slowest carousel, and were on our way to ice creams, so we decided to forego yet another possibly pointless and potentially dangerous kiddie treat costing five euros. That was when we were still multiplying every euro by 1.5 in our minds and subtracting it from the difference between the rent we were earning in Brooklyn and the rent we were paying in France. This math inevitably made us want to stop doing or eating anything at all, and just sit quietly in a chair. Before we eventually adopted the conceit that a euro might as well be a dollar, we followed an austerity plan that extended even to kid fun.

That day in Aix we smashed The Rule of We're Here into little pieces, and held up the grail of Next Time. "Next Time you can jump on the trampolines," we promised. Before Next Time, we would look online to check on the safety of AcroBungies. We might even get ourselves a pediatrician before Next Time, just in case. We would bring the right shoes Next Time. It was so hot we could barely stand to be standing there in the street arguing with children any longer, and wanted to get inside the ice cream parlor. We had to fairly drag the girls away, and only the carrot of Next Time got their feet moving.

Two weeks passed. Summer was closing up shop, and our girls were about to start a year in French school. I was distracted and worried, chewing on my nails, bustling around picking up the house, and organizing our tiny number of belongings.

Luckily, Bill had his idea generator on high, and came up with an idea. We would drive out on a random road and stop the car for any picture that anyone wanted to take. No matter what. A We're Here day in the classic tradition.

While I had a plan secreted away in my mind, I pretended to choose our destination on a whim. Although I didn't reveal my goal, I planned to get us as far as the excellent roadside vegetable stand with its to-die-for peaches and orange tomatoes. We would pass the sunflowers on the way, and Bill could snap to his heart's content. While pretending to be carefree, I would rack up another merit badge through excellent planning, as long as I kept my intent on the down low.

We made our first stop in a vineyard just outside Sillans-la-Cascade. Rows of green vines. Heavy clusters of purple grapes. Tiny white snails clinging to the leaves of dead and dying grass. Blue hills in the distance. Orange earth drying towards peach. Snap. Snap. Snap.

Every town we passed, every landscape, was made up of hues of just three colors. Orange. Blue. Green. Green plane trees. Blue hillsides. Blue Sky. Green vines, green trees, green grass, green plants growing out of the sides of the orange rocks. Orange houses, darker orange roofs, with shutters painted delicate and individual shades of blue and green. Snap. Snap. Snap.

Then we came upon the field of sunflowers.

Rather than a sea of plants drying in the sun, we found an empty field of dry brown beheaded stumps. Every sunflower had been mowed down and harvested, off to become useful: snacks, oil, or chicken feed. So much for Next Time. So much for that photograph. So much for my merit badge.

To Bill's credit, he did not say a word.

In our newness in France, we assumed that everything we were encountering was permanent, the way things *always* are. The sunflowers always loom over together in the same direction. That man always sits outside the café. That dog lives under the tables at the pizza place in Tourtour, where there is always live flamenco music and African drumming at the *Mairie* on Saturday nights. The river that runs by our house and falls into the waterfall is always a perfect clear shade of turquoise blue. It is always sunny and eighty degrees.

Not so. Each time we returned somewhere, assuming we would find more of the same, we found that the world had changed, not always for the better. On a return visit to Tourtour, no music and no dog. The river turned a mucky brown by a sudden rainstorm. By the end of August, it sometimes got downright chilly at night. Millipedes invaded our house, got fat, then died and dried up.

The moon continued to wax and rise in a different patch of sky every evening.

So when I saw the mowed down sunflowers, and right after admitting, in no uncertain terms, how right Bill had been about that photo he wanted to take, he and I hatched a plan in French so the girls wouldn't understand. We wouldn't just get the vegetables. We would drive all the way to Aix and put the girls in the AcroBungie. So what if Abigail was wearing a dress: we'd buy her some pants so her undies wouldn't show when she flipped. So what if I hadn't showered and was wearing elderly flip-flops: while Aix is overrun with glamorous people, I could survive the day looking smalltownishly draggy. So what. Tomorrow would be school. Today was for the AcroBungie. Time for a little We're Here.

It was remarkable to me how much easier it was to drive, to park, and to find where we were going on a second visit. We kept the Bungie a secret, and went to Monoprix, France's answer to Target. We picked out some back-to-school clothes for both girls, including a pink pair of pants in which Abigail could flip. We moved ourselves gradually towards the AcroBungie.

Maybe my foreshadowing with the sunflowers has given it away. We got ourselves to the far end of Cours Mirabeau, where the AcroBungie was meant to be. We were there, prepared. AcroBungie was not: just an empty space on the sidewalk next to the newsstand. I looked around once more, insisting that they must be here somewhere! No such luck. AcroBungie had packed up and moved on to somewhere else.

The girls were no worse for this, since Bill and I had so carefully kept it a surprise. They were truly excited about their new school clothes, and scarfed down ice cream while we drank wine at a sidewalk café. On the drive home, we stopped to photograph many more things that were blue, orange, and green. While the sun poured its fire on the trees and the orange roofs, the cool moon rose up huge and fully round in front of us, reflecting its white in the blue sky.

Over dinner, Bill and I told the girls about the (botched) plan. He said that he was thankful that I had had such a good idea, and I apologized for its failure. The girls turned smiling in my direction, sweetly grateful and almost proud that I had had something like a whim. According to the three of them, the day was a success anyway. There had been two ice creams, not just one, and new clothes to wear to school. There was tortellini for dinner, and *The Hobbit* to read before bed. The girls' little cameras had run out of batteries halfway through the trip, but they took mostly pictures of themselves and each other making faces, anyway. There would be other faces to make, and almost certainly some sort of Next Time.

How had we gotten ourselves there, and what lay ahead? These were questions I had asked all my life, yet I found myself letting them slip quietly away. Instead of learning from the past or planning for the future, I was living in the present. That evening in early September I took off my watch, and simply neglected to put it on again for more than a year.

As each of us shut down the day and dropped off to sleep, the night whispered its cool truth through the wide-open windows:

You are here.

CHAPTER TWO:

Le Portail (The Schoolyard Gate)

"IT WILL BE GREAT FOR THE kids to experience another culture while they are so young," we said before we left for France, as people love to say. I would often throw out this line just after letting people believe I was such a great wife for selflessly making my husband's lifelong dream come true.

Talking about the kids in this manner allowed us to suggest that the trip was some sort of benevolent gift to them, even though we knew we were going for ourselves.

"Your children will be so grateful to you," people gushed at us. Gratitude was not, as it turned out, their first emotion; and when it came to parenting in France, I often felt more awkward than enviable. Reality frequently stomped all over our hopes, and sometimes all over our American girls. While before I had been fully in charge of their school experience — the principal of the school both girls attended — in France I had very little control. And while I had always longed to have more time to spend with them, my abrupt shift to full-time motherhood brought me face to face with my limitations.

For the first ten years of my children's lives, the only merit badges I earned in the domestic sphere were for efficiency. I was a whirling dervish, providing just enough attention to each portion of my life that no child ever went hungry or uncuddled, and no task or appointment was neglected. But after parceling myself out, covering all those bases at once, I had little left.

When I came up with the geography cure, I did so believing that quitting my job would make everything hard suddenly easy. At work, I had had several hundred children (and their parents and teachers) to care for. With our move to France, I would chop off my professional life and focus squarely and simply on our little family of four. The girls had reached an easy age, I believed then — no longer needy babies or toddlers and not yet moody teenagers. I anticipated a luxury of time and ease. I looked forward to long, lazy talks and lots of cooperative enterprise. I imagined us doing chores together, just like in *Little House on the Prairie*. We would sweep, and chop apples. We would likely even sing while doing so.

Abigail, at age 7, found all kinds of ways to relish my presence. (She of course disappeared the second that any domestic chore was to be done.) She looked up at me with intense love, held my hand gently and quietly, or grabbed onto me with all the force of her powerful little muscles. She checked in with me to see how I was feeling, and let me know what I could do for her. Nothing pleased her more than having me put a band-aid on the most minor of her injuries. She would brag to anybody she met that I had run her school for as long as she could remember. With Abigail around, I felt like God on Sunday morning.

But even that level of Mama-worship gave her lots of time to herself. Even after I stopped working, there were hours and hours when we each were on our own trajectories. She was busy watching the ants as they cut up a leaf and dragged it across the floor. She was busy dancing around her bedroom to Steve Miller Band's "Abracadabra" on her iPod. She was busy scrubbing her retainer clean with soap, or yet again washing her hands slowly and fastidiously. Although domestic chores were always out of her sphere of interest, there was never any soap or time spared in the washing of Abigail herself.

While Abigail was doing her thing, on her own terms, 10-year-old Grace was also busy, embroidering with royal blue thread on an egg carton. Or she was busy lying on her unmade bed with her dirty clothes all around her, looking up at the ceiling. She was busy watching *Xena: Warrior Princess*, on a tiny screen. She was busy breaking a baguette into tiny, crumby pieces that she left on the counter and on the floor while she dragged the rest back to her room. These tasks were all very important to her, and she did not wish to be disturbed.

When I first had the time to watch all of this up close, it was more than a little strange. Funny how I imagined that just flying my children to France would change their basic interests. Instead of being glued to screens, the girls would suddenly take up baking, or hooking rugs, or making historical dioramas of Ancient Rome — you know, the kinds of things I thought were fun when I was a kid.

No such luck.

Of course, my preoccupations made no sense to my kids, either. While I was spending entire days pulling together delicious meals from the market, they just wanted a nice box of Kraft Macaroni and Cheese. Their childhoods were taking place within their own private worlds, and I was a stranger there. We lived so close to our children, but their feelings and preoccupations were opaque.

I was confused by this difference and this distance. Should I feel guilt? Pride in their independence? Or simply accept as natural that we were in different — even foreign — worlds so much of our days together in the same small space?

Like the afternoon I walked into Grace's room to try to find her to tell her for the quadrillionth time to brush her knotty, straw-dry hair. She was somewhere else in the house. But lying there on her bed was a paper with a short list of words.

Feelings: (she had written)

scared
sad
lonely
wondering

I was struck with a desperate sadness. I had no idea things were so awful, and I went straight to guilt. She had spoken with us on a few occasions of her fears about starting at a new French school. For Grace, it was not the idea of French that terrified her, but the idea that she might become a bully magnet. Moments of anxiety about French school came and went, so I assumed this must have been why she had made her feelings list.

This whole trip was an awful idea, far worse than I thought. I immediately hunted her down and asked her what was wrong.

"I'm fine, Mom," she told me, looking blankly in my direction. She blinked a few times, then went back to tying very small knots in a piece of yellow thread.

I don't know — I will never know — what those feelings listed on the page had to do with the thoughts in my own daughter's mind. At first I thought I was an awful mom not to have insight into her feelings or to be able to help her think things through. Gutted, I snuck back in to take another look at her notebook. On the next page, I read a second list of feelings:

scared
terrified
confused

… followed immediately by a short poem she had written about being chased and eaten by a vicious tiger. The poem perfectly evoked the list of emotions she had catalogued. Reading her poem turned my maternal guilt over her state of mind into the pride of a writing teacher. She had imagined a series of feelings, then described them in poetry. No longer a sad little girl, she was a brilliant writer. I was awash in pride, an imaginary Mother of Poet merit badge stitched on to my imaginary green sash.

Or so it seemed. There was always a gulf between what she felt and what I could know. One night, I kissed them both to sleep, reminding them to wait to open the windows until their lights were off. They hated bugs, and had learned their lessons about windows without screens the night before when the entire insect kingdom, including a praying mantis, came in to visit while they were reading.

Abigail flopped her head on her cool pillow. "I love you, Mom," she breathed, nesting down into the bed. "See you in the morning." Only months before, she could not get through the night without coming into our bed. What happened to seal her off from me, to help her grow into someone who could spend the whole night with the windows open in her own little bed with such a long hall between us? What was this moment of division between my child and me?

Was this resignation to her own bed my success? Was it my failure, my loss? Was it her loss? Or her success?

I went in to say goodnight to Grace. As I kissed her, Grace murmured the sounds of French words, gleaned from a slim volume of phrases that "real French kids use." Who knows where her mind had taken her — to the terrifying first days of school, or perhaps to a fantasy of great social success now that she could happily say in French, whenever it occurred to her, "I dig your new website." She had not yet been plunked into a French school, but at least for this moment, she seemed to have a linguistic plan for conquering it. On her own.

"I love you," I whispered to my oldest girl, my heart full for her and with her.

"I love you too, Mom," she whispered back, and returned to a land of her own making and her own experience, of books and thoughts and embroidering on egg cartons for hours at a time.

I fed them in a timely fashion, made sure that they were clean, well-rested, and suitably clothed. I kept them far away from real tigers. I gave them fresh fruit, plenty of exercise, writing paper, monitored internet access and adequate dietary fiber, and made sure they had done all the assigned homework.

I reveled in their stories, in their random curiosities, and in their few true strong friendships in this world. But I could not protect them from the schoolyard bully, the lonely pain of being misunderstood. Ultimately, after all the goodnight kisses and band-aids on knees, our children would have to live their own lives, separate from the worlds we built for them. Ultimately they would sleep in their own beds, and we rest alone in ours. We spent all of those hours in the same house, but we still lived apart in the worlds of ourselves.

From the day of our arrival, even as I watched the girls enjoy slowing down to the pace of France *en vacances*, a drama was cooking in the back of my mind. For a while, I could ignore not only the hour, but also the day of the week. But by the tail end of August, we faced an obvious countdown to when the girls would start school. When it got to that last *dimanche*, and school would start on *jeudi*, the free days were fewer than the fingers on my hand, no matter how French people say "four."

The drumbeat on French talk radio intensified my worry. They call Back to School "*La Rentrée,*" and it puts the whole country in a funk. Once again I wasn't quite sure whether or not I was as worried as the situation would warrant. If actual French citizens were all panicky talking about it, why had I left so much up to chance? I was sending my two children into a totally unknown situation without adequate language skills. Between decadent bites of buttery croissant, I was pestered by the buzzing of a deeply uncomfortable thought that somehow had not occurred to me before:

What kind of mother sends her children to a rural public school where they can't speak the language?

Nearly everyone we knew had expressed concern about our kids and their fates, particularly those who had reason to know better, like people whose children had actually lived overseas or learned a second language. The books we had read about being a family abroad told us, in great detail, that what we were doing would be valuable in the long term for our kids, but extremely difficult in the short term. The books instructed us to hire tutors, to be familiar with the curriculum and figure out, ahead of time, what they should wear, and in what sort of paper they should wrap their textbooks.

We did none of these things. I knew only that they probably should speak a lot more French.

People questioned Bill and me, very quietly, but they loved to tell the girls "You'll pick up French so easily. Learning a new language is easiest when you are young." Americans without actual life experience with children and foreign language tend to believe that a few months of immersion does the trick. The girls came to believe they'd have French down pat in a few months, and we neglected to disabuse them of this notion. Which, now that I come to think of it, was yet another of my self-serving lies.

Almost no French. No friends. We didn't know whether their teachers would be saints or monsters. They knew how to ask to go to *les toilettes*, but we had no idea if this is even a question that French children are allowed to voice. The school in Aups looked fine from the outside, but we had never been in.

I never learned the class size. I couldn't predict the math curriculum. I hoped that at least part of their day would be required English lessons, the one time of the day when they would be superstars. The nice woman who registered them at the *Mairie* told us all would be well; they need only to bring a pencil case and a backpack. Or at least that was the 30% of the conversation I understood.

Although I could admit that we had let them down in the language department, I told myself that we had given them what we thought they needed in lots of other ways. We fortified them with ice creams, downtime, baguettes and lots of swimming. And love. Lots and lots of unrushed and unhurried love, which is the very best kind, and which we hadn't always made time for before.

I recalled my own memories of magically learning French at age 15, and I conveniently forgot the years of French classes that had preceded those five weeks. Before school started, I veered between moments of quiet panic and a stupidly sanguine theory that everything would be fine.

I love to use my theories as screens against life's unpleasant facts. At the time, I was taken with the theory that everything would be fine because we had only three goals for the girls' education.

First, we wanted them to learn a second language, not because there is any particular magic to French, but because learning to speak something new felt like a worthy end in itself. We also wanted them to learn simply how to *be* in French school. We wanted them to experience, through all five senses, that the world does not run in only one way. We wanted them to sustain themselves in the face of not knowing, and thus to become stronger and more confident people.

Plus, there was that whole concept of raising hardy and independent children Bill and I loved so much. We reasoned that if we threw them into the deep end of the school, they would have to learn to swim. In Aups, our Nowhere-ville, where the hordes of English tourists were beginning to make themselves scarce, our girls would be the only English-speaking children for miles. They — and we — would have to learn.

Second, we wanted each of them to make at least one good friend. Of course, there were many, many things I could have done to make this more likely. Finding children to force on them would have been the most obvious.

However, that would have been my making them a friend, rather than letting them make their own. Bill had strong feelings about this. During his family's sabbatical year in England, his parents once took pity on him because he couldn't find anybody to play with. It's also possible, given what I now know about parenting, and about Bill, that little Billy's incessant questions, stories, and wild plans had started to irritate his otherwise calm and gentle parents, and they wanted five minutes to themselves.

Bill's Dad Gus looked around the playground and found a boy Bill's age for him to play with: *and then he offered him money.* The little boy readily accepted Gus's offer, and then spent the next hour essentially trying to babysit Bill, as Gus's offer had made him assume that Bill was — as we called it back then — retarded. When he discovered that Bill could read, play games, and do math problems, he walked away in disgust and kept the £2.

The moral of this story, one of Bill's favorites: let your kids find their own friends. We had stuck with this policy no matter what back in Brooklyn, even when all the other parents were scheming to engineer their children's social lives. So in France, as at home, we decided that the best way for them to meet another kid would be for them to go in cold and see what would happen.

My third goal, which I didn't worry over too much, was to let their brains keep growing by making them do regular old American grade-level math online, and by supplying them with lots of books in English to read in their scads of activity-free time. Because they had both done fine in school academically, and because they were still so young, I wasn't worried about their grades. I could convince myself of this because I was a principal, but perhaps I should have thought twice about the cobbler's children with no shoes.

So we had only three goals, two of which they have to accomplish themselves, and one I would be carrying out. Since I have never met a goal I could ignore, I thought success was assured. I even reasoned that anything that happened above and beyond those three goals would be gravy with *herbes de Provence.*

In retrospect, this seems like the overconfidence of an idiot, but it was also a reaction to the sort of mom I had been. I went from knowing absolutely everything about their school experience — actually running their school — to knowing absolutely nothing. Back home, even before they would walk in the doors in September, I knew more about their teachers, the curriculum, and the ins and outs of the lives of the other children in their classes than the most eagerly over-involved parent could ever fully process.

As a principal, and as a mom, I had the same mantra: trust the school, and leave education to the professionals, who care about it more deeply and more subtly than parents can know. I assumed that any parent who was overly concerned about his or her child mostly needed to relax. In that vein, I did my best to worry only when the teachers specifically asked me to do so.

As the Mom Who Knew Too Much, I took it as my challenge to do what I could to stay out of the way. I never achieved this goal quite as well as I might have liked, and I am certain that I meddled when I couldn't help myself. But I always trusted the girls' teachers to more than make up for my errors and meddling, and they invariably did.

Sending my kids to an unknown school in a foreign land was perhaps the ultimate experiment in hands-off parenting, an AP course in the school of let-them-learn-it-themselves. We knew nothing about their school, and had no way to learn. We did vastly less than we should have to prepare them. We believed they would be okay, based only on our theory that challenge is always good for kids. Everybody says this, so it must be true.

I clung to the idea that Grace and Abigail would, could, and should find their way, even when there was ample evidence to the contrary. I couldn't quite admit it to myself then, but now I can say it: ours are not the simplest and most straightforward of children.

Grace had just finished the fourth grade back home, her eighth year in our cozily loving school community. But she had never shown a whole lot of enthusiasm or affection for school. She had always been a bright and verbal kid, asking terrific questions and expressing unique insights about the world around her. But school wasn't always — or ever — her place. She had always been more interested in her private time back at home than in the social scene at school, and this tension became more prominent with each passing year. Most of the time at school she was deeply distracted. But other times she was just plain anxious. Her nails — like mine — were bitten to the quick. But while I thrived on my nervous energy, hers plagued her.

She liked it better when things were quiet. Really quiet. Like one-other-person-in-the-room quiet, and ideally the other person would be knitting while she stared out the window. Socializing drained her. She wouldn't come out of her room at her birthday party when she was 3 because one of the six people there — all of whom who she had known from birth — had a *beard*.

She found the threat of other people vomiting intolerable. That happened once at school, when her pre-K classmate Nicolai had eaten a bad tuna sandwich. None of the kids enjoyed that episode awfully much, but our Grace remained terrified of Nicolai for six more years.

But what Grace really, really, really hated was the sound of other people coughing. During nursery school, she spent most of February and March holed up in the cubby room away from all her classmates rather than playing at the sand table. We realized years later, after many more awful winters, that this had all gone down during cold season, and the other kids' innocent coughs were terrorizing her.

Why don't children come with an owner's manual, so I could look up her entire early childhood in the index under F for fear?

Grace grew into Bartleby the Kindergartener, as her favorite phrase was some 5-year old version of, "I prefer not." She couldn't understand the school schedule, so when the other kids got ready for recess, she would hopefully pack her things for home.

When she would not follow directions, line up with the other kids, or otherwise do what she was told, her Kindergarten teacher used to try to discipline her by sending her to the hallway.

Grace would say, with enormous relief: "Great. Thanks. It's quiet there."

The poor teacher would try again. "Well then, you can't go out to recess."

"Okay."

"No P.E.!"

"Okay."

And then the teacher would have to bring the big guns: "Grace, if you don't behave yourself and stay in the line as I asked, you'll have to go to the principal's office and sit in a quiet room with an adult all afternoon."

"Great. Because I sometimes miss my mommy."

Aside from coughing, and being in her classroom, her other dislikes included: doing things in groups, following rules, doing things with her hands, sports, games, toys, doing things on time, circuses, birthday parties, amusement parks, and noises louder than you might hear in a library.

Her preferred activities included: doodling, losing things, and talking about things that would make people look at her funny.

When we realized that other children were not exactly flocking to her side, we gently suggested that she might tell another child something she liked, and then ask a question. Later that day we were thrilled when she approached another 4-year-old on the playground. We stood just close enough to hear her idea of a good preschool pick-up line: "I have enjoyed thinking about death lately. What are your ideas on that subject?"

When other children were begging for the zoo, the circus, or a trip to Coney Island, her favorite weekend activity was to go to the Brooklyn Museum to stand in the deserted Egypt room and stare at the sarcophagi.

She was blonde, wide-eyed, and bewildered, hence the nickname of Andy Warhol. But in terms of her topics of discussion, she was more like Wednesday Addams.

Despite my belief in laissez-faire child rearing, and my great pride in her originality and intelligence, her quirkier qualities worried her teachers. When they asked us to try to figure out what might help her do better at school, we dutifully took her to a few experts. It turned out that being evaluated in a quiet room by a polite adult expert one-on-one with no time limit was another one of her preferred activities. Then, she would really open up. The experts we took her to for advice about how to help her at school thought she was a fricking genius.

Life might have been slightly easier for all of us if her younger sister Abigail also enjoyed the quiet life. We could have moved to Nova Scotia or Iowa and lived out our lives watching soybeans grow tall. But our second girl craved stimulation. Kiddy stuff! Candy! Street Fairs! Yay! The fun must never end!

When we made the mistake of trying to get both kids to do something at the same time, Grace would be cowering, pulling hard on my arm so that she could flee in terror and take me with her. Abigail would be pulling my other arm, equally hard, bolting towards the center of the action.

Plus, unless Abigail was asleep *and* strapped in her car seat, she never stopped moving or making noise for the first three years of her life. Rather than reflect quietly, she would wriggle and caterwaul, and seek out the object nearest her body to rip apart. Life with Baby Abigail was like having a raccoon in the house. You can imagine how Grace felt about all this.

While Abigail became a conventionally good student, eager to do what her teachers had requested, the self-control this required took its toll. She could hold it together all day at school, but when she came home, she needed acres and acres of downtime to unwind and relax by ripping her toys and other people's belongings into shreds.

She too always preferred to remain just a little bit disconnected from most of her peers. But Abigail's approach was different. She maintained her distance by turning the social parts of school into a contest. Her usual approach was to pick out the prettiest, most active girl in the class. On the first day of Pre-K, while the other children were busy weeping and hanging on their parents' arms, Abigail was scanning the room. Soon she found her mark and whispered in my ear. "Who is that girl? I *will* be the boss of her."

Everybody these days thinks that their kids are interesting, special, weird, or extraordinary. We tried really hard to buck that narcissism of our generation and believe our kids were typical. But we actually went too far in the other way, lulling ourselves into believing that they were perfectly normal. When our kids did truly weird stuff, we'd scoff, showing no respect for the concept of developmental milestones.

When our children turned out to be persistently different, super stubborn, and somewhat difficult in school, Bill and I weren't quite sure what to do with these facts.

Eventually we started to wonder if there was something *we* could do to help them to love school, or at least act more like regular human children. Perhaps if we would try some other approach, they would become more easygoing and have an easier time making friends. We tried earlier bedtimes, healthier lunches. Eventually, and after a great deal of prodding by her teachers, we sought the insight of learning specialists to help us figure out what would work best for Grace, and their advice was enormously helpful to her and to us. Still, school remained a mystery, and a challenge, and often a royal pain.

We expected our kids to be more like we were as children: busy little achievers with lots of energy and enthusiasm. Whether or not this is what we were actually like as children, it was certainly how we recalled ourselves in the rosy glow of memory.

As a career educator, I have seen lots of parents work through this problem. If their kids do not find success in the first school they attend, they sometimes shift them to another, believing this to be the answer to their prayers. Sometimes it is, of course — like when a noncompetitive kid switches to a Quaker school and suddenly makes Friends. But usually the parent discovers that no matter where their kid goes to school, she is the same quirky little bundle she has been since birth. Just older.

We did not admit that to ourselves just then, but behind our move to France was the untested theory that changing our school environment would fix what ailed us. In some other more wonderfully bucolic environment, our kids would be easygoing and carefree. They would have tons of friends, almost magically.

We sold the kids a bill of goods on this score. Before we left, Bill told the girls endless stories about how, as the sole American at his British school, he had captivated his second grade teachers and classmates all year long. Although he broke all the proper British rules, he somehow made everyone love him. He rode his bike two miles one way to school unsupervised, and got himself into loads of very fun-sounding trouble. And then, when he returned to his regular public school back in New Hampshire, he was far ahead of his classmates and could multiply circles around them.

To hear Bill tell the story, going to school overseas was a guarantee of social and academic success. AND would be wicked fun.

Perhaps this is why we so easily allowed ourselves to latch onto the belief that the challenge of French school would somehow change things for the girls, and they would become relaxed, easygoing, self-motivated little citizens of the world. "It will be great for the kids to experience another culture while they are so young," we kept saying, in increasingly fervent tones, as though this would make it true.

I certainly anticipated anxiously missing my job at that great school in Brooklyn, at least initially. But then, I imagined relaxing into a bucolic village idyll, with Bill and the girls in tow. We would drop the girls off each morning at the entrance to the school. They would skip down the lane on the way home. During our trips to the schoolyard gate, Bill would be charmed by a collection of colorful characters, and I would charm them in return. Our daughters would chatter fluently in French with adorably Gallic BFF's.

Yet another ship in the distance.

———

The first day of school arrived. The French are famous for their affection for just the right documents, and we had bravely faced down bureaucrats at the consulate in New York on multiple occasions in order just to get there. Thus we imagined that to shoehorn the girls into school might require an interview, perhaps even an exam, and we had no idea which one(s) of us would have to take it. On the appointed day, Bill got out the nondescript white notebook where he kept multiple copies of every important paper, but at the last minute we realized that we had used up our supply of copies of the girls' birth certificates. We shouted at one another in our panic to get everything right, then crossed our fingers, hoping that passports would suffice instead.

Both girls carefully picked out their clothes and combed their hair. Worried that we might be late, we sped to Aups. As we drove, we practiced asking and answering the question, *"Comment t'appelles-tu?"* How do you call yourself? I thought this might be the question that would be asked to get them into the correct classrooms.

The scene outside the school was familiar in some ways, totally strange in others. Parents and children milled about, the kids dressed in their new clothes, and the moms in little dresses or diaphanous white outfits. It was apparently quite stylish in Aups to dress all in white well into September, maybe because there is no Labor Day. There were lots of dads on the sidewalk, several of them smoking.

The girls were wearing the same short-sleeved dresses they had been wearing for weeks, but they were shivering. I asked Grace if she was cold, and at first she said yes. Then she admitted that she was actually just nervous. Abigail burrowed into my body, and pulled my arms around her as though I were her sweater. My hands rested right on her pounding little heart.

We all were blocked from entering the school by a tall green metal gate. After a minute or two, a man walked over from his place by the gate. He shook my hand first, then Bill's, and without so much as a "*Comment t'appelles-tu,*" called the girls by name. He leaned over and gave each baffled little girl two kisses, one on each cheek, then began speaking much faster than I could understand.

Bill caught the whole speech, and filled me in later on the details. This was M. Souris, the school's principal. He told Bill that along with being the principal, he also teaches full time and therefore could not answer any of our questions except on Mondays. We should bring the girls at 8:20, and leave them at the outside gate, which he called *le portail*. No parents were to come into the school. Ever. Our girls could stay for a delicious three-course lunch each day, but should we wish to have them eat with us, we would pick them up at 11:30 AM, and have them back for afternoon classes at 1:20 PM. Bill asked where, exactly, we were to pick them up, and the man looked at him, baffled. Outside the *portail*, of course.

Someone must have given him the memo on American parents, because he hit all the power chords. Leave them at the gate. Do not meddle. Ask all your questions on Mondays and let the school do its work in peace. And that was that. No exams. No documents. A school principal who kisses children he has just met and already knows their names. Two hours every day home for lunch.

And no French? According to *M. le Principal,* no big deal — they have several kids each year who can't speak French, and they run special classes for them, but the classes become completely unnecessary by the spring.

Of course, at the time, I didn't catch any of this. I had no idea who he was, and neither did the children. As he walked back to *le portail* and pushed the button, I assumed that we had just been given a dressing-down by the man in charge of the gate.

Bill tried to speed-translate some of what the principal had expressed, but it was clear that we had to get the kids inside before that gate shut again. Each child kissed his or her parents twice, once on each cheek. The mothers of the smallest ones looked slightly stricken, the parents of the older ones utterly relieved by *la Rentrée*. Children drained down into the schoolyard in little cliques.

I leaned down and whispered into the space between the girls' heads. "Remember, it's '*je m'appelle Grace. Je m'appelle Abigail.*' You can totally do this."

Of course, we learned months later that this is not something anyone ever actually says in a small village in France. You are either known, gradually become familiar, or might-as-well-be-dead-to-me. Introducing myself with the *Je m'appelle Launa* I learned years ago in French class made me sound like a total imbecile.

Nothing like planning ahead *and* making mistakes — undertaking their French instruction in the car, on the way to school, and teaching them to say something stupid. For someone who prides herself on being so organized, this whole "neglect to teach the kids useful French" thing was of course awfully strange. We had tried, if fitfully. However, I think that the language had not taken hold because it had simply not registered with the girls they might actually need to *try* to learn some French. When the realization hit, that morning outside of the school, it fell like a ton of *croque-monsieurs*.

While the other children disappeared into the schoolyard, I suggested to the girls as gently as I could that it might be time for them to go. I tried to get them to hold hands and leave together a few times, but they stood firm as the rest of the kids walked past them. I was wondering how much of a fuss I would have to make to get them to start walking, when Abigail turned to face me and said, steely and emotionless: "I'm going."

She turned towards the gate, then reached over to grab Grace's hand. "She's coming with me."

I have no idea what got her from using me as a sweater to deciding it was time to walk away. Abigail will always be a mystery, despite her pose of being all normal and straightforward.

The girls looked up into my face solemnly, unmistakably asking me to give them *bisous*, just like the rest of the kids. I kissed them gently and slowly on each cheek. Or they kissed me. It was so strange, yet so right for where we were, and when. They walked down the ramp beyond where I could see, Abigail dragging her big sister behind her like rolling luggage.

I told myself that I stood there for them. But it was all me. I wasn't quite ready to leave until I saw them rounded up into a classroom along with the other kids.

I left, not sure whether to feel despair, guilt, pride, or simple relief. They had walked in on their own two feet. I had abandoned them in a building where they knew no one. I had no idea what the girls' teachers' names even were, and no way to find out. The principal had asked us quite clearly and firmly to stay on our side of the *portail.*

Mostly, I wanted to cry. So much for that hands-off parenting lie I tried so hard to believe. I was a mother of my generation, after all.

With no job of my own to worry over, it was the first time in my life I was a 100% Mom on a school day. I had spent all of their other first-day-of-school mornings so occupied by other people's kids. I rarely worried at all those days about my own girls, so focused was I on making everything okay for several hundred others.

I spent the morning getting ready for lunch, believing firmly that if I served just the right midday meal, they would survive the day. I staved off anxiety by buying food for American-style lunches: white sandwich bread and individually wrapped slices of cheese.

I returned to our little apartment in Sillans, so empty without the kids in it. Bill was fully absorbed in other things, but I couldn't think about anything but loss. I felt separated from the girls, and now separated from him by my anxiety and his own more pressing concerns. I also felt separated from myself — at least from the version of me who used to have more to do on this important day. I had a queasy feeling and could not settle my mind on anything useful aside from watching the clock. I was so relieved when it was time to go back and get them.

I was there ridiculously early, and forced myself to walk around town for ten minutes before pining away pathetically at the gate. They emerged at 11:30 AM, with a small group of the other 20 other kids who had parents at home in the village to cook for them. When they emerged, they both looked relieved. Happy even. Abigail told me that she had had running races. Grace said that her teacher spoke nearly every language on the European continent, but not English. She thought he was funny. They were both fine. Absolutely fine. I tried not to reveal just how surprised I really was that they were so much more than just okay.

Back home, we fed them and listened to their stories. Bill and I drove them back to school for drop off, then spent the afternoon milling about Aups and reading at a café while drinking a single beer each, for about two hours. It felt like the most decadent thing we ever had done, to sit quietly in rural France while the rest of the world was hard at work, but I kept checking the clock after turning each page.

While I was reading and wondering about them under the town's 400-year-old plane tree, what were they doing? They both had said at lunch that nobody expected them to do anything at school: they just had to sit quietly while the teacher talked. What were they thinking about, those six blocks away from our table at the café? Were the other children being kind? Were the teachers?

When, exactly, would the sounds of the language start to unravel themselves so that my girls could join in the life of the school? And when would their French skills go zooming past my own?

By the next new moon, Abigail would be 8 years old. It would be time to move to our new house in Aups, a short walk from school. The girls would have become adept at their little routines.

I felt so separate from the girls for those hours, alone in my worry, wondering how they would make their way, torn between fierce pride and lingering fear. Since I was the one doing all the leaving, why did I feel so left behind?

When we first arrived in France, we slept as though we were drugged. Back in Brooklyn, all four of us had been running at full speed through a desert on nothing but inertia, and suddenly we arrived at a big fat wet oasis. We soaked ourselves in sleep and blue water, and stared at the orange dirt, the green trees, and the blue, blue sky. We buried our tired brains in old movies and new books. We ate a ton of ripe fruit. We did nothing of any use to anyone aside from our own little family, and immersed ourselves in human-scale, meet-able responsibilities. Our wedding vow about making everything meaningful rather than easy drifted right out the open windows.

Once school started, we gave up our slovenly 9:30 AM wakeups. Before school, there were usually one or more tanties. We refused to legitimize these little family fits with the proper name of "tantrum." While legitimate anger is absolutely acceptable in our family, tanties are baby stuff. There was hair and there were teeth to be brushed, retainers to be put away in the proper place, and breakfast to be set in front of both girls, then picked at grudgingly and eventually thrown away mostly uneaten.

By the second day of school, the drop-off drama had all but dissolved. Grace still hung back a little as we walked towards *le portail,* but she was also listing off the names of some of the kids in her class. She is some sort of language savant, has an incredible ear, and can reproduce the sound of her classmates' English perfectly: "*Gr-AY-AY-sse.*" She immediately began correcting my French pronunciation.

Abigail's day one jitters completely vanished as she skipped towards the gate, ready for action. I even had to remind her about the *bisous* she owed her Mama. Grace still went all grave in lifting her face to mine when it was time for the ritual kisses. They then turned and walked down the ramp without a backward glance.

In the schoolyard they began the important work of making friends. Abigail did exactly what the textbooks tell you that children should know to do. She stood on the edge of a group of children and watched what they were doing. She mimicked their movements. She waited for an opportune moment to join in the game. Soon enough she was on the edge of a game of tag, or perhaps a French version of the old standby "smack the foreigner." I couldn't easily tell.

Grace, shockingly, was even more socially successful than Abigail right off the bat. It's possible that in France things are just different, and that her habit of gazing blankly at people was what drew them all in. Grace has never had this bizarre American tic of oversmiling. So she collected friends like flies, while the rest of us languished in social purgatory and tried too hard. Children came up to her, took her hand, and led her to interesting things going on in the schoolyard.

One girl even asserted, before she could protest that she spoke English, not Spanish, that they were "*amigos,*" and would be so forever.

I learned all this by spying on them, and then later interrogating them. I spied alongside the skinny, bespeckled woman I met at the Aups Tourism Office. While the girls were trolling for new friends down in the schoolyard, I was doing the same. At first I thought I would French-ly pretend not to recognize her, but then I realized that I had the opportunity to meet a fellow Mom, one who knew a lot about the town and had already spoken with me, if only in her professional role. Perhaps she had been trained by the French government to be kind to foreigners, because when I hovered nearby, she made her hands into binoculars then made a joke that she and I were doing "espionage." I even laughed, once she slowly repeated the joke for me.

I could not make friends in France by being funny. I recognized early on that it was going to be a long year of asking people to repeat their jokes, then laughing too heartily several beats too late.

Tourism lady tired of my over-hearty laughter pretty quick, then left with a flat, "*au travail*," which I took to mean "Time for work." Apparently she was only required to be extra kind to boring unfunny foreigners while on duty. Or maybe this is what I sounded like when I had too much job and not enough time.

After I dropped off the girls, I spent an hour at a café combining four separate worlds into a proper address book. In the past, I had my address book at work, my fancy little gift shop book of Christmas card addresses, a list of the 30 numbers of my friends and family, and then a Xeroxed-and-scrawled list of telephone numbers we regularly called in the business of our family life.

Part of the pleasure of making a new address book that day was also deciding who would get the boot. The address book is just a grown-up version of the 7th grade friend list. As I drank my *café au lait* in the sunshine, I had the quiet thrill of crossing off people, places, and institutions that no longer held meaning for me. Specialist MD's who had long since left Brooklyn for Manhattan. The friend who told me I was becoming too bourgeois for her — as though I had ever been anything else. The tone-deaf child psychologist someone referred my way. The babysitter who more than once fell asleep while watching my children. The other babysitter who called us drunk late at night to pick a fight.

I sorted out what was still a part of my life, and what I could wash away forever. But I had nothing much new to add. I punched in my three French contacts — one of them my own cell — with the strange two-digit Morse code structure that made them seem much longer than U.S. numbers.

I wondered how I might add a few more, or even learn the name of somebody who lived in town. I wish I could say that I spent the morning with the town historian, or perhaps with a visiting author, with whom I could share a few *bons mots* about Balzac. I wish I had met a local character, a funny old olive grower, or perhaps even the Mayor. It would also be nice to say that I had coffee with another mom of a child in Grace and Abigail's school, someone who could potentially become my friend. But that would require me to have broken the obvious barrier between me and anyone French who actually lived in the town. That social *portail* might have been invisible, but it sure held fast.

Aups was more like my memories of the 1970's in the hamlet where I grew up. Back then, newcomers were expected to be humble and quiet for a while — say three or four years — before being invited into the social whirl of Church potluck suppers, school potluck suppers and — well, there wasn't a third thing.

I didn't have three or four years at my disposal, so I put my hopes in Jessica, the owner of the house we would be renting in Aups. Jessica and her children had mailed us very sweet letters of welcome in the spring, and we were eager to get our kids to meet hers, so we made plans to meet up at a café one day after school. While we waited, we studied the pictures Jessica had sent us of her kids so that we could recognize them: 8-year-old Louise, 6-year-old Zach, and Cameron, almost 5. Jessica and her partner Gerard weren't in the photos, but I thought I recognized the kids already.

When they arrived, we shook hands and shared *bisous,* and the kids gave Grace and Abigail drawings that they had made for them. Jessica is British but grew up in Provence. She and Gerard, who grew up in Aups, live on a farm and raise donkeys, chickens, rabbits, ducks, and geese, and bees. Louise and Valentine are his daughters, and Zach and Cameron are her sons; they are a British-French Brady Bunch with a lot more animals, and tons of lavender honey.

We took a walk through town together, and Jessica showed us the road to the house we would be moving into in mid-September once the visitors who pay summer rates had all left. It was a five-minute walk from school, even closer than our house was to school back in Brooklyn. Jessica even told us that school in Aups meets only four days per week: kids have off every single Wednesday.

When she said this, the girls looked at each other in delighted disbelief.

The girls enjoyed being with Louise and Zach, who were adorable and sweet and just on either side of Abigail, agewise. Cameron had held my hand crossing the street. We had been there several weeks, but these were the first French people we had actually socialized with. And they were smiling, unguarded.

As we walked back to our car, an unfamiliar sense spread through me. I am pretty sure that the French call it *bien-être*. Well-being. Perhaps if I were okay with Jessica, I could become, through the transitive property, okay with her French friends and family. I was essentially hoping for her to do the equivalent of sharing her 7th grade friend list with me, despite the fact that I had nothing much to offer in return.

My wish came true the Sunday after school began, when Jessica invited us to her friends' house for lunch. We sat for hours in the welcoming shade of a big leafy tree while sipping multiple bottles of wine. Our hosts were Mathilde and Laurent, and their children Elise and Clement. From them I learned that once you actually meet someone French and share *bisous*, the smiles open up and the laughter runs free.

Still, it was painfully and horribly clear to me that my French simply wasn't up to the challenge of extended conversation. I spent much of the day with my eyes glued desperately to the mouth of whomever was speaking, hoping that somehow more than 34% of the words would come clear to me so that I could follow their meaning. When I had to say something, I rehearsed the first few words inside my head, but then always got marooned mid-sentence, hoping to be rescued by a stronger swimmer. Laurent and Mathilde, who own the big grocery store in town, had each spent time in the United States, and they were as generous with their English as they were with their food, wine, and crunchy snacks. Jessica moved smoothly and swiftly between the two languages, and while Gerard didn't speak a word of English, I could sometimes follow his rueful and very funny jokes.

While we drank our *rosé* and shared stories (mine in caveman language), the kids created a *spectacle* for the adults, with the 5-year-old-girl juggling two red *boules*, the 4-year-old doing flips on the mini-trapeze, and Grace bouncing a ball on a racket while singing the entire *Marseillaise*. I wish I could say I were just the tiniest bit blasé about this achievement of hers, but it was all that I could do not to burst with pride as she hit the crucial phrases with r's a-rolling and a closed-mouth "*ehew*" sound. Even the laconic and confident Laurent had to comment that Grace could sing his national anthem much better than he could sing *The Star Spangled Banner.*

Lunch ended with *bisous* all around, and all of us sloshing back home to finish up the kids' homework. And once again as it got dark, I settled in to write.

And there, while sitting in my chair and recalling the stories of our day, I found it again: that unfamiliar sense of well-being. It was settling in around the muscles in my shoulders where I had previously stashed all my discontent and anxiety. I was getting nothing done, yet finding my life in France was making me incredibly, reliably, and quite fully satisfied rather more frequently than my old life ever did.

Peaceful, settled happiness is a taboo topic, particularly if it feels like the deep and real kind. How can you not sound like a horrible jerk telling somebody how happy you are? Usually it's a kind of pathetic humblebrag, a masking of some deeper well of loneliness when somebody goes on and on about how *happy* they feel, how *at peace.*

But there it was: peace in my life, after a long and difficult absence when I had managed to forget what it felt like. I was plenty happy a lot of the time back home, certainly moved and often deeply shaken. But now all that movement was stilled. I felt the 3,000 miles of distance from Brooklyn somewhere deep in my stomach, but also felt a new closeness to my family. Perhaps this feeling was the deep relief that follows when one's fears are dispelled and one's fondest hopes come true. It came floating in the windows at night on the cool air and was reflected back and forth between the huge sun in the day and the equally enormous moon at night. It's what I was waiting for, and there it was.

For the first time in years, my family was starting to feel more like a refuge than a burden I could not properly carry. As the air grew chilly, I drew them around me like a shawl.

After a week of school, I decided to join the town women in their diaphanous white outfits. Perhaps because of my enormous white shirt, or perhaps because I was becoming just a little more familiar, I received several "*Bonjours,*" each with a tight little nod. I did best when I fought my overfriendly urges, and kept my hand down and didn't wave. French people find cheerful waves just as threatening as you should find their strident one-finger waggle.

Of course, just as Grace settled in with her amigos at school, and Bill and I got to enjoy running into our new acquaintances from lunch on the lawn, Abigail started to feel left out. We first started to notice that she was going wild during the two-hour break at lunchtime, jumping up from the table to draw our attention with a crazy dance. French school doesn't provide a lot of opportunity for jumping around and repeatedly smacking one's own butt for laughs, so I initially guessed this was just her getting her wiggles out.

But then she started to fight us on everything: getting up in the morning, putting on her clothes, taking them off, sitting down to breakfast, clearing the food away uneaten. Our usually sunny kid was giving us lip, while the moody one was suddenly giving us a hundred smiles a day.

One kid falling down, the other one rises up. At the playground, the girls' favorite activity was always the see-saw. But they never just played a gentle up and down, back and forth. That would have been too simple, and taken all the edge out of their play. Instead, they each liked to take turns stranding one another up in the air, then swiftly dropping her down to the ground without warning. I always saw this game as a spinal cord injury in the making, but they found it hysterical. The harder the drop, the more they would laugh. They called this game "Kill Farmer Brown," and seemed to enjoy tormenting one another much more than they would ever take pleasure from one another's hugs.

Grace has a big heart, and I wished that she would see Abigail as someone she could reach out to at times like this when she was so sad. Instead, she intellectualized the problem, pointing out that even though she was making friends, she thought that French kids could be a little mean. She once saw a little girl sitting on the wall of the playground crying, and looked around to see when someone would step in to help. She didn't know the words herself to say, "Are you okay?" Her new friends walked right by, telling Grace that they didn't want to stop and help. And since this was French school, there were no teachers to come over and dry her tears. Presumably, at some point the bell rang and the little girl had to go back to class. I wonder if there were tearstains on her little dusty face. I wonder if she hopped up a minute later and went back to her game.

Clearly I was more torn about this hands-off business than I had previously thought. I had always believed it healthy for kids to work things through on their own as much as possible, with plenty of love, fresh air, sleep, and healthy food at their backs. As a teacher and a school principal, I had seen the ways that too much adult attention on children's feelings could get invasive. With someone watching and worrying over their every step, how could they gain the confidence to make a leap when one was required?

Still, when it was my kid sitting on the wall at recess, I couldn't help but wish for a fairy godmother. The teachers certainly weren't going to help. When I went to pick up Grace, her teacher (a dead ringer for a 50-something Peter Fonda) had lit up his cigarette and was on his motorcycle before he had seen whether she was safely back with me. Abigail's teacher made a cursory glance in my direction, but she never met my eyes.

I tried to love *le portail* and the way it gave the kids a whole new kind of freedom and challenge. But some days, it felt like we had dropped our kids off at jail.

The things I took for granted in my old life were gone, and new rules applied. I was luxuriating in the slow unfolding of French time, but when the girls suffered bad days I berated myself about the losses we had foisted on them. How, in gazing at our new distant ship, we threw away some of the things they had most wanted to keep.

I can sometimes remember that there is a usual cure for what ails Abigail. She gets better with a steady diet of little toys, extra candy, some TV, reading aloud, and extra snuggling. We do what she wants, and let her play in the bathtub for extra-long stretches. Since the French school week was just two bursts of two days, with Wednesdays off, we were never more than two days from a sort of weekend.

I even packed chocolate bribes for when I picked her up at school, something I never in a million years would have done back home, because I could see that Abigail needed recompense for what she had lost. I had to remember that she was the one most on top of her game when we packed up all her stuff and threw her on a plane.

Early that summer, before we arrived in France, I thought that it was me who was giving up more than I was gaining in my desperate grasp for a simpler life. But once the girls started school, I could see that it was Abigail who had the least say in the whole decision.

"I just wish I had tried to learn French," she told me again and again, rueful and unfairly angry at herself.

On some of our early days in France, three wheels of our family shopping cart faced in the same direction, and just one of us needed a little boost to roll awkwardly along with the rest.

On other days, we nearly drew and quartered ourselves pulling to the four cardinal directions. Grace pulled towards quiet, Abigail towards stimulation; Bill pulled towards adventure, and I towards structure.

One day it was raining, so there was nothing to do outside. We drove back and forth to school, heated up the leftovers for lunch, mooned around and picked up dead and dying millipedes. Internet access inside our rental was patchy, so we jockeyed for position within the two-square-foot space that was still indoors and could receive a signal.

I can't recall what I was doing online that day, but Bill had an exciting new project: finding a used car. Our special lease on the Renault would last only 180 days. In his new role as family manager, he spent hours researching used cars and putting in endless numbers of details into a sort of European Blue Book website to determine what each one was worth.

It's bad enough trying to understand car language without translating it into French, sometimes in and out of British English (lots of expats selling their over-fine automobiles at the end of the summer season), and then translating prices in and out of giant-size pounds, middleweight euros, and our piddly little pint-size dollars. He was becoming obsessed.

On our way to pick up the girls from school, the rain cleared for a while and clouds started racing high and fast across the sky. Open blue spaces appeared in the clouds, and the sun moved in and out of them. As we drove between Sillans and Aups, high over the far hills there appeared a rainbow like nothing I have ever seen. Rather than being high and semicircular, this one was low, hugging the hills, and was fat, wooly, and almost flat. It was hard to see behind the dense green trees edging the road, but every once in a while we would speed past an open patch and get a glimpse.

We like to believe that signs in the sky like well-timed emerging sunshine and oddly pudgy rainbows mean something. A vestige of our cavemen-in-the-hills-of-Aups days, this peculiar tendency to look up to see into the future works only so well. You might think that the clearing sky and a big fat wooly caterpillar of a rainbow promised smooth sailing for the little displaced family in a speeding Renault wagon. But no. We might have all been in the same car, but we might as well have been speeding in rockets to different planets.

The kids were whiningly hungry. In France, we ate only at meals, and it took months for us to get used to the sensation of eating because we really needed to, not just because we're sort of bored or distracted and "Oh, look, there's another place selling food!"

The kids had also just been through two grueling 3-hour sessions of *le blah blah blah* and wanted to go back home to decompress. Bill and I had been through a full day of feeling crowded and cramped indoors, and sorely wanted a piece of sky. Abigail was longing after Brooklyn "where everyone is so joyful," as she remembered it, and Grace couldn't stop talking about how badly we needed a French guinea pig to sub in for Samson, the sweet lab hound we left at home with my in-laws. It wasn't long before someone's pathetic longings would turn into actual tears — particularly if we put John Denver on the iPod. "Leaving on a Jet Plane" could set off any of the four of us at any moment.

I tried for a plan to bring us all back together. We would drive over our favorite mountain just north of Aups, to Moustiers, the super-cute and pretty-colored town where it was so sunny and bright and where I had first found that rhubarb sorbet. It would be full of little things to look at, and we could have an early dinner. I would get more rhubarb, and wouldn't that really be so much fun, everyone? Keyword "mountain" pulled in Bill's vote instantaneously, while the vague promise of food staved off the girls' complaints long enough for me to turn the car hard north. Mama would save the day.

The Verdon valley, soaked with rainwater, showed its colors more brilliantly than usual. The orange earth glowed both darker and brighter. The rain had washed all the dust off the green trees, and the blue water of the lake was positively electric.

We wound around the corners, past the gorge. Abigail asked if she could jump off the bridge, and we briefly pondered whether she would be killed instantly, or merely maimed and then drowned in the cold water. The open-air restaurant on the lakeshore where we had eaten just a week before was closed, *fermé* for the season. There were no boats out in the lake, only one or two lonely people sitting on the shore, wishing that they hadn't been so cheap and had just paid the in-season rates when planning their vacations.

When we arrived, there were still tourists milling about the little picture-perfect (but now chilly) town, but they were upper-middle-aged and sharply dressed French couples, rather than in throngs from all over the world. All the *faience* stores were open, *faience* being both an outmoded technology for making fine china and Moustiers-St-Marie's claim to fame. They have *faience*, and also that gold star strung by chains between two high mountain peaks just over the gorge and the river running through the center of town. We parked and wandered, looking for something to cheer us up, to distract us from the entirely minor losses of the day, and to fill up our bellies.

But despite the fact that the early birds were circling each establishment like vultures, there would be no dinner served at 17:30. And not at 18:00 or even 18:30, either. Dinner will be served in France at 19:00 and not before. There is almost no amount of window-shopping in fine china shops that can distract two children and two red-blooded American adults with rumbly tummies for that long.

So all at once, the four wheels of our cart tried to set off in different directions. Grace needed an immediate advance on her allowance so that she could buy yet another beaded keychain. Abigail needed to dawdle around the water fountain, and Bill set off to find the W.C. I thought that perhaps I would just pop into the store with the *provençal*-printed bathing suits. The streets were a warren of little shops, galleries, and lots of closed snack shops. They were twisted and narrow so that you could only see promising signs, not actual establishments. We would look down a street and see a sign that indicated a store that might have calories or trinkets. We would walk down the street, hopes up high, and inevitably: *fermé*.

Sometimes the right of weight wins in our family. Bill took charge, and decided to pull us all along on a hike. An 11th-century chapel high in the crook of the cliff was calling him. And somebody had to break the stalemate to get us to the magic hour of 19:00 when we would be allowed to dine.

After a few false starts to find the trailhead, we were climbing up pebbly stone steps into the sky. We walked past the first few stations of the cross (rendered, of course, in *faience*) and then the miracle occurred. Not a ray of sunshine or even a fuzzy rainbow. Jesus did not step out of the sky to help us sort out our petty human problems. Instead, our miracle was a little sign on a tree reading "*Zone de Silence.*" We suddenly had earned a free pass from whining, complaining, or asking for non-existent snacks for the duration of the hike: this sign was a harried parent's dream.

And, of course, from the girls' perspective, this also meant a moratorium on all those pointless things adults can't seem to stop themselves from saying: "Hey, would you look at that amazing view?" and "Look out, you're too close to the edge" and "Would you please stop walking on the edges of my shoes?!"

In France, away from our friends, without jobs and extracurricular activities, the four of us spent a lot of time together. A lot. We were coming to see that this was actually the whole point of the adventure.

That said, as much as we loved one another in our little family, there were moments when we all needed a break from so much family togetherness, and we had a hard time letting ourselves make it happen. A long stony pilgrimage up to the Chapel of Notre Dame turned out to be the perfect ending to our day. The sign took away our need to constantly talk to, around, and at one another, while the path took away our need to tussle over constant decisions without adequate information. With up as our only option, we would not have to fight it out over north, south, east, and west.

There on the path, we could march along at our own pace, sometimes holding hands when we wanted a companion, and sometimes walking along alone. I could stop and look out over the hills to the lake when my shoes started to bother me. Grace could stare down at the interlacing patterns on the orange tile roofs. Bill could imagine himself into the world of J.R.R. Tolkien, climbing the stone steps to Mordor. Abigail could dawdle and scour the ground for fossils and sparkly treasures.

At the very top of the mountain, the path ended at the chapel. By the time I got there, Bill had gone into the dark stone church, lit only through six tiny stained-glass portals high on the vaulted walls. Abigail and Grace hung back and waited for me, too anxious to walk inside. They each grabbed onto one of my arms as we entered the dark, but they leaned in rather than pulling out.

We walked down the aisle to meet Bill. At the front of the chapel stood a gilded altar full of cabinets, cubbies, and dozens of candles burning at the feet of Notre Dame, the original Supermom. Little signs on the side of the church thanked her for her protection at various points in history, mainly clustered around the two world wars. Inside was peaceful and quiet and just the tiniest bit gothically creepy. We stood together holding hands, still in grateful silence, as our eyes adjusted to the dark. Our little family, back on the path, all together, and all alone.

CHAPTER THREE:

Enchanté

I N A SURPRISE MOVE, THE GAME of Kill Farmer Brown once again
upended things. One morning when I dropped the girls in Aups, Abby
went skipping down into the yard, her high ponytails wagging in the wind.
Grace could barely drag herself past *le portail*, and kept glaring back at me with
pitiful, guilt-inducing looks.

Mid-morning after I had dropped her off at school, it finally hit me — she
was either anxious or sick. To her, they feel like the same thing. Grace, like
her father, often confuses physical and psychological symptoms; she thinks she
is sad when she is sick, or sick when she is sad. I try to remember that when
members of my family feel sick, they probably need some other sort of comfort,
like an ace bandage or some downtime away from other people. Sometimes Bill
has actually gone off to bed thinking he was feeling ill, only to be cured by a
single telephone call, a band practice, or a beer on the stoop. But when Grace
or Bill complained of feeling homesick, or told me they missed me, they were

undoubtedly having some sort of physical problem.

My role in crazyworld has often been to sort through the denial to help them figure out the real underlying malady. When we were in Brooklyn, battling Bill's chronic fatigue and Grace's intermittent anxiety, I dedicated part of my brain to diagnosis and treatment. In France, with less to distract me, I was getting better at my diagnoses. I just wished I could more quickly read these patterns and help everyone back to balance and health. Whenever possible, I prefer to magically look around corners and pre-solve problems before they occur.

Once I realized what was going on with Grace, she and I spent two days in the world's most boring holding pattern. I kept her home from school, and read her *Harry Potter* aloud until I talked myself into a nap. She perked up and got close to normal when I gave her French Tylenol, but went back to drooping around when it wore off. Bill and I took turns ferrying Abigail back and forth to school, where she was still not speaking any French, but regularly playing with the kids, and appeared to have attracted several little girls as potential friends.

Watching children and tending to a house requires the same set of repetitive tasks and quiet focus in any language. It's like the quiet steady boredom of practicing scales or memorizing the conjugation of verbs. It feels like nothing is happening, while just under the surface, shaky situations are transforming into something more solid and secure.

Grace didn't have a fever, and really had no symptoms other than lassitude and a headache. If we had been back in Brooklyn, I would have stuffed her full of Advil and sent her to school so that she wouldn't miss anything and I could go to work. Part of the reason that I let her stay home was that I thought she would be overwhelmed by all that French *le blah blah blah* in her sickly state. Fishing for meaning in a new language made us both awfully tired. We might pick out a word here and there while the rest flowed by us. Just as we were trying to attach some other word to that one, some other nugget of meaning would pass and disappear.

I worried about overtaxing her when she wasn't feeling well, but I also kept her home because I was terribly afraid to be blamed for bringing an illness into the French school system. And even though I was certain it wasn't *that* virus — no coughing, no fever — swine was on my mind.

Mine and everybody else's. A school a few towns over closed for two weeks on the second day of school because one child had one suspected case of flu. They were simply not messing around where the Swine Flu pandemic was concerned, and had very grave-sounding public safety announcements on the radio. In the context of the totally blasé French attitude towards traffic safety, playground supervision, and cigarette smoking, the cultural anxiety about the flu stood out as particularly fervent. Perhaps only *La Rentrée* was more feared.

I understood that the flu — any flu — is dangerous to people who aren't healthy. And I understood that while H1N1 was acting like a regular flu, it had more than the usual potential to mutate into a more serious illness. I had done my reading on that one. But I remained sort of amused by the overly-serious way that the French were treating it, freaking out over some chills and a sniffle.

While I didn't worry that Grace had H1N1, I did worry enough to keep her home. Then I worried that keeping her home would undermine the essential process of her learning enough French to feel she belonged. Bill's French was rapidly improving. He cared about it, he worked really hard on it all summer, and took every opportunity available to him to speak. Not so for the rest of us, who moved more slowly and strangely towards our shared goal. I was now up from 30% to 37% comprehension, although Grace was kicking my butt on pronunciation and Abigail on the words for numbers.

To get us to try a little harder, at dinner we played a little game that I called "Can You Say?" As Bossy Mama, I acted as puzzlemaster, and did my best to challenge the kids without ever stumping them. I would ask Abigail, "Can you say blue?" because I knew she'd get "*bleu*" right away. I asked Grace about harder words like "glass" or "pear," but she nearly always nailed them. Sometimes I asked Bill a word that I was confident that he knew, then I asked the girls the same word a few beats later. They were delighted to be able to give the right answer and rarely noticed that we had just taught it to them.

But mostly I stumped Bill intentionally, because it was so awfully gratifying to the girls to see Mr. French Traveler struggle as much as they were struggling. I might ask Bill the French for "sleepwalking," and then he would get it wrong, and we'd look it up in the little dictionary, modeling proper learning behavior. But unless they were doing homework, the girls would never look up a single word of their own accord, even in the new picture dictionary I bought at the grocery store in a fit of misguided optimism.

I knew even then how they would learn: Grace would wake up from her sick funk and be miles ahead of all of us in her comprehension and her precise, elegant accent. Someday Abigail would finish building her wall bit by bit, and would just jump up onto it and run along the top, scampering and leaping along with a brand new tongue. I also knew how I would fail: when I have to learn something that I can't read about, I tend to languish in ignorance, angry at myself for not already knowing it. I wait impatiently for meanings magically to reveal themselves.

How were the words starting to seep into our consciousness, so that "*verre*" was not "the French word for glass," but the thing itself? How were the waiters starting to sound to me as though they were speaking something as utterly clear as English?

As I drove back and forth from home to school, I listened to French talk radio when the girls were not in the car. I tested myself to see how long I would have to listen to a broadcast before I could figure out what they were talking about. Having heard the H1N1 Public Service Announcement several times, and knowing all of the crucial facts, I gradually came to understand the whole thing, in its ringing and dangerous tones.

Sometimes I drove the whole way to Aups without understanding more than a word here and there. Then, suddenly a crucial term would reveal itself, and the whole meaning was suddenly clear like a sandy puddle on the shore as a wave pulls back towards the ocean. One day they were all *blah blah blah le blah*, and suddenly they were talking about the number of French women who watch pornographic movies independently of their partners. And then, later that day, the *blah blah blah* with dark and significant musical accents was suddenly the story of the murder in Miami Beach of Gianni Versace. In this case, the phrases "Miami Beach" and "News Café," spoken in poorly accented English, were my runes. From there, I could follow nearly the entire sad and gory tale.

The voices on the radio would eventually become like the waiters in the brasserie, and sound as though I had always understood. The smoke would clear in an instant, and suddenly and miraculously I would be healed of my pathetic leprosy of total confusion and dismay. There was not knowing, not knowing, not knowing until I hated myself, sure that I would never learn. And some new truth would dawn on me — Grace is sick; the French are being over-anxious about this flu; they are talking about women and pornography — and suddenly I knew for sure.

The town we only sort of accidentally chose is not far from the Gorge du Verdon, a deep canyon with a mineral-rich aqua blue river slowly splitting it in two. The river spills out under a high bridge into the Lac St Croix. The weather was glorious well into September, so one weekend we drove there and rented white plastic pedal-boats, drifting up and down the canyon with other happy families.

The road to the lake wound up the hill from Aups through a series of switchbacks, rising to a peak from which we could see a long stretch of blue and purple mountains in the distance, layered below with all of the bucolic green hills, then the flat roofs and ochre walls of villages and farmhouses packed into little pockets of towns.

At the crest of the hill, the landscape became moonscape. A huge flat plain loomed, wrapped around the edges with dark, sharp-edged mountains jutting upwards. The brush turned scrubby and dry, unwatered and virtually unplantable. The mesa rolled along towards the Gorge du Verdon, and dipped into a deep blue lake ringed with rough orange sand.

Cresting that hill gave us the sensation of being lifted up gently along the most beautiful Green Mountain pass, and then dropped without warning into the dry mountains of Utah. We were tootling along in something familiar and adorable and friendly, then suddenly slammed into a stark, forbidding, shockingly beautiful and unfamiliar new world.

When we arrived for dinner at Jessica and Gerard's farmhouse in the evening after our boat trip, we discovered that their house had been built directly on the crest between the valley of Aups and the valley facing the Gorge. As we drove along their rocky driveway, we looked one way down to Aups and the other way towards the high dry hills. Their stone house sat in a sloping bowl of land overlooking the high mountains that eventually turned into the Alps.

As soon as we arrived, their dogs Alba and Goya came out to greet us with the greatest of enthusiasm and slavish joy. The shepherd Alba immediately attached herself to Abigail, and laid herself at her feet, hoping to have her belly rubbed until the end of time. Louise, Zach, and Cameron took us out to the barn to show off their geese, the ducks and little black-and-yellow ducklings, the chickens, and the big, high-sided enclosure of rabbits.

The girls adored watching Louise and Zach pick up the rabbits and bring them over for inspection. They would pick up the wooden box under which fifteen or twenty rabbits were huddling and hiding together, then grab one under the shoulders and lift him up for our entertainment.

Zach preferred to lift bunnies by the ears, although we would warn, "*Doucement!* Gently!" hoping, but not really believing, that this was a safe way for a farm child to lift a rabbit. We were a little giddy: translating rabbit and *lapin*, watching the bunnies hop away in fright, watching Zach clowning for us. Little Cameron couldn't see anything, and Bill set him on the edge of the high wall. After a bit, he jumped down and tried to pick up a rabbit himself, laughing and complaining as the rabbit scratched him then scrabbled away. I was worried about Cameron being inside, but I tried to relax. After all, the girls were beside themselves with laughter, and all five kids looked as though they had never been happier. I can't say the same for the rabbits.

We were all looking at one fat rabbit that Louise had picked for us, and all laughing in a few different languages. But then the heavy wooden box that Cameron had been lifting up to pull out a rabbit fell down with a thud, and I began to hear a sound that I first thought was a child squealing. I just couldn't tell which one. But then the children's voices stilled, and even though the sound was coming from where Cameron was, his mouth was closed. I asked, "What's that sound?" already knowing what had happened. It was a rabbit's high-pitched terror cry, pealing out over and over again.

Louise picked up the heavy wooden box, and an auburn colored rabbit lay still, no longer crying, as the rest hopped away. She picked it up, thinking its leg was broken. The way its hindquarters dangled showed me that its back had been broken by the heavy wooden hutch. It was calm when she held it, but when she set it down, it could only hop with its front half.

I felt as though we had been driving along in our bucolic happy postcard of Provence, and suddenly dropped without warning into an alien and terrifying landscape.

Louise, normally sunny and tremendously engaging, turned on Cameron and grabbed at his ears in anger. "*Doucement,*" I said again, although I don't know why I thought the word that had failed earlier would work then. The kids looked stricken, and tore off for the farmhouse, leaving Bill and me staring at one another, knowing that we had failed the kids, failed the rabbit. I had no idea what Jessica and Gerard would say, but I was nearly as afraid and embarrassed as were the children. It was an awful moment.

We trudged back up the hill, slow and guilty, but Gerard was already coming out towards the barn. He looked purposeful, but not particularly angry. This was a farm, after all. Cameron and Zach had run in opposite directions to hide, Cameron with tears of shame and frustration streaming down his face. Jessica came out to collect him, to caution him, and to console him all at once, in that way that we moms do. He shouldn't have been in the rabbit enclosure, she reminded him. It wasn't his fault, he had to be much more gentle, he shouldn't be so upset, and yes the rabbit had been hurt.

And now it would have to be killed.

This was what I had feared, but I wanted it to happen as fast as possible. Gerard came out of the barn carrying the rabbit, hanging limp, by his ears. I wasn't sure whether it was already dead, or whether Gerard was taking it off to kill it elsewhere and hang him up for later. Gerard joked in his farmer French, "Time to eat it now." Seeing our frowns, he reminded us, "He was going to be dinner next week, anyway. This way it's just a few days sooner."

Jessica's and Gerard's children cried a little, Louise and Cameron for a very long time. Louise was angry that the rabbit had been killed, although she must have known long before that these rabbits were not pets, but meat. Cameron didn't stop wailing until Bill assured him, in his best French, that this was Bill's fault, not Cameron's. He should not have let him into the rabbit pen. Having been absolved by this strange man speaking pidgin French, Cameron stopped crying.

As I was trying to process our role in the tragic end of M. Lapin, we were graciously swept up in *apéritifs*. We drank Jessica and Gerard's ambrosiac homemade quince wine, then a liqueur made from walnuts that made me wish I could take a bath in it, not just drink it. We ate Gerard's homemade patés, one with *herbes de Provence*, another with truffles dug on their farm.

Yet, even as we made our polite conversation, death was everywhere in the air. Hunting season would start the next day, and Gerard spoke of killing tiny thrush that Jessica would put on a spit and roast. We talked about hikers being gored by wild boar in the mountains, and Gerard's friend who shot and killed a man poaching truffles on his land. Bill, not to be outdone, told Gerard stories of my father shooting a hole in the ear of our neighbor's dog when the dog had been harassing his sheep. Somehow my childhood stories were more interesting when told by Bill.

Gerard told of the time he had been hiking in the Gorge and bitten by a viper. He put a tourniquet on his arm, then lacerated the wound to suck out the venom. He told another story of fishing in the same river we had been blithely pedal-boating on earlier in the day, when a huge rock, the size of a dining room table, broke free without a noise and fell a foot from his body.

My favorite Gerard near-death story, however, was his story of fishing in the Gorge when the water suddenly and rapidly rose about ten feet. He pulled himself up the side of the canyon with a rope, which worked nicely until an enormous wave came down the Gorge and slammed him against the rocks. He woke up 500 meters downstream, face down on a sandbar.

So much for my sense of ease here in the mountains of Southern France.

So maybe I should have learned my lesson from Gerard and told Bill "No, thanks honey," when he offered a hike the next morning. He had been scouring the Michelin guide, unthwarted by Gerard's tales of tidal waves, angry truffle-mad landowners, the start of hunting season, and viper bites. After an overly quiet month, Bill's hiking hunger finally unleashed itself with a vengeance, and he led us to a hike up a mountainside to Tholos de la Lauve, to visit some monoliths. Whatever a monolith might be.

Bill led us past Salernes to a nondescript parking space along the road I had driven a dozen times. We started up a rocky path onto the hillside. Once again, the view behind us was supremely pretty: verdant hills and earthen farmhouses tucked into their sides. Purple-blue mountains rose up behind the hills. The sun moved in and out between clouds and sky, showing off with lots of sunbeams and mottled light-and-dark patches on the landscape below.

As we climbed higher, the mountainside became dry and scrubby, all loose gravel, yellow sand and ochre rock. Abigail found a rock with the obvious outline of a stone snail, finally finding her first fossil. We walked past a dip in the earth, rocks piled around a place four feet by seven feet that had been dug out a few feet deep. It was now filled in with plants, but was still an unmistakable shape. A few yards higher, there was another, then another and another. Pit after pit surrounded by piles of rocks, sitting in this barren moonscape of hill. First we were on a sweet little hike. Then we were walking through a bleak rocky path past shallow graves.

We tried to generate other possible interpretations for the holes. Perhaps there were stone carvings in each of these pits, Bill suggested, but they had been taken to a museum. I thought briefly that these were the abandoned foundations of little shepherd huts. But then there were just way too many of them. How many shepherds does one hillside need?

By the time we got to the top of the hill, and the eerie laid-out rock circle altar, I was sure. A sign at the top that reinforced my worst fears: not only was this an ancient burial ground, it was An Ancient Burial Ground. Like 2,500 years before Christ Ancient. Like same time as the Egyptians Ancient. It had been discovered and excavated in the 1950's by a curious pharmacist in Salernes.

All this creepy dead people ancient-ness failed to faze the girls, who were competing in their usual triathlon of whining, complaining, and lagging behind looking for sparkly rocks. The reference on the sign to Ancient Egypt caught Grace's attention, but it was the group of men, walking around their trucks not too far away from the top of the hill, that caught mine.

If I were an animal, I would be a sheepdog, one eye always on the dangers up ahead.

Just as I had dreaded the rabbit death just a few seconds before I could actually have prevented it, I started to be just the tiniest bit concerned about the truck guys off in the distance. Here we were, in an ancient Neolithic Burial Ground, which was creepy enough. What if it were also on someone's private property, and perhaps they weren't that excited to have us there? I called to Bill, trying to get my three little sheep herded up and started back down the hill. It was, after all, the first day of hunting season. They ignored me for a good long time, as they are wont to do, until a whine not unlike a dying rabbit's started to enter my voice. Time to go home. Now. Like right now. *I mean it.*

They had just started to walk towards me when we heard the first gunshots.

Close. Now, not only were we in a scary old place with ancient graves, but also, people were shooting at us. Or at least near us. Bill, now moving rather more quickly, loudly reasoned that we were all wearing bright red and pink. I reasoned back that that was fine, but that we were on someone else's land, and that someone was now shooting guns. It was time for them to come with me, and I couldn't really wait for Bill to decide to agree.

It's probably not a great idea to run down a mountain of scrabbly, loose gravel and rocks. It's also probably not a great idea to scare one's children unnecessarily. I had no actual proof that we were being shot at, as opposed to shot near. But there is a fine line between pastoral and disastoral. I had crossed it as the cute farm animal turned into a paraplegic, then into dinner; then re-crossed back and forth several times during our bloody, death-tinged conversation. This time, on the way down the hill, I skated along its edge, moving my little family as fast as our feet could carry us without breaking our own legs, without being swept against the walls of the canyon.

Only when we were in the car could I turn on the music, roll down the windows, and exhale. And only once we had parked back in our own driveway could I joke with Bill: "We just got shot at in a Neolithic Graveyard."

We spent the rest of the evening close to home. Safe in the house, happy ending assured, I could admit — to myself if not to Bill — that for once I *liked* the adventure. Our day on the cusp of danger had been exhilarating.

Here is a fairy tale that is at least partially true:

Once upon a time there was a lucky girl who married an extremely enthusiastic prince. They moved to a beautiful city with parks and trees and lived in a narrow brown castle with their two princesses and a big black goofy dog, and they worked to make the world a better place. Sometimes dragons came out of nowhere, but the two bravely fought them until they were vanquished. The city was awfully busy, and all their high-minded hard work and dragon slaying sometimes made them tired and cranky, but they could always order takeout and sit on the stoop of their castle at the end of the day.

Then the little family decided to pack up to go on a long journey, a big adventure they would take together. They left the city they knew and the people they loved for a different country far away, where they discovered delicious new foods, and a proud people who loved their land fiercely, who gave each other bisous, *and who spoke in a strange tongue with a lot of extra vowels.*

There, they would find mountains and valleys and fruit trees. There they would find peace.

It dawned on me as I was again down on my hands and knees using a little bit of paper towel to wipe dried up millipedes off the tile floor of our rented cottage: nothing enchanted remains so forever. Eventually everything that first appears to be magical reveals itself as real, often when things start to really make sense. Or when it's time to clean up.

As I got comfortable there in the magical world of *bien-être*, some of what at first appeared to be unreal started to make sense and become my life.

What was I learning from France's many enchantments? Like the nice ones, rather than the scary ones? And what was I learning from the subsequent disenchantments that came our way? Like the moment when I realized that no matter how incredible that last meal may have been, somebody would need to wash all the dishes. As I transformed from the bold and beautiful heroine of my own life story into the mama of my family's story, I also took on the duties of a millipede-slayer and scullery maid.

I used to wonder about the story of the Garden of Eden. Having grown up on a farm, I knew what animals and gardens required. My favorite joke as a kid was about the moment just after Adam and Eve had finished naming all the beautiful new creatures, and started wishing that the elephants and zebras had been created with some zookeepers to pick up all the big piles of dung they were leaving around the garden.

Or heaven. While I was loath to be rude to God by harping on ungrateful thoughts, I couldn't stop worrying as a child: wouldn't heaven get boring after a while? Eventually? How long can something perfect continue to entertain us fickle human beings?

But then I discovered a new question lurking inside the mystery I thought had deflated. What if this real earth, with its dirty dishes, dead bugs, full parking lots, disappointments, and horrible wars turns out to be heaven itself? What happens if we start to see it and treat it with the majesty it so clearly deserves?

Abigail turned 8 years old on the day we moved from *Les Baumes* to *Bastide de la Loge*. On our last full evening at the mill, we wanted to enchant things as fully as possible for her.

We celebrated with all her favorites: lots of plastic toys, *pistou provençal*, a CD ranging from Jackson 5 to John Denver to Journey to the Black Eyed Peas, a download of *Harry Potter V*, and a big old yellow cake with chocolate frosting — the traditional birthday cake of all the lucky princesses in my family.

This was the first birthday cake I made from scratch in my ten-and-a-half years as a mother. I always told myself that Betty Crocker made it better as an excuse for not having made cake baking a priority. To make the cake without an accurate teaspoon measure, I had to improvise some of the measurements into the metric system, and I invented the chocolate icing recipe myself from butter, melted dark chocolate, heavy cream and powdered sugar. The cake was incredible, way better than Betty's. We liked it so much that we ate it again at breakfast. I felt a sudden and unearned kinship and rivalry with Julie and Julia.

Abigail's eighth birthday marked a high point for my baking career, but also the end point of a few crucial enchantments. For one, she had recently recognized that her mother is her tooth fairy. That summer, Grace's molars had dropped out like they were going out of style, and the tooth fairy had a lot of work to do.

Abigail found a baby tooth in my wallet jangling around with the coins, and turned towards me with a cautious, dawning awareness.

"Mama. There is a tooth with all your quarters. Is the Tooth Fairy real, or are you leaving Grace all that money?"

"Well, since you asked, I am going to tell you the truth. I give out the money."

The news fell like a brick on her head.

It is my policy — both personal and professional — to tell kids the truth when they ask a direct question. Since she hadn't asked directly about other enchanted creatures, I didn't out E. Bunny and S. Claus. Children ask only what they need to know only when they are ready to hear the truth.

When I was straight with her about the Tooth Fairy, she looked relieved and wounded in equal measures. She had been freed of the burden of forcing herself to believe, but also robbed of the miracle of something for nothing.

A few weeks before, some American friends traveling through Southern France had been visiting us. She revealed the tooth truth in close confidence to them, as soon as she had them alone.

"I know about the Tooth Fairy," she confided in a low whisper. "And now I'm pretending to believe in everything else."

Our friends swore themselves to secrecy, but she still saw fit to add, "Just don't tell my mom. I don't want her to be disappointed."

I found it touching — heartwrenching even — that she couldn't bring herself to tell Bill and me that she no longer believed. Perhaps she thought that it would hurt our feelings, much as I had worried about offending God by wondering about the entertainment value of the heaven he had made. Perhaps she wasn't quite sure what she believed, and worried that her doubt might be dangerous to the fairies' health. She's a responsible sort, and would hate to be the last child who stopped clapping to save Tinker Bell.

But more likely she kept mum because she did the calculus and realized that the end of fairies might mean the end of childhood treats. I hoped all the plastic toys we bought her for her birthday reassured her on this score.

I loved having her be 8. I have loved every one of her new years, but it felt particularly wonderful to have both girls in the same developmental stage for the year we were spending all of our time together. Neither little kids nor tweenagers, they were whole and perfect and complete in themselves as children. As girls. The enchanted years of Early Childhood were over, but this new phase felt so right.

Even French was becoming less mysterious. On the day we spent shopping for Abigail's party, I found myself confidently ordering breakfast for the four of us. I didn't need to translate the menu before speaking. My speech was poorly conjugated and poorly accented and required a lot of *quelque chose* "somethings" to fill in for vocabulary I didn't know, but suddenly I was speaking French. No drama. No problem.

But at the same time: no drama, no problem, no more enchantment. Precisely as I got so comfortable with the language that it came spilling out, reality came thwomping down around me. Before the French wormed its way into my ears and out of my mouth, I had been in a magical and incomprehensible land.

There was a mythical blue waterfall and a soft green olive grove, and there had never been such beautiful weather in all of eternity. I had found somewhere that nobody else had ever been, and it was nicer than all of my old someplaces jumbled all together. We were standing together holding hands in the garden, ready to give new French names to all the creatures crowding around.

But then, once I settled in enough to get familiar with the words and with the place, the enchanted parts fell away. I found myself sitting in a mall, having a mediocre breakfast with my cranky little family. We had spent the morning locked in quiet disagreement with used car salesmen trying to find something safe and pretty to drive, and had ended up in a shopping mall. We were about to go buy plastic toys, carrots, and pickles.

The setting contributed to my sense of the magic falling away. Unlike other brasseries we had encountered on the sidewalks of Aix or the town square of mountaintop village Y, the place where French suddenly felt natural to me was the awkward and artificially-lit hallway of a shopping center.

Picture the location of your favorite Kay Jewelers in a prime corner spot. Instead of poor-quality diamonds, this location was hawking *café au lait* and *croque-monsieurs*. They had set out little tables half into the open space of the mall, each set with the standard brasserie table settings and bell-shaped wine glasses.

Just a few dozen yards away was a V.I.P. Jeans store, with a supremely weird ten-foot fiberglass statue of a bison standing guard outside. On the statue had been taped a hand-lettered sign (written in French, which I could read just fine) asking us please not to sit or climb on the bison.

It was all so real, so strange, and so tawdry. It was France with all the mystery and style squeezed out. All the way home, the weather was dreary and chilly. I despaired of ever finding a decent used car. I went to bed early, feeling deflated.

I woke up the next morning, fully expecting to feel awful once more. But the sky had gone back to bright blue. There was heavy mist on the mountains as we drove to school, as though the hills were defrosting. And speaking of frosting, it was time for me to bake that cake and get the party started.

First, my world was enchanted. I was 5, or 16, or 34, and I believed all sorts of magic tales and feared all sorts of imaginary dangers. Nothing had a name, and anything was possible. I tested out ideas in the world of fantasy, groping in the dreams and the dark to try to catch onto something solid and real and sensible. I learned so that I would be ready when the dragons come to call.

And then I was 8. Or 18. Or 38, and suddenly the magic peeled away to show me things as they really were. I stepped out of the gates of that big garden and felt the weight of knowing: the weight and the privilege. I wondered how I could have been so blind. I was angry at the old lies, and mourned them at the same time. Everything decorated with *fleurs-de-lis provençales* was suddenly smushed down to earth in the brasserie in the mall.

But then. Then I turned 11. Or 27. Or 39. Or maybe someday 92. After the magic part, and then my subsequent cranky disenchantment, there was a moment when the realness of the world took hold, and I no longer mourned or sought the old stories. I began to sort the world I had named, to alphabetize it and file it according to a system I made for myself. I began to make good use of the world. Realizing that nobody was going to keep the garden for me, I started tilling it myself.

The world itself was animated and growing, rather than magic and enchanted, and I got the privilege and the challenge of living in it clear-eyed. The dragons often revealed themselves to be dangers that I could fight myself. Sometimes I could see that they were horrors of my own making. And sometimes, they came barreling down out of a clear blue sky with a force from which nobody could protect me or the people I love.

But thus far fortune has given me more smiles than I deserve. The handsome Prince Charming became my husband of sixteen years, someday fifty if we both continue with our luck. The princesses turned eight and ten, smart and sassy and sweet, sometimes impolite and always imperfect, not unlike like their mom and dad.

At Abigail's birthday party, we ate our pasta and laughed at all of her jokes. She ripped open the wrapping on all of her toys in three minutes. Grace started to hula hoop in the front yard while Bill opened her tubes of toxic plastic goop that they all blew into translucent bubbles with a little straw. Abigail blew out her candles and we laughed some more.

Then we sat together on the sofa, warming ourselves around the screen of the MacBook. We ate popcorn and candy and watched *Harry Potter*, a movie in which digitized actors pretend to be enchanted. And it was all way better than magic, to be hugged that close together, safe and warm in the dark.

PART TWO:
JOUER À LA MAISON
(PLAYING HOUSE)

CHAPTER FOUR:

"You Live Here?"

W HEN I WAS A LITTLE GIRL, my grandfather made a dollhouse for my sister and me: a replica of my family's big white farmhouse with its green shutters. I would play for hours, setting the furniture, the food, the family members, and the always-in-season Christmas tree in place, moving everything around, and then setting it back. Often our crazed orange barncat would climb in and terrorize the interior decoration, sometimes chewing on the mother or the baby of the family. But his depredations just gave me another pleasant and welcome opportunity to sort and put everything back where it belonged.

Since way back when, my dreams have been about houses. In scary dreams, there is a fire and I can't get outside. Or I dream that someone is coming to get me, and while I'm hunting for a place to hide in closets or even drawers, I panic, realizing that not one lock works. In more benign dreams, I visit places I knew long ago, and rediscover each knob and cabinet and door in great detail. The most exciting dreams are fantasies of enormous rooms with ceilings sixty feet high, sometimes with a giant freshwater pool with a fountain in the middle.

Other people dream of flying, finding rubies, or getting it on with the captain of their high school swimming team. My dreams are nearly all houses. It's not just fancy real estate porn, although there is a certain amount of lusting over that giant indoor pool. Rather, my dreams reveal my deepest craving: a white linen, chocolate chip cookie, deep bathtub, puffy comforter, soft sofa, stone gate, everybody's together feeling of being fully at home.

In the darkest days of my life, I would dream that entire new wings were hidden in a house I was living in at the time. I might open a door in my crummy graduate-student rental, and there would be room upon room of new beautiful spaces, full of old velvet and mahogany furniture. "How did I not open this door before?" I would inevitably wonder, my deepest wishes fulfilled by new open space and great old dressers and sofas. When I woke up, back in my old familiar room, with my old familiar problems swimming back to the surface, I would try to hang on for as long as I could to that sense of the possible lurking just inside the real. If I could only find the door.

The spring before we left for France was one of my low moments, and I had a whole lot of looking-for-home dreams. For months, those dreams would take me back to my grandparents' farmhouse. Upstairs and way back on the south side of the house, I would find a door, and open it again and again to find room upon room of old carpets and big wooden antiques. Each new room felt eerily familiar and birthday-present new at the very same time.

These house dreams skate the thinnest possible line between the metaphorical and the literal. I crave the feeling of home. Houses make me happy. Their symbolism is so immediately apparent as to be almost embarrassing: why do I always have to be so damn transparent? The truth is simple and straightforward as an old foursquare colonial: houses are important to me in a way that my family is, that writing and thinking and teaching and sunlight are. That love is.

I say all this so that you can see what it felt like for me to walk into *Bastide de la Loge* for the first time. This new old house plunged me fully and giddily back into pure enchantment. All of the wish-fulfillment extra wings of houses I ever discovered in my dreams had been put together by some sort of genius dream-architect. And then I was given (if only for eight months of off-season rates) the heavy iron key.

When we were planning this trip, we rented both of the places we would stay based only on internet marketing and our budgeted price point. When we found the first place to land, that olive mill so dreamily named *Les Baumes*, we thought it was the most luxurious and impressive property we would ever in our lives inhabit. Over the course of the spring before we left, I had developed increasingly cold feet about moving overseas at all; Bill knew that a great first impression would win over my confidence, and he was relying on *Les Baumes* to be the house of my dreams.

Bastide de la Loge, in contrast, looked pretty nice online, just somewhat less impressive. In our minds, we were going from a fancy Hamptons rental back to a realistic sort of place in which to spend the longer spread of our time. We liked its location right near the school. We liked the fact that it was big enough to have guests visit us. The phrases "washing machine" and "American-style refrigerator" may have played into our decision.

Our last day at *Les Baumes* was one long, shameful, and sad little episode of packing and tidying up, yelling at the kids, final dead-millipede rounds, and eating through the last bits of leftover yellow cake with chocolate frosting. The rain wouldn't stop falling, and everything I stuffed into bags felt distressingly damp. Tumble dryers are either illegal or blasphemous in France; I was afraid to ask which. We left Sillans for Aups for the final time, snapping a picture of the sign with the red slash through the town's name that told us we were at its edge and moving into new territory.

I knew I would miss *Les Baumes*, a place with a name rather than a number for an address. I would miss the view over the valley to the cliffs. I would miss our waterfall, and the sweet little bedrooms and (yes) even standing at the edge of the yard and gazing up at the sun while hanging all our clothes on the line to dry. There might never be a full moon like the one we watched rise in the east and set in the west.

We arrived at *La Bastide* with battered boxes, bursting luggage, and supermarket shopping bags full of old groceries, damp laundry, and new birthday presents, and knocked at the heavy oak door. Jessica welcomed us into the house's courtyard, with its deep blue stone saltwater pool, stone lions and turtles and tables, and enormous potted plants and glass bottles everywhere.

From the side of the house I had seen, it appeared to be just one and a half stories, with almost no windows. However, as I walked into the courtyard, I saw that the hill had camouflaged the house's true scale. Jessica explained that *"bastide"* does not just mean "house" — it denotes a great big fortified house with an impressive position in the town. A dozen and a half big blue-gray shuttered windows were stacked three-high along an enormous western-facing yellow wall. The courtyard was about four times as grand as I had thought, given the photographs online, and it made me inordinately happy just to be inside its walls.

Jessica and Gerard had just finished cleaning the house after the final summer renters. The doors and windows were thrown open wide, and Gerard poked his head out to greet us from within, welcoming us into the cool, dark interior. As High Priestess of the Church of Perpetually Delayed Gratification, I was still taking in the scale of the courtyard, and almost wanted to wait outdoors and stare for a while before allowing myself inside. When your dreams are about to come true, it's important to take in the magnitude of the moment.

Grace named it first: the House of Wonders. She disappeared, swallowed up into its many rooms, and instantly took to opening every drawer and finding hidden keys, old candles, fancy cut glass, piles of ancient stationery, and yellow-and-blue stoneware platters stacked 20 high. Abby scampered out to the garden, looking for snails and fossils. As Bill listened to Jessica tell him about the quirks of the plumbing and how to work the keys and the washing machine, I just wandered from room to room alone, taking it all in.

Every surface of every wall — up and down the entryway staircase, along the halls and inside each of the bedrooms — was hung with eclectic and stunningly quirky original artwork, stacked almost floor to ceiling wherever there was an open place for a hook. Most pieces were askew a little more than slightly. Aside from the frames on the artwork itself, there wasn't a right angle to be found in the place.

Off to the right, the kitchen was stuffed with enough pots, pans, stoneware, colanders, platters, spice jars, honey pots, wooden spoons, teapots, English cookbooks, Moroccan pottery, coffee cups, and old baskets to stock a kitchenware store. The kitchen walls were lined with green and yellow tiles, and there were two wall ovens, four gas burners, and two electric. A big stone sink sat in the window between the enormous wooden kitchen table and an even more enormous stone one just outside, under a metal trellis hung with a green canopy and wild climbing vines.

I thought to myself: it's the food, stupid. And this time, I was going to be the one making it. My survival-mode days of heating up leftovers to keep my family alive were officially over, and I would let the kitchen turn an average Josephine like me into the Barefoot Goshdarn Contessa. I felt as though I had stepped off the little scooter I had been pushing around for years and had hopped into the Formula 1 racing car of kitchens.

On the other side of the hallway was a dining room with dark red walls and Moroccan art. Jessica's mother, the remarkable personality who reveled in the project of decorating the house, lived in Morocco when she wasn't in London or the South of France. The table was very old and grandly scaled, with embossed leather on top. Beyond the dining room was a great big room with an enormous stone mantel, low coffee tables, and big plump sofas covered in big shaggy Berber blankets. Joy of joys for the other three members of my family, there was also an enormous TV hooked up to a satellite providing them with hundreds of shows. In English. This for the children who had been deprived of cable TV their entire lives, on principle.

I stopped there, just for a minute. I wanted to savor the sense of there being more to discover. I bet Lewis and Clark felt sort of that way, say in Ohio. They had already seen so much, and there would clearly be more. They couldn't have predicted the Grand Canyon, or the Rockies, or even the alternately scary and soothing feeling they would have in facing the Great Plains. I knew there were bedrooms upstairs, probably with more art and big square pillows and enormous stoneware lamps with crazy chintz patterned lampshades. I was thinking there would be a bathtub, maybe two. I was looking just then for stability and ease, so to me a really good bathtub might as well have been the Great Salt Lake.

I hadn't banked on two full floors of more bedrooms. The place kept swirling upward and onward forever. More tiles, more rugs and pillows, and extremely beautiful, quirky, and arresting original art everywhere. The house just kept expanding in front of me, filling itself up with strange old puppets and a treasure trove of books, and an enormous crazy-quilt of women's hats hung over the master bed.

I was suddenly and deeply in love. With a house no less. I had that sense of home, but also the thrill of discovery I had when I used to poke around the back bedrooms of my grandmother's attic, full of old toys and papers and photographs from decades of my grandparents' lives, before any of us were born.

When I first got to *Les Baumes*, the air whispered to me through its open nighttime windows — you're here — welcoming me to time, to reflection and attention and sensation. At the *Bastide*, the walls and the windows and the hundreds of secret drawers and corners called to me anew, promising something like the safe place I had dreamt about all those years.

Actually leaving the house was a different story. Outside of the fortified stone walls of the *Bastide*, I was still in bumbling American mode with any establishment except a restaurant, where I could read from the menu instead of generating words myself. *Je m'appelle la stupide américaine*, I could have introduced myself, if I could ever get the courage to open my mouth. I was overwhelmingly self-conscious about everything I so obviously didn't know.

Back in Brooklyn I could read all of the signs in all of the stores, and I frequently knew what time it was. I knew which sketchy looking guys on the street were harmless, which were shabby hipsters, and which were to be avoided at all costs. I could type on a computer for seven minutes or so, and then boxes of predictable groceries that I knew how to heat up in our microwave would be delivered to our kitchen 24 hours later. I didn't have to worry that they might bring me horse meat or strange kinds of mushrooms if I made a mistake. In Brooklyn, I had earned my place. I gave help, others provided help; we helped each other, unless we were too busy getting more coffee or running off to work. In fact, I prided myself on being one of those super-bossy helpful New Yorkers who walk up to strangers and give them directions whether or not they are actually lost. I took for granted these accomplishments and skills, so much so that I didn't even give myself merit badges.

There in France, I was a city slicker in someone else's country. None of my skill sets applied, and I didn't even know who to ask for help. Thus, in France, all four members of our family became fully dependent on the kindness of strangers, as we were clueless idiots hitchhiking a ride on someone else's community. Like Blanche DuBois, alone in a strange town with lots of French speakers, we had to use our charm to get by. Bill, the only one with reliable access to language, could employ his wits. The rest of us just had to trust in the goodness of other people, hoping we were adequately adorable, which is easier if you are under 35. I just made like Blanche and kept the lights dim.

Instead of being impressed with myself for helping people all day long, I had to learn to be grateful while letting myself be helped. Back home in Brooklyn, I took my pride and self-sufficiency to illogical extremes, even trying never to go to the doctor without first diagnosing my own illnesses. But when I pulled a weird muscle in France, I had to rely on the French medical system to tell me whether I was broken or just bent. The nice doctor I met with in Draguignan amply rewarded my faith in humanity by instantly shifting out of French and into English at my first blank stare. He was born in Greece, moved to Belgium, was educated in Germany, and spoke in an almost perfect American accent. All that and a doctor too; maybe he had superpowers. He asked me pertinent questions, probed where necessary (literally and figuratively), and reassured me in full, and in English, that all was well with my insides. Full price cost less than a co-pay back home.

Even hardy traveler Bill sometimes needed help in France. When Bill was gearing up for the epic hiking adventures he had planned, Gerard insisted that Bill would need an epi-pen to protect himself in the event of a snakebite, and directed him to the town pharmacy.

Old Rugged Bill would have blown off this suggestion and gone up to the hills in his flip-flops and some old cutoffs. He would actually have gotten a viper bite, then lived, then told an amazing story about it at dinner parties forever after. But something was gradually changing in Bill's approach to adventure. In France, he was the only one who could take care of us. He recognized that he was the only one who could use verb tenses accurately, or communicate with immigration authorities. Aware of his responsibilities for his displaced, helpless family, a new Careful Bill was taking fewer chances.

At the pharmacy, when he asked after the epi-pen, a cadre of pharmacists conferred among themselves for ten minutes or so before determining that an epi-pen would not be necessary for a standard-issue human being on a standard-issue hike. They also delivered a lengthy disquisition on the symptoms of anaphylactic shock, the physiology of allergic reaction, and the different sorts of snakes in the region. Imagine that: he went into a store, looking for help, and the people there selling things actually concluded that he didn't need to buy what he came in to get. This level of conversation simply never unfolds with the disaffected teenager you are likely to meet stocking band-aids at your local CVS.

Every single interaction the members of our family had with physicians, pharmacists and insurance companies in France reassured us about the essentially helpful nature of socialized medicine. A doctor's visit cost 22 euros (about $35.00) *without* a social security card, a cost that would be reimbursed to citizens of the European Union. We got appointments right away, and were seen by qualified and efficient doctors who seemed actually to care about our wellbeing. When we needed one, we got a specialist without having to make supplicating telephone calls to our insurance company. Everybody gets equally great care: rich and poor, young and old.

People can be complicated, messy, and difficult to talk with. But then again, when you join several million of them in a nationalized health care system, you spread out the risks and the gains so widely that everybody feels they've gotten a good deal. You are not a consumer, but a member of a community.

Unlike us Old Rugged Americans, French people are not making the awful choice between paying massive percentages of their salary for medical care and health insurance and going without. They don't have to save and borrow to send their kids to college, either. Instead, they share. Nobody gets the enormous piles that our billionaires pile up. But the French seem less invested in protecting their billionaires than we do: instead, they protect their own.

As I was beginning to get the hang of listening to French NPR, I heard that Nicolas Sarkozy was in Pittsburg at the G-20 trying his darnedest to get Americans to understand what they are missing in their insistence on holding capitalism as the highest possible value. It was the top story that day in France, and got extended press. Apparently the French were done being all irrationally angry with us about the second Gulf War, and wished to share a few of the things they had learned.

Sarkozy, never one to shy away from drama, was nearly on the verge of tears trying to explain the lessons of enlightened socialist societies. I wasn't sure whether to feel sorry for him or sorry for Americans when I looked at that day's American newspapers and realized that this top story in France was buried deep in the back pages of *The New York Times*. Likely the story never made it out of the Metropolitan papers and into the small town dailies. The article I found wasn't so much about Sarkozy himself as the hero (that was the story in France) but rather about a more fundamental question: what is the proper measure of a nation's strength: its GDP, or the quality and strength of its communities?

He (and the French people) invited us to ask not how much political and economic *freedom* we have, but how much "*bonheur*" — a specifically French version of happiness that is not actually the same as happiness — is enjoyed by the members of our communities. And by communities, he means *all* the people who live in that community, and not just the ones lucky enough to have a MasterCard currently and recently topped up with yet another home equity loan.

At the pharmacy, we not only got great assistance, but also a recommendation for where to get a haircut. When you are cursed with really bad hair like mine, the prospect of making it worse sometimes induces a sort of anxious avoidance. I knew that my roots had grown out to a ridiculous sort of four inch-wide mousy brown stripe over the top of my head, but I was even more fearful of saying the wrong thing and ending up with frosted tips or a reverse Mohawk or a military buzz cut. But when I saw a pharmacist with a particularly excellent dye job, I gave Bill the difficult task of chatting her up to get the name of her salon.

She was duly flattered to have the tall American asking her how she got so damn beautiful, and ponied up the card for *Pascale Coiffure*.

It's one thing to rely on strangers who speak your language, which is essentially what you do every time you go to a new hair salon. It's yet another thing when you don't know the words for "blonde but not so blonde that it looks white or super-trashy, but not so subtle that I feel cheated when I walk out of your shop" or "short but not like puffy on top or too layered, with little wisps by the ears but none at the nape."

Pascale turned out to be extremely kind, and we weren't strangers for long. She and I communicated through the language of those weird books of hair photographs and franglais. "*Comme ça, mais* not *comme ça exactement* here on the *haut* of *la tête*." I was relieved when whatever I said caused her to bring out the highlighting foils and a purpley-blue sort of mush that looked just like what the hairdresser painted on my head back home.

We chatted, and she filled in words I didn't get. She was French and averred that she rarely leaves the Var. However, she was born and lived in California until she was seven, so she could follow my English when my French broke down. We got on famously, laughing knowingly about the *provençal* accent when a man came in and twangingly asked if he could get his hair cut "*demang*," rather than "*demain.*" We talked about French homonyms (*verre* for glass, *vert* for green, and *vers* for something else I couldn't quite follow. All are pronounced "vare" but with a little attitude in the r.) And I ended up with a perfectly serviceable cut.

There is nothing like a good haircut to improve one's sense of *bonheur.* Perhaps it is only a matter of time until France socializes the beauty industry as well.

House? Check. Medical Care? Check. Dye job? Check. We were no longer floating vacationers, but slowly were becoming grounded residents. Or at least playing at it.

The basics dealt with, we moved on to a more challenging purchase: the car. Our 180-day rental was ticking down day by day. Of course, when I went to count, it occurred to me that not only was I not crossing days off the calendar, but also I was actively wistful to see each and every sunset. It was amazing how good my head felt once I removed the anvil of responsibility that I had been balancing so precariously.

Following the vein of this sort of hedonistic mindset (I will wear no anvils for a whole year!!), I was hoping for something exciting to drive once we ditched the underpowered Renault. My goal was to have a lust-worthy automobile for the sweet short time we were in France; not a Porsche or something crazy like that, just a sweet and sensible cute German machine. I shalt not covet my neighbor's house, despite my penchant for real-estate porn, but I sure as heck covet nice cars.

Back home, I was much less of a spoiled brat, recognizing how lucky I was to have a car at all. I don't love ours, but I am certainly resigned to what is reasonable, and there are few cars more reasonable for a family like ours than a doggy-smelling, parking-battered Toyota RAV4. But in a year away, when the rules all added up to unreasonable, why shouldn't I give in to my baser automotive desires?

Bill had his own goal: to lose as little money as possible in the short span between purchase and resale. As he frequently points out, with impeccable logic, a dollar saved is way better than a dollar earned, since you pay no income tax on the saved one.

After we looked at a few used cars in Draguignan he nearly memorized Argus, the French version of the U.S. Kelley Blue Book. Once we realized that the standard dealer markup on a used car in Europe was *ridicule*, and that no used car dealer would bargain with him, Bill locked himself inside for three days and used our spotty internet service to set up a cage match among pricing, availability, and options. He took numbers from Argus.com and cross referenced them with "*Autos D'Occasion*" (which sounds really fancy, but is just French for "Used Cars").

And this is how he ended up calling a certain Mr. Chanson. He actually spoke to Chanson's wife first, but got flustered and called her an Audi. This didn't make a great impression. But things got even weirder after that.

When Bill expressed interest in his car, Chanson insisted that Bill meet him at a wine store parking lot, which was the first thing that made Bill nervous. Chanson was a few minutes late in arriving, and this made Bill even more nervous. He thought the women in the wine store might think that he was stalking them, so despite the fact that he had no service, he pretended to talk on the iPhone. When Chanson still didn't show up, Bill started to get worried that the store's staff would call the *gendarmes*.

When Chanson rapped on the window of Bill's car, he started to worry about other things. Suddenly, having cops around seemed like a good idea.

The thing that sent Bill from regular old car-buying nervous to full-on panicked was the fact that Chanson's rainwear had a snugly cute kitty cat theme. As everyone knows, items with cats on them are just wrong for a man of any age to be sporting, especially on an umbrella.

Bill also has a thing about cat people, especially kitties where they don't belong, like near an extremely tall, angular, super-fancily dressed middle-aged man. Chanson's hair was a bottle auburn, and both very thin and very done. His head was sparsely populated, but each hair was in exactly the right place.

Here's something else to know about Bill: he's not exactly a metrosexual. In fact, tidiness in other men gives him the creeps.

Chanson's shoes had a pointy toe that came to a severely acute angle. With a little ball on the end of them, they would have looked like jester's shoes, except they were black leather. He smelled of cologne and wore all kinds of necklaces.

Inspired by the low, low price Chanson was asking, Bill went and sat in the car anyway. Chanson showed him all the gadgets, of which he was very proud. In particular, he liked how the cupholders flipped out and then turned up at an angle, and showed off this feature several times.

Bill may not have appreciated Chanson's excessive tidiness, but he appreciated that the car was beyond clean inside. He liked the idea of a fresh start, because any car Bill touches invariably becomes filthy.

When Chanson asked Bill if he wanted to take the car for a test drive, Bill said, "*Oui, bien sûr.*" But even though Bill really liked the car, he wasn't feeling so "*bien sûr*" about Chanson himself.

It was pouring rain that day. As Bill started the car out of the parking lot, he realized that nobody, not even his family, would know where he was if he did disappear. "Oh my God, I'm going to be murdered and left in a French ditch," he started to worry, as scenes from *The Vanishing* ran through his mind. To fight off his unease, Bill started nervously chatting with Chanson about where in France he had bought the car.

"Well, you see," Chanson hedged, "the car is not actually French."

Bill paused, then said, "Really."

"Yes, it is from Belgium. And the license plates as you see are German. I really only insured it in France these two weeks, so I must sell it quickly. You understand."

Bill pretended to understand, as though this is just how things work here in the E.U. But the worst case scenario, bubbling up behind Bill's usually relaxed exterior, was that this car was not only hot as in pimped out with gear, but hot as in actually stolen.

Then, breaking the sacred rule of all good tourist-residents of France, Bill asked him what he did for a living. There was another long pause.

"You see, I am now expanding the operations of my business."

Bill should have left well enough alone. Perhaps because he was nervous, he pushed on in a way that is utterly common in the U.S., and utterly taboo in Europe.

"Really! What sort of business, then?"

Chanson answered quietly. "Well, it is a sex toy and adult video company. I drive a lot for work."

This was the only time that Bill saw Chanson looking anything but totally self-assured.

It dawned on Bill that he was now purchasing for his family a possibly-stolen car with uncertain national heritage from a man who also sells things we tend not to discuss in polite conversation. Unmentionable things that might at one time have actually been in that car.

I'm not sure whether it's a good thing or a bad thing that Bill didn't tell me all this until the strange man and his wife had come and gone from our terrace, and the car was wearing French plates and parked in our driveway.

When he did happen to allude to some of the circumstances of its purchase, our discussion got heated.

"You mean to tell me that not only did you buy a car from a porn dealer, but also that you aren't sure he actually owned the car? The guy with the white jacket that looked like a marching band uniform, with decorative safety pins down each sleeve? The teeny woman with the spike heels and the gold-plated cell phone that made the sound of a music box the six times that people called her during our conversation? Those super-strange strangers who showed up in our courtyard, took your check, left the car, and squealed out of the driveway?" I was using that high-pitched freaked-out tone that sometimes creeps out of my mouth when I'm not careful.

Bill defended Chanson as though he were his attorney: "I had no reason to believe it was stolen. Nor do I know whether the car was used to transport merchandise, whether legal or illegal. I was merely describing the facts as I heard them. You draw your own conclusions."

"No wonder that guy made everything he touched suddenly look like stolen merchandise. Do you think they were talking to X-rated video stores when they kept taking calls during our conversation and looking up prices in his notebook?"

Bill thought about this: "You know, once he told me what he did for a living, everything fell into place in a weird way. For some reason, realizing this allowed me to see him in a whole different light, and made his kitty cat umbrella seem less weird. I realized that he was just coming from a place I don't know much about. Probably in the sex toys and porn video world, he's known as a really stand-up, super-organized, and great guy."

I stood there with my mouth open. Sometimes this also happens when I am not being careful.

Bill took this as an opportunity to keep talking. "And you really shouldn't refer to them as strange. They are a lot more like us than you would like to think. They may not act like us, or dress like us, or talk like us, but they were really incredibly helpful."

"Bill, we are not helpful!"

"No, Launa, Jean-Paul was really kind to me. Or perhaps just desperate to unload the car before his two weeks of insurance were up. Sometimes it's hard to tell the difference when you're in a new place talking to someone from a totally different line of work."

I was willing to give him this. We were learning a lot of strange new things while relying on strangers. "I think I may just be reacting to his wife, as her dress was just a little more like lingerie than I am used to seeing in the middle of the day. And his shirt? I didn't know that they could even make fabric in a shiny black alligator print. And there they were on our beautiful rented terrace. I'm so glad Jessica didn't drop by. She might have evicted us right then and there."

Bill was quick to defend his new acquaintances: "There you go again. These are superficial differences. You have to admit he was very nice, and awfully polite. He printed out all those forms for us. But I was still freaked out by how tidy they both were. Her signature was the tiniest one I had ever seen. Who knew: dirty movies can be sold by tidy people.

"And you gotta admit, Launa. I got us a really great car."

It was true: she *was* a really great car, probably the nicest car I will ever get to drive. We even gave her a name, in honor of her German ancestry and her fuel cocktail of choice: Diesel Liesel.

Bill might even have been right about Chanson and his wife being two of the most stand-up members of the adult entertainment industry.

While Bill and I rarely think alike, and it often takes me a while to admit it, I love finding the method in his madness. His decisions are governed by a logic all their own. And when you get right down to it, he's right: based on his completely sensible decision-making process, we got a great deal on exactly the car we had hoped to find. I would have dumped way too much at the dealer with my squeamishness about negotiation, then lost even more on resale. When you're buying a car using your business mind, it really doesn't matter how strange, or how strangely dressed, the strangers are who had it first.

I also realized that this was yet another string in a series of ways in which Bill was using his wacky genius in a new way. His enthusiasm generator was still operating on high, but instead of dragging us on wild goose chases, he was taking awfully good care of us. His means may have been unorthodox, but it was hard to argue with his results.

Thus we welcomed to the family our hot blue friend Diesel Liesel. All of her adventures with us were strictly rated G. But while there were no more dirty movies in her trunk, her life was about to get a lot less tidy.

One afternoon, before I picked the girls up from school, I walked into town to the tiny market to buy enough butter to cook both French Onion Soup and Quiche Lorraine. I bought French butter of course, a substance that bears almost no resemblance to Land-O-Lakes.

While I was waiting in line, a sunburned man in a t-shirt and board shorts was using serviceable yet poorly accented French to ask the woman at the counter when the butcher shop next door would be open. Apparently there had been quite an awful injustice, in that there was an "*Ouvert*" sign, but nobody there to sell him any meat. And for this, the woman at the grocery store would apparently have to pay.

Our dear girl at the grocery store just looked at him blankly. There was no commerce between his question and her comprehension, and the fact that he merely repeated the question, louder, was not producing the response he desired. I decided to help both of them, first in French, then in English, telling them I thought it would likely open in ten minutes, just after school let out. I had seen the butcher's wife picking up her child at school, and then seen the shop open up again afterwards.

My little comment broke their stalemate, and when I spoke to him in English, he thanked me in British. That explained his rudeness to the French woman; the French and English aren't as fond of one another as you would think. I cautioned the British man, revealing in confidence a complaint I would never make in French in front of the shopkeeper: "You'd be amazed; it's hardly ever open."

The young man turned to me and asked, wonderingly, "So you live here?"

I learned the answer to this question, quite by accident, by hearing myself answer it: "Well, yes, I do."

He looked at me completely wide-eyed, and said with a kind of awed and completely friendly envy in his voice: "Well that's brilliant! However did you manage to pull it off?"

Flattered and pleased, I blamed and credited Bill both for the idea and for the execution. Then I confided once again, "The best part is that we're spending the whole year *without jobs!*" He congratulated me heartily on this impressive anti-achievement, and went back to not buying his meat while I joined the butcher's wife in waiting up at school for the kids to be released.

I finally saw it. Often the most obvious things escape me, and I was pleased to know that our exchange had revealed a new and important truth: after a long summer of staying places, there we were, living somewhere. We had left home so long ago, and finally come to live in Aups, our funny, sometimes-picturesque, sometimes merely down-at-the-heels little village.

The day after my conversation with the British dude of the board shorts, I ducked back into the grocery store to buy the girls a little snack for after school. There at the counter were three Americans, immediately revealed by something unmistakable in their dress: the cut of the chinos, the button-down shirt, the shiny shoes. We all imagine we look simply like ourselves, but really we are more strongly marked by our nations than we imagine. When one of the three spoke, and I could be sure of his U.S. bonafides, I butted into their vacation, "Oh, you're American. It's so nice to speak face to face with an American. I haven't done that since we moved here."

He admitted cautiously that yes, he was American, but looked a little guarded, needing to place me before taking the conversation forward. He was quick to pull out one of the rigorous questions that we Americans are programmed to ask (usually right after "Where you from?") in order to cut to the chase:

So what are you doing here?

The story of our trip had a title for situations like these. When we needed to impress somebody, we referred to "our sabbatical year," even though that wasn't what we originally called our plain old year off and away. It was shorthand, and while nobody officially granted it, the term conferred the positive connotation of doing something marginally useful within a career somehow related to the life of the mind.

Our American, of course, was a smart man. He wasn't buying my bill of goods. Rather than praising me for my brilliance in electing to live for a year in such a beautiful place, like the impatient young Brit had, he gave me a knowing look. "Ah, so you're an academic. So what is it that you're *supposed* to be doing, then?" He gently chided me, "Are you really getting anything done?"

Instantly I was snapped back to a New York memory. For almost a year, despite my great lie about *why* we were going, I found myself persistently unable to effectively answer the question that New Yorkers asked us hundreds of times when we spoke of our plan:

"But what will you *do*?"

They asked this as though without at least one job to anchor us, we might become babbling lunatics or lose all purchase on our right to continue to inhale and exhale the world's dwindling supply of oxygen. New Yorkers generally use doing, rather than being, to define a life, and couldn't imagine that anything would "get done" without paid work being involved. As we were leaving, it seemed doubly sinful that we were choosing to give up perfectly good positions at exactly the same time that so many people we knew were losing jobs against their will.

I had a hard time answering this question, not because the question was unfair, but because I felt so uncertain, and so guilty myself. When you go so long defining yourself by your work, it's hard to shift to the opposite tack. So when answering the American's more hostile line of questions, I did not, I as I had done with the Brit, brag about my treasured year of nothing.

"Seems like very little work gets done here," my new friend went further, and I had to agree that he was completely right. If any Americans had even heard of Sarkozy's proposal to start measuring a nation's success by the length of its lunches, vacations, and naps, they weren't letting on. They just focus on the hours of leisure as though the French are lazy.

But then I remembered to defend my adopted home, saying, "Yes. It's quite wonderful that the French have such different priorities." I then offered something about writing fairly regularly, but I might as well have told him I was spending the days making then burning a succession of paper kites without ever getting one into the air.

As we move from one place to another, we move from one self to another, and we ask ourselves different questions. When we change our where, we change our how and also our why. Back home, the question was always about work. The self I left behind worked a full day, every day, then spent hours past when I was required to be working sorting computer and paper files in a frenzy to get it all done. I worked to achieve the safety of certainty, which nevertheless remained out of reach.

How could I make things better? How could I get more done? How could I solve the insolvable problems? I worried all those nights, wished I could have done simply everything better. Somehow the laundry got done, food found itself on the table. But so much was poured into doing that we forgot to leave much time for being. Or being together.

When we moved to France, the questions poured in from an entirely different and unexpected direction. What vegetables were freshest at the market? What sort of wine might go with that? What should we make for lunch in order to cozy the girls through yet another challenging day of *blah blah* recess *blah*? What story would I write to seal in the memory of that new day? What sort of person was I becoming by asking all of these new questions all day long, instead of my old familiar ones?

———————

Of course, because it was such a small town we lived in, the American didn't just go away. We kept running into him, and his continued questions quickly put me on the defensive and got under my skin. After he saw through my "sabbatical" story, he kept pressing me on what I was really up to.

In my own defense, I decided that he was just another work-obsessed American, all button-down shirt and shiny shoes. Unlike *that* American, I was freeing myself to a new and higher calling: the holy purity of doing nothing. Unlike my straw American, I was seeing the *true* Europe, while he could only visit for his two week required vacation. And I relished all my judgments about him, all lip-smacking with the righteousness of the truly at ease.

But boy, was I wrong about him. Could not possibly have been wronger.

During our usual Monday morning shopping excursion, Bill and I walked past the outdoor café where the American, his wife, and his friends were having a cup of coffee. We missed him on the way out of town, but on the way back, he saw us first, stood in the middle of the street, and asked me how my day was going. Was I still successfully up to nothing? Did I do my vegetable shopping every day? Where could he and his friends get a decent breakfast around here, anyway? His friend joked, "Yeah, like an Egg McMuffin." At least I was pretty sure he was joking.

Up until this point in the conversation, I was hanging on to my initial impressions. But then the talk turned, slowly and with lots of warm smiles. Would we like to see his sketches from the day before? He had drawn his first cat, sitting under the plane trees all afternoon.

"*Très mignon,*" I told him – very cute – and he asked if *mignon* meant cat. Had we been inside the beautiful place in the center of town where they were staying? No? Well we would absolutely have to see it; it was unbelievable. Then wouldn't we like to come over at six? And bring the girls? Please, it would be their absolute pleasure.

He also asked if I had had success with my writing the day before, and he hoped that I had written about meeting them. I was instantly stricken, having in fact done just that, but not with such a *mignon* portrait — more a caricature of a much uglier American than the one I was facing.

He wanted to know even more today about our year away. His friend Harry was ready to move right into town, and having spent the afternoon at the café and thought over mine and Bill's plan, he thought that idea wasn't half bad. I realized that the posture I had taken as combative — all those difficult questions

— was instead truly, fully curious, and perfectly friendly. They invited us for a drink later that evening.

I dashed home to take out the more hostile sentences and soften my impressions. I wondered about the ethics of what I was doing — not only smearing a complete stranger, but then going back later to cover my tracks with a sweeter portrait as I came to see him a little more clearly.

At 18:00, we put a bottle of *rosé* in a bag with some ice cubes and wandered over to their big wooden door. Harry and the American were actually waiting outside for us, eager to usher us inside and show us around.

We got the grand tour, and the girls were received like princesses of the realm. Grace's "Nice to meet you" stunned me with pride — her directness, the sweetness of her smile, the confidence in her tone, and the openness of her eyes. She had transformed somehow in the weeks when we four had been so alone together.

The wives of the two couples could not possibly have been nicer or more generous, welcoming us to poke around all the many, many rooms of their rented palace and asking us gentle, friendly questions about our plans and our experiences.

The longer I spoke with the American, the more I saw myself in his questions and his half-teasing, fully-generous curiosity. Hadn't I always been the one asking the too-direct questions with an expression of total innocence and interest? Didn't I often skate straight over polite and into more dangerous territory without a second glance? We bantered about his children, our trip, our children, his 30-year friendship with Harry. While we all shared our grimaces about the weakness of those puny sad little dollars relative to the more solid euros we were spending, nobody referred to work, or one-upped anybody else.

The easy story of our trip is that we got there and realized that everything was different, and *so much better*. The food, the schedules, the schools, the philosophy, the people. The easy story is that Americans are dull and boring and midwesternly close-minded. It's the story that ex-pats tell themselves all the time, and often write in their romantic memoirs.

The real story I found was too complicated for any either-ors to find purchase. Our new world was better, and worse, but could only be evaluated and measured according to its own values, not mine.

The longer we stayed, the more comfortable the girls got with all of their new grown-up friends. Abigail started up a game of tag with Harry and the American, causing Harry to wipe out and fall down on the grass. The American showed the girls great magic tricks with a euro, and Abby didn't hold back on her giggles or her eye rolls.

Part way through the evening, the American took me aside and asked me, disarmingly and quite in earnest, if honestly our children weren't really quite remarkably bright. He praised their self-assurance, their vocabulary, their sunny and friendly and direct way of being with adults. He was fascinated by them and spoke with them without a trace of that condescension of adults talking down to a mere kid. If he hadn't won me over before then, I was suddenly putty in his hand.

A big long table was pulled out under an enormous spreading plane tree in the courtyard. Everybody got a glass of icy pink wine and sat down over bread and cheese. If we all just squinted our eyes a little bit, we could have been their children and grandchildren, and they our proud and doting parents, with midwestern accents.

Soon the girls and their new grandfathers were playing *boules* together under the trees. The girls would tease the grandfathers, and they would tease back, only a little more gently and warmly. The grandmothers told me stories of how wonderful Harry and the American are with their grandchildren — how the American has been telling an ongoing story to his grandchildren for the last ten years, and only now is the oldest one, at age 12 and on the cusp of adolescence, getting too old for it.

I gazed over at Grace, still grinning at the American's magic trick with the euro. How many more years could she stay perfect like this — caught just on the wire between goofy little kid and too-cool-for-school? If we are lucky, she will somehow take her store of experiences like this one and launch herself directly and confidently into the adult world without that awkward "adults are lame" stage. As if. Or perhaps even while she is finding me and her father unspeakably lame, overbearing, and horrible, she can still connect to the Harrys of the world: grownups like her grandparents and her teachers and her aunts and uncles, adults who remember to talk with her directly, to take her seriously, to find her as compelling as she truly is.

In my defensive posture, I was wrong about this American, and I'm probably wrong about a lot of us. I just had to fly a few thousand miles, and then see my girls — and myself — through someone else's eyes.

———————

Back home while Bill and I were working full time, all of our best social events involved a restaurant or a potluck. There are sacrifices that must be made by mere mortals when they work full time and raise kids. Unless you are one of a very few super humans who don't ever yell *and* crochet their own Christmas gifts *and also* run a successful company, you eventually get used to being disappointing in one or more categories. Life becomes all about choosing wisely what to suck at.

But during the magic year, while I was punching a big gaping hole in my resume, I did not need to split myself. Whole days went by when there was really only one thing to do, and thus I could do it with all my heart.

Around the end of September, I decided to invite all the French people we had met — Jess and Gerard, Mathilde and Laurent, and the nice couple who lived next door, along with all their children — for a lasagna party. To pull it off, I would need to become the kind of person who has exotic aperitifs on hand, who presents several courses at three different tables, who serves things like goat, sheep, and super-stinky cow's milk cheeses, and then remembers to make and pour espresso at the end of the meal. Previously, I might have been able to manage some of those tasks individually, but I had never had the luxury of six hours when the kids were at school in which to plan and execute such an endeavor.

But there was an additional degree of difficulty with this particular high dive: figuring out what exactly makes French people happiest at a dinner party. Our guests were all parents of young kids, completely devoid of pretense or snooty attitude, so I wasn't concerned about impressing. I was, however, eager to make them feel as at home in our house as they had all made us feel in theirs.

The menu cornerstones were easy to devise: lasagna is one of only two things I make reliably and well for crowds, and I picked that because it was still too warm for stew. Grace wanted apple pie. I planned the rest of the meal to include all the little French touches I had gleaned from eating there for a month and a half.

Buying the ingredients, setting the table, making the food, and worrying assiduously about whether I would be able to pull it all off took most of the day. To start off, I threw all kinds of cheese, tomatoes, vegetables, and butter into a shopping cart. Mostly, though, I bought alcohol. I wasn't sure what my guests would want to drink, and thought it would be best to have a lot of each of the three different colors of wine to serve. *A lot.* But there were the drinks before dinner and for that I would need to have on hand *pastis, crème de cassis,* and a few more obscure things like fig wine.

To figure out just what was meant by "*apéritif,*" I consulted my favorite fake book, *Joie de Vivre: Simple French Style for Everyday Living.* This book, a gift from Bill's colleagues on his departure, was written by Robert Arbor, the chef of the Le Gamin chain of restaurants in New York. His tone is pretty much Classic French Insufferable, but the book is full of direct and practical information and great simple recipes. He generously decided to take all the mystery out of the daily routine of French people — and I found by following his rules that he was actually telling the truth. He became my go-to-guy when I was puzzled by what exactly I should be doing, desiring, or thinking about as I visited the market, drank my coffee, or gazed off into space.

Our guests all arrived precisely 40 minutes after I expected them. If I had been back at home, this would have been when my pot-lucky guests and I would have been wallowing around in various cheeses, but I knew better than to serve cheese so early on. Instead, with the *apéritifs* we would have salty little snacks, like thyme-flavored pepper-crusted sausages, and little cornichons. Following Chef Arbor, I also scrubbed off some very pretty pink radishes, put out a bowl of soft butter and another bowl of salt, and watched my guests rub the first in the second then dip them in the third.

While we sat and drank and ate little treats, the kids ran around and screamed their heads off. They fought with plastic Star Wars light sabers, played tag in and around the garden, and required separation and forced apologies now and again when things got too physical. French and American grownups may do a lot of things differently, but kids will be kids will be *les enfants.*

Americans invented fast food, dining and dashing, Early Bird specials, and whole cookbooks just for things nuked in a microwave. France takes its time, and moves even more slowly if there is a table involved. The evening of the lasagna party, we sat outside for nearly two hours as the day turned to full-on night. After a while I pulled the lasagna and the takeout pizza from the oven (why waste good lasagna on kids who aren't going to eat it anyway?) and set the pizza out on the big solid kitchen table.

I then faced my first roadblock as a hostess. With the lasagna cooling on the sideboard, and our French guests smoking and enjoying themselves on the terrace, and my own limited command of French, I couldn't quite figure out the right moment or sequence of words that might indicate to my guests that dinner was served. I would wait for one cigarette to burn down and be snuffed out, and suddenly there was another lit at the other end of the table. The French men drank glass after glass of *pastis*, a milky-looking liquid tasting like anise-flavored poison. The women (and Bill) drank *kir* — white wine colored ruby with *crème de cassis*. Nobody looked even remotely interested in eating anything but buttery salted radishes and little rounds of wild boar.

When the rules between cultures are dramatically different, you can make some fair-sized social faux-pas without having anybody hold it against you too awfully. Here, I couldn't quite figure out the proper unfolding of time. Being the sort of person who rushes through too many things anyway, I couldn't quite get the rhythm of an evening unfolding in my (rented) house on someone else's only-partially-adopted cultural timetable.

I tried to translate, "Is anybody hungry?" into French, but my new friend Laurent only gestured appreciatively at the boar sausage. I tried to catch Bill's eye for an assist, but he was deep in conversation with Gerard. I asked the other three mothers, "Do you think the children should eat now?" but they didn't think that needed to happen at any time in particular. My administrative habits were getting me nowhere.

After several false starts, I simply interrupted, awkwardly gathering our guests around the table. I provided the tiniest bit of structure to the seating by asking the women to choose the orange napkins and the men to choose the *aubergine*. This meant that I ended up with women at both heads of the table, which is probably wrong in both America and France. *Faux-pas* number two for the night.

Serving and eating dinner turned out to be the easiest part of all — just a big old pan of lasagna and a multicolored salad with lots of little herbs mixed in. I assumed that the only remaining challenge would be to keep the wine glasses full all night long.

But then I hit cultural *faux-pas* number three. While I was rushing around getting the kids' plates filled and Bill was serving squares of melted-cheese and pasta goodness, I neglected to sit down at the table and give the proper "*Bon Appétit,*" which is French for, "Gentlemen, Start your Eating Engines." Our guests sat politely, but clearly uncomfortable, just looking longingly at their plates. Soon Bill figured out that something needed to take place, and tried the "*Bon Appétit*" himself. But without me at the table, the magic words were useless. Until my butt was in the seat, no eating could be done.

To my high dive of hostessing, with a double somersault for making stuff French people like, I added the twist of ESL: entertaining in a second language. I juggled plates and cups with remembering to put out the grated parmesan while also trying to follow a conversation that zoomed in high speed French between familiar subjects (the rambunctiousness of 4-year-old-boys; the difficulty of finding a good contractor; our kids' crazy teachers; sibling rivalry and what to do about it) and totally new and complicated conversational territory, including a lengthy discussion of criminal cases in which the Mistral wind had been accepted by a judge as an extenuating circumstance in a murder trial.

Over dinner, I offered my little opinions and jokes when I could — and earned at least three unforced laughs. I could hold forth most effectively when both the subject and the language were in my areas of strength, so I did my most impressive communicating with the children, using the imperative. I would say "*Ne fait pas ça avec le sabre de lumière!*" and bingo, the boys would cease whacking one another with their plastic Star Wars weapons. I could also ask the children questions, like "would you like *plus de pizza, mes petits?*" and "*veux-tu de la salade?*" (Not surprisingly, they did want another slice, *merci*, and no salad at all).

When the adults got on that familiar topic of rambunctious 4-year-old-boys, I could effectively reassure the mothers in attendance, as long as Jessica speed-translated me as I held forth. Yes, I said, many teachers misunderstand boys; yes, they will grow up into perfectly lovely children; and no, their kids probably wouldn't get kicked out of nursery school. Unless of course they bite, I tried to say in French. I found halfway through my sentence that I didn't know the word for this, so I grabbed Laurent's nearby arm and pretended to take a chunk out of it to illustrate my point. So much for my impressive professionalism and gracious, ladylike ways.

My bad manners were not the only danger in the conversation. Gerard entertained us with more Gorge de Verdon. It was re-determined that the pharmacist was wrong and that Bill *should* bring a snake-bite kit with him while hiking, and we were instructed to keep our children well clear of wild boars.

Twice Bill and I landed on a topic of conversation that created firestorms of controversy among our French guests: grammar and *pastis*. The grammar war began when I asked, as innocently as possible, about the intricacies of determining whether to use "*tu*" or "*vous*" when meaning "you" as opposed to "y'all." I was doing this, in part, so I would know what to call my new not-yet-friends. According to one guest, you use the formal "*vous*" at work, both up and down the chain of command. According to another, you "*vouvoie*" your mother-in-law no matter how much you think she really loves you, just to show your respect and deference. One member of our party asserted that he is above or below no man, and therefore he can "*tutoie*" everyone he meets. I wondered briefly how his mother-in-law felt about this, then recalled that he was divorced.

After this scintillating disagreement on authority and *politesse*, there was near-shouting on the topic of the correct ingredients for homemade *pastis*, the home-making of which is illegal. Apparently politeness and aperitifs get French blood boiling in the same way that real estate and the endless discussions of schools get New Yorkers really worked up.

The cheese course was served, during which I had what I hoped was my final *faux-pas* of the night: cheese courses require a separate knife at each place, like the extra salad fork at an American dinner. This time, the guests were comfortable enough to just ask for more cutlery, avoiding another long stretch of longing looks at their plates.

The kids got out of control, then corralled with yet another movie. Grownups took their smoking breaks out on the terrace, adding yet more scads of open and happy talking time to the evening. By and large I managed to follow the thread of the conversation at the most general level, until I got too tired and my brain got way too full. At that point in the evening, we had poured many, many bottles of wine into our happy guests (*all* of the many I had purchased, as well as the many they had brought), so it is entirely possible that they also were making a little less sense than usual.

By the time I served the pie and got espresso on the stove, I had worked out the grammar for an important announcement for my guests:

"*Ce n'est pas une tarte tatin*," I told them imperiously. "*C'est* American Pie." I don't know why it was so important for me to assert the American-ness of my dessert, to distinguish it from the loveliness that is *tarte tatin*. I had done so well in keeping them all happy, in (mostly) sitting down when I was supposed to, and (by and large) keeping everyone's wine glass full and (even) keeping my cool when the kids poured nearly an entire giant-size bottle of Orangina on the chairs and the kitchen floor. (My flip-flops were sticking before they flipped or flopped for the rest of the night.) I think I just I wanted them to know that this wasn't a bad *tarte tatin*, but a really great American pie. I could accept that they might question the hostessing skills of this new American in town, but could not bear for them to think ill of my pie.

They ate it politely enough, and exclaimed loudly about its deliciousness and its exotic difference from *tarte tatin*, but I caught their kids scraping off the top crust before leaving most of it on the plate. French people do not eat pie.

By the end of the night, all the kids were in various states of breakdown and exhaustion, if not already flat-out asleep on the sofas and the floor of the living room. French parents don't fuss over early bedtimes, relying instead on long restorative naps the next day. Nearly every napkin, plate, glass, bowl, and platter in the house was dirty, with a mixture of tomato sauce, red wine, beet juice, vinegar, incredibly smelly streaks of oh-so-ripe *Epoisse* cheese, and little bits of honeyed apple. There were bits of pie crust and crumbled pretzels everywhere, and a big sticky orange-smelling mess on the kitchen floor. Nearly every glass in the house was glazed with just the residue of *pastis* or kir, *Cinqueterre* or espresso, but there was not one partially-full glass. Apparently, in France, it's all good till the last drop, no matter how many drops are poured. We put away the food we hadn't eaten or mangled, got a full load of dishes in the machine, then crashed into bed.

We all slept in until after 9:30 AM, then it took us most of our free Wednesday (which we had taken to calling *Mercredi Libre)* to clean up. Without somewhere else we had to be, we could take our time, brew some coffee, share the washing, drying, and putting away, nibble on leftover bread and cheese, and get the wine stains out of those placemats with salt. Usually after a big party, I have to spend at least part of the next day worrying that maybe I said the wrong thing after one too many glasses of wine. In France, I hardly spoke at all, so I didn't have to worry on that score. Even after all my *faux-pas,* even with all those dishes to do, Bill and I enjoyed being together, and we both felt awfully proud.

Around midday, our very sweet new neighbor arrived to deliver our mail. She told me my French was really just fine, that it had been a "*bonne fête*": a great party. We were reassured that, yes, with this group, we were among friends, and therefore "*tu*" was the only way to go. I had laughed with a new friend about the American habit of smiling all the time, and he told me that among friends, one can't help but smile — his face lit with a big grin.

CHAPTER FIVE:
Traveling Without a Guidebook

I HAVE A PROBLEM WITH GUIDEBOOKS: THEY raise my expectations so drastically that reality inevitably disappoints.

Guidebooks encourage travelers to long for, prepare for, and pay for experiences that they fully expect to be glorious and wonderful. Some plan for years, coming to fully expect that their trip to Tahiti will not only be sunny and warm, but also served with a bottomless cup of sweet, icy drinks. In a word, perfect.

When they arrive, the sand is smooth, the hotel is newly renovated, and the people are five-star friendly. But what happens when they are 20 minutes late for the Tahitian dance class, or plagued with two or three nasty mosquito bites? Given how very long those travelers have longed, how high their expectations have taken them in advance, can that wonderful experience ever be exactly and everything they dreamed?

Can any human be spoiled without overhigh hopes spoiling the experience?

Once we were settled into our house in Aups, I was sucked in by the house's stash of guidebooks. Guidebooks help travelers avoid bad stuff and not miss the good, and better readers probably use them in precisely that way. But for some reason, whenever I spent too much time with my nose in one, real life felt impossibly tawdry — full of bad pizza restaurants, gas stations, and mini-malls. Which is sometimes what real life looks like, even in France.

Convinced by the guidebooks that I would have to leave town to find the *real* France, elsewhere, I began planning a series of trips to dreamy places with names that did not sound like "Oops": Paris, Avignon, Aix-en-Provence, St. Paul de Vence, St. Tropez.

Or rather, I began not planning those trips. Confusing The Rule of We're Here with the idea that unplanned travel would somehow feel more "authentic," I decided to leave my trips distressingly open-ended. My baby steps towards spontaneity made my travels occasionally transcendent, but all-too-often haphazard and strange.

For my first trip, I took the TGV from Aix-en-Provence to Paris to meet my college roommate Jackie and her mom, Loni. I had enjoyed having so much time with my family, but I also enjoyed the feeling of sitting on a TGV, zooming away from them at 200 miles per hour. I was ready to ride the coattails of Loni's plans and let somebody else be the mom for a while. Loni is a classic savvy traveler and memorized her Paris guidebooks, carefully curating the perfect visit. She had found a sunny apartment in the Marais, had chosen all the best restaurants, and had planned her museum trips and shopping expeditions with precision. I relished the idea of getting all the guidebook benefits without the pressure of making decisions.

I arrived just in time for the lunch that Loni had planned at Guy Savoy, the three-star flagship restaurant of the famous restaurateur. For Loni, this lunch was fully loaded with guidebook promises. She had been planning, reserving, and dreaming about this lunch for months. There was a lot on the line.

But as three-star Parisian restaurants had until that point been pretty much out of my league, if not out of my general awareness, I probably didn't long or expect enough to get to the heights that lunch achieved. It's like I just came along on the trip to Tahiti at the last minute, hopping on the plane as a tagalong without really knowing where we were headed.

As I drifted near the door of the restaurant, several people were on hand to receive me and begin meeting my needs before I realized I was having them. A doorman in a brown Guy Savoy uniform was there to spare me the trouble of opening the door all by my lonesome. Just inside the door stood a small receiving staff. Although they were French, somebody must have told them that I wasn't, because several of them were already smiling in my direction. This squadron received my umbrella, sussed me out to be sure I had a reservation, and then sent me through the second set of charmed doors, past several nervous young men whose only job seemed to be to say "*Bonjour, Madame*" to me.

As I learned later in the meal, a discreet and friendly staff member was also delighted to accompany me to the bathroom at any time, even on my second trip, perhaps to prevent me from feeling lost. In fact, they wouldn't really even *let* me go on my own. At Guy's flagship restaurant, all I had to do was let a desire cross my mind, and suddenly someone would arrive to fill it and then some, doing everything just a little more nicely than I might have even thought to request.

This led to an interesting phenomenon of Loni, Jackie and I — three deeply competent adults — being treated as helpless children. There were almost as many waiters as diners, and this ratio of help to helpless made me feel deeply tended, even just the tiniest bit controlled by a benevolent but ever-present parent.

As I was waiting for Loni and Jackie to arrive, I practiced my French bored stare while enjoying a government-issued reverie. I had skipped breakfast, and I must have looked a little hungry, because one of the nice men in charge of my personal happiness stopped by with a one-tined silver fork on which he had skewered *foie gras* and toasted bread. *Foie gras* is the silk of food, in that it involves both luxury and animal suffering, but is nonetheless irresistible.

There was only one other diner in the room at that moment, a middle-aged man sitting alone at a table and eating while checking his BlackBerry and reading the paper. He looked genuinely bored by the whole thing; I could compare him to the guy who does Tahiti's taxes, gets comped vacations on a regular basis, and has tired just a little bit of the whole lie-on-the-beach and be-super-pampered plan. If he was in Heaven, as I was, he didn't seem to notice. Although his lunch was as good as or better than any of ours, he was not at Guy

Savoy in the way that I was at *Guy Savoy*.

When Loni and Jackie arrived, they were fussed over just as I had been. Guy Savoy is renowned for deeply friendly service – almost un-Frenchly friendly. Nobody said, "I'm Kelly and I'm going to be your server!" but the smiles were not parceled out any more than were the rolls or even the desserts.

And then, almost as soon as we had been seated, Guy himself arrived to welcome us personally to his restaurant.

Yes, that Guy Savoy, one of the most famous chefs in Paris. In sports terms, this was like Peyton Manning coming to your seat in the stadium to say hi just because. Loni, never one to be shy, asked for a photograph to be taken, and Guy, never one to be stand-offish, brought in the official staff photographer and napkin folder to do Loni's bidding. Immediately following the several snaps, he invited us back to the kitchen. I was at first taken aback, then charmed and fascinated by the way his enormous staff stepped aside from their purposeful endeavors to allow us to feel special.

The wait staff initially spoke to us in French, assuming by our nods of assent that we understood every word. I was by then understanding 41% of what was being said, which I assumed would be enough to get me from the entrée to the dessert. Jackie's French was even better than mine. But Loni had many questions to ask, so our exchanges with the staff quickly and gracefully shifted into English.

There was much discussion over our order, and much helpful advice provided by the order-taker Hubert. Clearly Hubert felt that he knew better than I did what I might wish to eat. I'm not the kind of person who asks the waiter his opinions on the food, so it was just the tiniest bit strange for me to have Hubert expressing such strong feelings about what I would enjoy. Eventually I just decided to go with the infantilization, and let Daddy Hubert tell me what I wanted for lunch.

Jackie and her mother ordered one of the most famous specialties of the house. When in Tahiti, you really should have the poi. The "*soupe d'artichaut à la truffe noire, brioche feuilletée aux champignons et truffes*" was (as further described on the translated and embroidered menu,) an "artichoke soup with black truffles, slices of black truffle and parmesan shavings." Alongside was an ethereal "layered brioche with mushrooms, spread with truffle butter."

In every wonderful experience, there has to be a high point. Here at Guy Savoy, the high point arrived early, in the form of a corner of Jackie's brioche. Mushrooms are the only forbidden fruit in my house, so I don't like to turn down an opportunity to have one when I am out on the town. When Jackie gave me a bite of hers, it blew me away.

My entrée was little pieces of fish, "*goujonettes*." They were perfectly cooked, and arrived on the edges of a plate with a well the size of a big marble in the middle, full of the appropriate dipping sauce. Dipping was encouraged at Guy Savoy, explicitly so with the brioche and the artichoke soup.

In order to further encourage dipping, one of our six waiters brought us a little hand truck full of nine different kinds of bread shaped into fantastical shapes. There was a stick of seaweed baguette, a circular chestnut bread with scales like a dragon, and a small-grained bread with dried fruit.

Jackie and Loni ordered the Turbot for two people. The meal had already provided us with copious amounts of butter and cream, much of it mixed with truffles, and a great deal of it in and on the brioche. Their enormous fish, split down lengthwise, was brought to the table with its head and tail attached, then sliced and diced on a special table alongside us to be further sautéed in more butter.

I ordered "*agneau croustillant-moelleux à la graine de légumes*." This was "*different parts of lamb cooked with various methods: thin-sliced roasted saddle of lamb, stuffed and braised shoulder of lamb, and roasted lamb ribs accompanied with vegetable semolina, chick pea purée, and lamb stock*." Oh, and a gracious egg-shaped spoonful of mushed up spinach, flavorful as could be, and cooked to the consistency of extremely fancy and well-seasoned Gerber baby food.

The little pieces of lamb could not have been tinier, and I could not have been happier to eat every little one of the nine bites, and even to pick up the lamb chops and chew the meat off (like the dipping, this was also encouraged, by the kind offering of a silver fingerbowl with warm water and a thick slice of lemon.) By the end of this course, I was a happy little infant indeed, although I did manage not to spread the spinach puree on my face and hands.

A few other little things were served post-big-plate and pre-dessert, including a little floating cloud on a tiny silver spoon. Jackie and I each retain a vague memory of Earl Grey-flavored sorbet. But we still had some serious eating to do, as our good man Hubert had — at least an hour earlier when we were ordering — talked us into the concept of two desserts each. He was eager to have us try their three fruit desserts: a terrine of grapefruit and tea sauce, the wonder of a perfectly poached pear hollowed out and re-filled with pear-flavored ice, and a figgy delight topped with a thin cookie and then almond ice cream. According to Hubert, he doesn't often get to serve three women dining together. His come-on was that we could share these three things, then have the dessert cart later, from which we could choose a second (chocolate) dessert.

We had seen the cart nosing around from table to table, its many pots and tarts and containers promising all sorts of sweet bliss. And the menu had promised a spread worthy of Willy Wonka: "*rice pudding, caramel cream, prunes in wine and spices, chocolate mousse, 'diamond' shortcake, chocolate-vanilla macaroons, marshmallows, ice cream and sorbets (green apple, salted caramel), cheesecake, pies, wafers, chocolate sweets, dried fruit, and almond milk cookies.*"

By the point it arrived, we were all so sated as to be barely upright, but happily agreed to the flavored marshmallows (mint made with real mint leaves, and lemon, and strawberry with basil inside) and the chocolate macaroons, and then little scoops of ice cream, sorbet, and chocolate mousse.

Paris always surprises me by being somehow ridiculous in its fanciness, and intimidating in its demands, but also completely above and beyond. There you are, and the apartments are incredibly small, the garbage workers are on strike and blocking the way of your taxi. Your dollars are worthless, and your clothes aren't chic enough, and even though you're already perfectly attractive as you are, you start to think that you really should lose about eighty-five pounds. Especially after a three hour meal with Guy.

You think that the Tour Eiffel is too kitschy to be believed, but then they put little sparkle lights on it, and somehow it can be both over-the-top and beautiful at the same time. There is the Seine, and the stunning flowers in the Luxembourg Gardens. For Americans visiting Paris, all this pleasure is overdetermined, outlined by the guidebooks in advance. But Paris never needs to be exactly what you would have ordered yourself to be exactly as it should be. It shapes your desires around itself; it takes control, and you are best off just letting that happen.

After spending a few days in Paris, Jackie and I sent a sad and wistful Loni back to New York, and we headed back to Aix-en-Provence on the TGV. Our assigned seats faced backwards. I watched the misbegotten suburbs of Paris float into the future, then field after field of white cattle lying down in the rain. The whole trip spooled out backwards, setting Paris back in its place of beautiful impossibility and bringing me back to the boonies. Just after we crossed the Rhône from Languedoc into the Côte d'Azur, the clouds cleared from the sky and I was back to our eternally bright sunshiny day.

Once we were back in Diesel Liesel and on our way towards Aups, we called to check in on the crew back home. We were excited (but also a little apprehensive) to hear that Bill and the girls had been working most of the day to make us a special dinner, theme *franglais*.

When I walked in the door, there were delicious smells already there to greet me, even before I got enormous hugs and kisses from the girls. Abigail had high ponytails in her hair, and was already standing ready to pour us glasses of white wine from our favorite local vineyard. Grace was wearing a long yellow gingham apron and seemed impossibly grown up. She had been sick, or perhaps anxious, while I was away, but appeared to be thriving and happy. Bill attributed her recovery to the big turkey leg he found at the Aups market on Wednesday and the amoxicillin prescribed on Tuesday afternoon.

The meal was quite the experience. Grace and Abigail had both applied to be waiters at Chez Guillaume, and were competing rather than cooperating in their desire to get things to the table to serve.

Bill had put little radishes on the outside table, as well as pickles and little sausages. I didn't ask what animal they came from. It's never a good thing to think about these things too closely unless you're actually shopping and therefore deciding among donkey, wild boar, and regular old Wilbur.

While Bill pushed hard for Jackie to try some *pastis* for the full *provençal* experience, she wisely stuck with the wine. Grace and Bill finished making the French onion soup, pushing slices of bread onto the top and covering the whole with *Comté* cheese. Abigail treated us to some stories, some more wine, and some backbends. She loves to show off her backbends. I'm glad that she did them, and equally glad that the staff at Guy Savoy refrained.

I helped Grace to set the big table in the crazy Moroccan dining room and we all ate our yummy gloopy soup. Our wait staff once again leapt up to volunteer to clear the plates. I began to wonder if Bill had given the girls something stronger than penicillin to get them to behave this way, then realized that I was on the receiving end of actual gratitude. They were as happy to have me home as I was to walk in the door.

There were, however, significant missteps in the second course. The mashed potatoes turned out to actually be boiled apples. When poor Bill started to carve the duck, it seemed somehow to wrestle him back, requiring him to take the dish back to the kitchen in order to eviscerate it with his bare (now greasy) hands. Through it all, Jackie maintained her composure, and stuck mainly to the bread and olive oil, always a safe choice at a potentially problematic restaurant. By the time the enormous apple pie arrived at the table (with one big slice already taken out of it) the previously attentive staff had all quit their posts and were either dancing around the table or slipping off to watch Sponge Bob before the proprietor noticed.

Impressed with his style, and curious about his methods, Jackie and I questioned Chef Guillaume to learn more about his impressive meal. I was eager to know exactly what guides he had consulted to create such an, um, *unique* repast.

"Sweetheart, how did you come up with that great menu? I overheard you mentioning something earlier about burnt toenails. They didn't make it into the meal, did they?"

There was a long, thoughtful pause before regular old Bill became Chef Guillaume, renowned chef of the Cuisine Franglais, speaking in a fake French accent.

"Launa, you don't decide on a menu. A menu decides on you. I mulled it over for days and days, waiting for inspiration. At first I was going to make Duck à L'Orange, in a nod to my Franglais roots; I thought that a dish that American housewives could make couldn't be that hard. But when I looked at the recipe, it had a lot of words I didn't know. Even in English."

Bill continued, "And then I wasted a lot of time reading this Elizabeth David cookbook to get an authentic recipe for onion soup."

Aha. Elizabeth David, author of the classic cookbook that first convinced English-speaking cooks that they might make something other than boiled beef and cabbage. Her guidebook to French cooking is the bossy sort: it promises perfect results, but requires rigorous perfection from its followers.

"Didn't I tell you how to make onion soup right before I left?" I asked.

"Your recipe is fine, but I didn't want to take any shortcuts or use bouillon or anything. So I turned to Mrs. David, who had strong opinions on the topic. She seemed to think nothing of spending five full days just making the broth to get to onion soup. This seemed like the kind of authentic meal I wanted to make."

Jackie added: "I can get behind that sentiment."

Chef Guillaume continued. "But it was harder than I thought it would be. If Elizabeth David's recipe were written in stepwise fashion, it would start with: 'Find a cow.' Then 'have your man render the cow.' Then 'cook the other parts in these other recipes.' Then 'cook the cow's feet off and boil those for two days with seven different specific kinds of vegetables.'"

I guessed then about the source of the smell still lingering faintly in the kitchen: "Is that how you ended up with the burnt toenail problem?"

"Almost. I went down to the butcher and asked for good bones for soup. The first time I went he told me I could have them, but I would have to return. The second time, when he told me he would be there, the store was *fermé*. The third time, he brought out an enormous bone that was from a kind of dinosaur. He put it under a saws-all and told me to boil up two chunks, promising me that it would make delicious soup.

"I thought, 'this country rocks.' I did what he said, then followed Elizabeth David exactly. I cooked it for two days straight, while the kids kept complaining that it made the house stink. And when I was about to put it in the onion soup, I had a moment when I finally admitted to myself that there *was* a funny smell in the kitchen. I had spent a long time on those onions, and thought that maybe I should listen to that still small voice of fear before ruining them.

"I poured some broth into a spoon, took a good whiff, and finally admitted to myself that the kids had been right: the kitchen had been smelling bad for two days. And then it hit me, I knew that smell: it smelled like when you cut your toenails off and set them on fire."

Jackie was incredulous, much less willing to get behind this sort of sentiment. "Did you use to do that?"

Guillaume, suddenly Bill, was momentarily ashamed. "Well, not every day." His chagrin was only momentary; he had a story to tell. "But then I tasted it, and first I thought I was going to throw up into the soup itself. Then I thought, maybe this is just an acquired taste, like andouillette or stockfish soup, or most cheese: things that taste good but have bad smells. Then I thought, don't bullshit yourself man, this is serious. So I poured it down the drain. I probably should have flushed it down the toilet, but I had to get it away from me as soon as possible."

I asked Jackie, "Do you think Guy Savoy has ever had a moment like this?"

She was philosophical, as usual: "I'm sure Guy has had his toenail moments, although they might not smell like actual toenails. There is no way to reach levels of genius without failure."

Bill turned back into Guillaume, and agreed. "In the life of every chef, there are always moments when you think, 'What the flipping hell was that?' But there can be no antithesis without hypothesis."

I corrected him, "Didn't you get that backwards?"

"Whatever. This toenail soup was antithesis, for sure. So I resorted to using bouillon from the store. I guess once again you were right. But you asked me about where the menu came from. Once I failed so badly with the Elizabeth David recipe, I just decided, I'm going to go down to the market and buy whatever looks good."

This was dangerous. Without a guidebook or a benevolent parent to plan our experiences, sometimes Bill and I can go way off the rails.

"I was going to get a duck, because I like duck. At least when other people make it. I wanted to make apple pie to indicate the Franglais nature of the meal. Also because it is the only dessert that I have ever made.

"I asked all around the market for a duck, and everybody said, 'That lady sells great duck. But you're going to have to ask her today and then come back in three weeks, when the duck has been fattened up.' Luckily, this turned out not to be true. She had a perfectly fat duck for me right away, and she was very happy to sell it to me. But it was not prepared at all. It had been plucked, but when she pulled it out of the bag, it still had its head on. She had removed the innards, which were sitting in a giant plastic tub on the counter. She pulled the duck out. She told me exactly how to make it, which was exactly the opposite of what the recipe said. And I told her it was my first time cooking duck, and she laughed and said, 'You're going to need a lot of good luck.'

"She chopped off the head, reached into a bowl full of innards with her bare hand, and filled the duck with duck heart and guts. 'You will love these,' she promised. 'These are delicious.'

"So you are also probably wondering how I achieved that dried out, paté-like quality in the duck. I scrupulously followed two completely different recipes simultaneously to cook it. One said to do it on high heat for 15 minutes at the beginning, and one said to do it at the end, so I did both. I completely ignored the old woman in the market. Her instructions probably would have resulted in a nice juicy piece of duck that you could get anywhere."

I disagreed. "I thought it was delicious. I was only surprised it proved so difficult to wrestle into submission. Speaking of submission, Chef Guillaume, what can you tell me about your relationship with your staff? They seem to be a high-spirited group; much more so than Guy Savoy's. What is your ethic of service?"

Guillaume stayed in character. "My ethic is that I tell you to do something and you do it. This was in conflict with their ethic, which is that I tell them to do something, then they whine about it and ask to do something more fun. There was also a big fight over who got to wear the apron. I tried to fire them several times, but they kept coming back."

Jackie and I were really getting into the fun now. I asked her if she had noticed any big differences between the staff at Chez Guy and Chez Guillaume.

"There was a major height difference, to begin with. And although it might have happened out of view, I don't believe that any staff at Guy Savoy quit mid-meal and decided that they had something better to do. This staff here also let you have your space. I had the impression that if I got up and left mid-meal, my napkin would remain where I had left it."

Guillaume, getting a little defensive, demanded: "Well, I'm sure that dinner at Guy Savoy was great and all. But how well would he cook if he had to feed his staff and put them to bed while cooking dinner? Anybody can cook; can you cook with Grace and Abigail whining at you?"

Jackie took the edge off by redirecting the conversation to dessert, her specialty. "I was a little surprised to see that the apple pie already had a slice taken out of it. Did the staff revolt and take a piece?"

"Actually, that was the second pie, after the disaster pie. There is a little problem, in that apple pie is an American dish. So only American measurements work. And then when I was making the crust, basically I screwed up on a metric conversion. And we ended up with a ball of flour eight inches wide. And very dry and crumbly.

"By then the staff was shouting for more water. They wanted me to put the dough in the sink so it would get more sticky, and I tried to roll it out, it was a total disaster, and there were two tantrums, and they both got sent to their rooms. Actually there were three. And then a fourth when I came back, and realized what a mess we had made."

Jackie mused: "I would like to see what happens when the staff at Guy Savoy has a tantrum."

I guessed, "Time outs, and then Guy keeps all the tips for the night."

A duck, sliced apples boiled on the stove, a radish dipped in butter and salt, a pie missing a slice. Two beautiful girls jumping around and singing to us and giving us their whole hearts and their best efforts. A setting sun, and the people I love around the table. I loved every second of that meal, even more than the perfection of Guy's three-star restaurant. It didn't matter that the boiled *pommes de terre* were actually *pommes*, or that the gravy wouldn't thicken, or that the beans were cold. I loved every little bite, every glimpse of the girls, every hug they would slip in between courses and serving and clearing.

When you have dinner at Chez Guillaume, the whole is so much greater than the sum of its parts.

After our meals in Paris and Aups, Jackie stayed with us for a few days. We ate well, we went for long walks, and we explored places new to both of us.

On our first daytrip, back to Aix-en-Provence for a day of wandering and eating, we followed Liesel's rather confident GPS directions, and found ourselves deeply lost in the tiny winding hills in and around Cotignac. At least I think we were near Cotignac, because we saw nothing but olive trees and flocks of sheep. I followed Liesel's directions dutifully, even after it became clear I really shouldn't. She was following some outdated map, perhaps, with the slavish devotion of somebody who doesn't know any better. And I, equally slavish, was following her.

On our second trip, into Nice via St. Paul de Vence, she once again directed us onto a road to nowhere. Just as all the signs were directing me to turn left onto the Promenade des Anglais, Liesel insisted on a right. She chucked us onto the off ramp, into an office park, and then twisting in and out of the access roads of the airport. There was swearing involved, and while Jackie very kindly kept her cool, I imagine she wished at that point she were back in Brooklyn.

I could damn that Liesel all I wanted; without a guidebook or an internal map to guide me, Liesel's guidance was all I had. I learned, only after two wild goose chases, to trust her G.P.S. only as long as it was in accord with what the signs are saying and with all the other things I know. Liesel was generally a great asset, particularly when she helped me follow a path already laid out in advance. However, when she suddenly took me in the wrong direction, I decided I should no longer assume that she'd found an awesome new shortcut.

Not to put too fine a point on it, but I really need to remember that it is always me driving my car, and driving my little life, no matter what kinds of expert advice comes my way.

But speaking of shortcuts, we were going to find Modern Art — that most excellent shortcut between representations that were merely realistic, and representations that reinvented the world. On our way to Nice, Jackie and I spent midday and the afternoon in Saint Paul de Vence, a tiny medieval city that turned itself, through the good graces of savvy art dealers Aimé and Marguerite Maeght, into a paradise of incredible modern art, in a setting purpose-built to serve that art.

The Maeght's Museum is at the town's core. Not a bit of their museum is contemporary art. Instead, Fondation Maeght has dedicated itself to the modern: that universe of beautiful and strange work made from the nineteen-forties to the seventies by men (and one or two women) obsessed with new ways of representing humans and animals. While the impressionists revolutionized the representation of light and color to shift the way we look at the surface of things, the moderns took us back to our roots in cave paintings and primary colors and allowed us to see the outlines of the world anew. They were not afraid of a wrong turn or two, but instead followed their guts to get to the soul of the world. Bonnard, Miro, and Picasso were not waiting for guidebooks or G.P.S. to tell them which paint brush to choose and where to put all that black, red, and blue. They had a much more personal conversation going on, one that changed not only the maps but also the actual landscape of art.

Femmes et oiseaux (women and birds) were clearly Miro's favorite subjects, and he re-shaped them in sculpture, in painting, in prints, in books, and in ceramics. At the time of Jackie's and my visit, the museum's extensive Miro collection was on display. The Maeght family has so much damn art that they have to rotate their collections and they tend to show just one genius at a time, with just a few little Chagalls or Giacomettis thrown in to remind you what else they must have lurking in their deep closets.

At the Fondation, we went straight back in time to an era when it seemed like a good idea to see in radically new ways. Due to my new acquaintance with the cavemen of Southern France, Miro's work looked primal to me, even tribal. He didn't ever paint a pretty woman, or a cute little bird, but rather struck at the heart of birth or flight. There would be just the outline of a head and a beak: *oiseau*. Or a sculptured egg sitting on a chair: *femme*. Centuries of decoration and depiction sliced away, leaving only essences in line and color.

This museum's insistence on seeing the world anew extended past the art into the architecture, which uses concrete, rocks, tile, water, and glass in strange shapes and directions.

The whole of Fondation Maeght felt like the 1970s — not just in its strange design, but also in that it was so deeply unsupervised. No guards warded us away from the art; precious few signs mediated between us and the paintings. I got right up close to the droopy Giacometti dog, and the one-off Miro prints, and the incredible swirling perfection of Chagall's monster mural-size work, *La Vie*. While we were there, a few guys in regular clothes kept taking priceless Miros off the wall and walking around the museum with them, sometimes leaving them on the floor. As we were leaving, they had even taken down the Chagall and were huddled together looking at the lower edge of the frame. And because the Maeghts were dealers, not museum curators, you can buy the real stuff in the gift shop, not just posters, just as long as you brought along many many thousands of euros.

Here, the art is both new and old. I realized there, with a stupid sort of shock, that to be "modern" is to be dated. In most cases, it is to be older than I am. Jackie and I spent several sunny hours wandering around the museum, backwards through Miro's life (I missed the sign, in French, directing me in the "sense of the visit," which was clockwise, rather than counter).

On our way, we saw a film of Duke Ellington playing at the Fondation, around the year that I was born, riffs improvised on the spot and at least ostensibly inspired by Miro's work. The film was old and grainy, turned all blotchy with the process of digitization. Listening to that music, under the colored light coming through a huge stained glass window, was the most movingly religious moment I have ever had in a museum. Ellington's music, Miro's art, and me: all born into the world at the same moment. The music, the art, and me: all growing older with the remorseless march of time. But as I listened and I watched, I could also see that that music, that art, and I myself were all still just as alive and powerfully vibrant as we were the days we were created.

Change. Growth. Improvisation. Adjustment. Finding the new path out of the old patterns and places. Everything I was encountering those days spoke to putting the new into context with the old. This new life demanded that I re-examine and put aside the old habits in favor of new directions. That I update the old maps, stay open to new twists, and trust my instincts when life showed me that it was time for a U-turn.

Being so open to change was entirely against my better judgment, and the way I had lived a safe life. It was taking me a while to get with the program, to see the shape and the map and the context of the path Bill and I had put ourselves and our family on, and not just to flee stupidly in terror into various wrong directions, or slavishly follow an outdated plan.

To get where I am going, and not just plod the road well-traveled, I had to continually re-negotiate my relationship to the world in the past and in the present.

Take Liesel, for example. She was all *au courant* in 2005, but by the time I had met her, she had certain limitations, her map of the world fixed, stuck on the old paths. I wondered about her wrong turns: were they programmed in from the start? Did every driver following G.P.S. instructions get diverted off the Promenade des Anglais at the crucial moment, as she urged me to do? Did that account for all those cars making U-turns at the next set of lights? Was I destined to do the same stupid things that *everybody* does when they get to the exit for 40?

Maybe the road to 40 I was looking for doesn't even exist anymore, and I would have to make my own. If there is a guidebook to the longer journey of life itself, I haven't been able to find it. Then again, if I did, I might be better off ignoring the wisdom of the ages and improvising my own route.

Leaving for a year somewhere else was teaching me that I didn't always have to stick to the straight roads and the efficient path. Instead, I could let myself wander, and even get lost now and again. As I traveled, I hoped to gain the wisdom to hold on to essences: to cling to the best relationships, to my primal love for my family, and to the crucial truths, even as I was gaining the courage to eat and see and drive and learn and live in new ways.

My parents, David and Carol, came to stay in late October, just in time to carve a pumpkin and bob for apples with the girls. We suffered more than a few bouts of homesickness during those first two months of school, and we were all eager to see them.

We took a few more road trips when they arrived. Having by then mastered Aix, I carried out a trip that was a big hit. But I can't say the same for Avignon. This time I did use a guidebook, which led me to make reservations at a little guesthouse near the Palais des Papes run by two Parisians, M. and Mme. Chocolate.

Mme. greeted us in English and sent us up to our little rooms as the Monsieur breezed out the door. Mme. Chocolate was friendly, sort of, but wanted to rush me through her usual spiel of directions while drying her big mop of hair. She warned me off the tourist restaurants in the Place d'Horloge we planned to find, announcing in a high-minded tone that these simply would not do. Mme. Chocolate reminded me of those guidebooks that are more warning than promise — the ones that make you keep one hand on your wallet, imagining that the world is out to rob and cheat you blind.

The cagey, suspicious sorts of guidebooks invite your trust by promising to keep you from grievous travel harm and canned experiences. But I find these to be even worse than the shiny marketing ones, as they imply that there is always somewhere cooler and better than where you are. It's really great, but it's always a secret, accessible only to the chosen few.

Powerless fools, we had no choice but to follow her advice. Before dinner at the cooler restaurant, we walked around the high stone walls of the Palais, which is really the whole point of Avignon. A month beforehand, we had prepared for my parents' visit with a reconnaissance trip, taking as long a trip through the Palais as the kids could stand. There had been neat little cell-phone audio-guide devices to fill us in on all the history of the years that the center of Papal authority had been in Avignon. But I don't recall a single fact I learned there. Mostly I remember Abigail complaining that her feet hurt.

The Papal Palace is not a place for kids. It is a series of enormously tall bare stone rooms in which various ancient Popes made their decrees, ate their state dinners, and brushed their holy teeth. I could have been convinced to get into the creepy Gothic spirit of the place if I had been allowed to pay attention for five minutes. But Abigail likes attractions where you can be terrified in more overt ways, like by water flumes, sharp drops and leering wax statues. To put it most obviously, she's a normal kid, and what normal kid wants to spend a second sunny morning of her life hearing about how many chickens, boars, and eggs it took to make the Coronation Meal for Pope Leonardianiotonio the Eighth?

So when she saw the soaring towers and the huge gold statue again this time, she went on strike. "No More Popes' Palace!" she begged. "Don't make me go there tomorrow! It's so boring."

And suddenly as she spoke it was 1976, but Bill's life rather than mine. When Bill was in second grade, on his family's famous year abroad, they spent several weeks in April touring England. His family drove from cathedral to cathedral, flying along from buttress to buttress and nave to nave. They saw endless organs, saints, and stained glass windows. After more than a dozen cathedrals, Bill fell to his knees in prayer in one of the pews.

"Please, God," his parents heard him plead. "Please make my parents stop taking us to cathedrals."

The Almighty works in mysterious ways, and eventually answered Bill's plea, although perhaps not as quickly as young Bill might have liked.

That night we watched the moon rise, looking up between the huge white towers as we walked down the tiny winding streets. We ate our lovely dinner at the non-touristy restaurant, went our separate ways to sleep, then woke up early to get ready for Mom and Dad to visit the Palace, and Abigail and me to do whatever it was we were going to do.

Breakfast was nice enough, but I kicked myself for choosing a bed-and-breakfast. It was too quiet, too fussy, with a little silver sugar bowl next to those awful red-wax wrapped gross little Babybel cheeses. As is the case in most bed-and-breakfasts, there were cat statues and little Victorian details everywhere. Mom seemed to think that it looked like a home for "ladies of the evening," as she put it. But in my view, the place had neither the pleasant anonymity nor the liveliness a real brothel would have offered our solemn little well-behaved party.

It was time for us to leave to go be tourists. But just as I was paying our bill, I heard Abigail from the top of the stairs. "Mom. Come quick. Something really awful has happened."

I couldn't have moved faster. I saw her face, relieved to see that she was still breathing and not bleeding, and couldn't figure out what was the trouble. She led me by the hand into the bathroom, where the beveled and mirrored frame of a huge mirror had fallen off its plywood backing and onto the floor. It hadn't shattered, she was fine, and so of course I went straight to the interrogation.

Abigail might be prone to boredom and mischief, and she might sometimes be a little less tactful than we would all like, but she is constitutionally unable to tell anything but the full truth. "I just brushed it with my elbow" she said (it was directly next to the toilet, not ten inches away) "and it broke. Mommy, I'm so sorry." And I knew, without a shadow of a doubt, that while something awful had happened, she had done nothing wrong.

M. Chocolate was in the middle of getting my change when I went downstairs to break the news. He was bewildered and confused, but I insisted he come up to see. "*Ooo la la,*" he said, his tone far cooler and angrier than I thought it might have been warranted. "You have no idea how much this mirror is worth."

There we were, in a foreign city, staring at seven years of bad luck on the floor of this tawdry little bathroom. My parents were hovering a little shocked and anxious on the edges of things, and Abigail was trying not to positively wither with embarrassment. I thought the mirror looked like an old sort of reproduction thing, its beveled pieces glued onto thin plywood. But according to M. Chocolate, they had paid dearly for its antique majesty.

And now so would we.

A bed and breakfast is not the sort of place you really want to get into a full-on argument. So I mounted my tightrope, strung tightly between protecting my family, meeting whatever reasonable obligations I had to Mr. and Mrs. Candypants, and getting the hell out of there with my daughter's sense of self intact. "What is it you need me to do?" I asked again and again, in as quiet and calm a voice as I could muster. "It was an accident and we are all very sorry." I said this series of sentences approximately a dozen times as they tried to get a rise out of me.

Mme. Chocolate came up to inspect the damage as well, and to inflict her own. How could the child possibly have done such a thing, she wished to know. This was a terrible thing, a terrible and a horrible thing that had happened. She bitterly blamed herself (but really, me) for allowing children in the house at all. "Never, never again," she intoned. "Never will there be a child staying here." Many nasty things occurred to me to say in response, including pointing out to her that if she had any sort of policy against having children in the house, she hadn't mentioned that when I wrote — with Abigail's age in the email of course — to request a reservation.

"This mirror has been in my grandmother's family for generations," she told me, despite the fact that M. Chocolate had paid so much for it in the earlier version of the story. And despite the fact that plywood was not so readily available those generations ago. I decided that my best role in this particular drama was the quietly boring and appeasing bad tourist. The more times I said sorry, the less I raised my voice, the more I leaned over to tell Abigail "It was an accident," the quicker we could leave.

M. and Mme. Chocolate, for all of their distress, seemed unable to come up with any sort of action plan aside from wringing all sorts of guilt out of me. I must have insurance, they insisted, and I refrained from suggesting that they might as well. M. Chocolate mentioned in French to his wife that cash on the spot would be preferable, but I pretended not to hear. They directed a number of rhetorical questions Abigail's way before I decided to set up a buffer and speak only in French. The candy couple could be as sourpatch as they wanted in their own home, but I wasn't about to let it spill all over my kid. Presumably some day they would send me an inflated bill for repair, and we would negotiate and eventually I would pay some or all of it. For now, I just had to leave. I wrote down my name and telephone number on a little post-it, I repeated once again my apologies, and we finally cowered our ways out the door.

The rest of the morning was more rough than Rough Guide, not at all what the book had promised. As many times as I reassured Abigail that she had done nothing wrong, tried to jostle her along with "*Ce n'est pas grave*" (No big deal), she couldn't quite get over her hang-dog expression.

I too was deflated, guilty for not standing up to them, and sick with the thought of any more contact. I kicked myself for not taking a picture of the stupid mirror, for making the reservation in the first place. Mom and Dad went through the museum on their own, perhaps wondering why their otherwise capable daughter had chosen such a strange trip and stranger hotel. And why this trip to the palace of the Popes, they must have wondered. We're not even Catholic. Poor Bill had to ask his parents to stop taking him to cathedrals; my parents were too polite to ask me.

Bill's buoyancy saved our day. As soon as I got him on the phone, he promised that he would take care of any further communication or demands for restitution from the Chocolates. He is particularly well-suited for this sort of thing, both by profession and by personality.

"Sweetheart, it's only money, and they won't dare ask for much. But when they call, I'll pretend that I can't speak English *or* French," he told me. "I'll get them for intentional infliction of emotional distress. I'll ask them why they hadn't affixed such a dangerous object more carefully to the wall. Don't worry, honey. I'm great at flummoxing people like this." The truth of this statement made me laugh, and suddenly things were okay again.

Things went from okay to really great when our American-and-British friends Zaro and Gareth drove down to meet us for lunch. Knowing the town better than any guidebook experts, they picked out a great old-fashioned restaurant — not the tourist kind in Place d'Horloge, and not the faux-sophisticated one Mme. Chocolate sent us to. Perfect ratatouille, a big chunk of salmon for Abigail, and lots of those great sauces for which French cooking is rightly famous.

Through most of lunch, Abigail was quieter than usual. There couldn't have been a politer or more gracious little girl anywhere in the world, but I could tell she would rather be running around in an open field someplace with dogs, playing tag, or jumping on a trampoline. The world was suddenly so very real, and there she was in it, trying to piece together her childhood from strange sounds and new smells and odd trips to boring and weird places. She was both open and self-contained; carefully balanced and always an inch from tipping one way or the next. A little toy top, spinning and wobbling along her way, but never falling down.

In guidebooks about Southern France, the sunflowers and lavender are always blooming. They do bloom, and nobody needs to doctor the photos to make them gorgeous, but only in the months we didn't actually live there: June and July. The rest of the year, sunflower and lavender fields are razor stubble.

This was just one of the truths my parents discovered when they flew thousands and thousands of miles to come and visit us.

They missed us, and the grandchildren we had stolen from them, and so they had ample reason to schlep all the way to see us, even without the lavender. David, known as Pops, sharpened all the knives, then helped to teach Abigail to ride her bike. Carol, known as Nona, stitched up the Halloween witch costume that had badly thwarted me. They pitched in, changed spent light bulbs, did dishes, and gave us all lots of hugs. They settled in quickly and comfortably, as though they traveled to the Continent all the time.

Of course by then, we had adjusted our own oxygen masks, and could see to helping others. We had a few purely scrumptious dinners down pat, and knew our way around the wine and cheese aisles of the *supermarché*. We had mastered the art of the A8 highway tolls and the parking garages, and had finally internalized the French meals clock. By then, we rarely got stuck on

Sundays with nothing at all to eat. And Diesel Liesel and I had come to a better understanding.

Perhaps we should have stuck to our most well-traveled paths with Mom and Dad in tow. But having visitors, however familiar, raises the ante for daily pleasures and tourguiding. Our little trips to medieval hill towns were all fine and good, but we wanted to show off by heading to St. Tropez to dazzle our lucky, lucky guests (most likely against their wills) with the finest treats France had to share.

St. Tropez conjures up visions of a pre-political Brigitte Bardot in a bikini, and luxury yachts moored at the port. Guys in Ray-Bans and white shirts unbuttoned to the navel. Champagne cocktails, beaches, clear water, and endless sunshine.

My own St. Tropez memories are nearly as glamorous. When I visited there when I was 15, my French family took me to a resort with a pool and palm trees and unlimited chocolate mousse. My French family spent a day on a sailboat cruising around the bay and looking at all the enormous villas, then another day on a nearly-nude beach where everyone but the five of us was topless and barely-bottomed. Then the 20-something resort activities director, the tall, French, and handsome Jean-Luc, took an interest in me, and we kissed late at night in a hotel corridor while the wind roared outside. I get shivers just thinking about it.

That was then, 25 years ago. This was now, six of us driving South in two cars. In the girl car, we played Abigail's birthday CD and all sang along. Presumably the boy car spent their trip reminiscing about their earlier European tours, 50 and 20 years ago. Bill loved telling stories about his trip with Alain almost as much as he loved hearing my dad recount the road trip he took from Italy to Morocco in 1959 with American co-eds named Ginger and Polly.

As we got further and further south, we hit a long stretch of road construction, and clouds gathered above the empty hillsides. We passed into Ste. Maxime, St. Tropez's ugly stepsister, with her waterparks and roadside McDonald's and endless poorly constructed orangey-beige concrete blocks of vacation apartments. The only good news I could really think of to add was, "Hey! No crowds!" I guess the smart money packs up and high tails it out of St. Tropez a lot earlier than that cloudy, menacing November first.

Bill's plan was for us to eat a picnic lunch on the famous Tahiti beach. We had the usual sausages and bottled water and a few coconut cookies. But this trip to Tahiti wasn't exactly what we planned and hoped for. Instead of great accommodations, a sunny beach, and sweet drinks with parasols in them, we saw only the sad backstage of the vacation melodrama.

It took forever for us to snake through the walls and high hedges of the fancy ocean compounds to find the parking lot, which, when we arrived, we found simply *fermé*. Not just a Sunday-afternoon sort of closed, either, but a final-seeming, end-of-the-season closed. You could walk onto the beach only through a few dissipated and nearly-abandoned beach bars, their only sign of life the chalkboards still advertising massively overpriced salads and fried bits of squid. We poked our heads through, but the water was high and angry on the shore. The whole beach was strewn with dirty brown seaweed, looking a lot more Cousin It than Brigitte Bardot.

It was then I that I paused to consider what lay before us. I don't know why people make such a virtue of being "undeterred" in the face of unpromising circumstances, particularly when it doesn't matter, like when you're on vacation. Looking back, I see that deterred is exactly what we should have been right then. We should have hopped back into the cars to soak up the sunshine and familiar medieval hilltown joys of the Var.

But we are fools, we humans, drawn forth by our stupid happy hopes even when reality is tapping us on our shoulders with an insistent, bony finger. Bill promised that a better beach, a prettier walk, and a better picnic all awaited us in town. I was holding out for a restaurant and a proper restroom. The poor kids and their grandparents became mere pawns in our chess game, unconvinced about the promised glories ahead, yet politely unwilling to point out the painfully obvious: Bill was almost certainly deluded, and I was becoming an awful grump.

Back in town, we found an overpriced car park. Then Bill marched us off towards his beach. I ain't too proud to beg for a restaurant, particularly when it looks like it's just about to pour rain. But I was soundly and firmly overruled, and we headed straight up the St. Tropez version of Lombard Street. Winding our way, we passed the walls of the fort, circling around a long cemetery, where whole families were stacked up in big square above-ground crypts decorated with real and ceramic flowers. It was Toussaint Sunday, and there were chrysanthemums for sale to the living to honor their dead.

It was getting colder and more overcast the further we got from the car park. Of course, nobody had an umbrella. Bill promised us, "Oh, just another half mile" just as I was ready to join some other happily dead family in their crypt for all eternity among the chrysanthemums. And I despise chrysanthemums. Bill had long since stopped listening to my pleas, marching purposefully up ahead. I was dramatizing my own distress, sulking unpleasantly in the background. Everyone else was just quiet and resigned, not quite sure how this stalemate would play out. We hovered in the pause that became the snit.

We finally arrived at Bill's beach. I'm sure that in August it's quite lovely and picturesque, but in the November gray, it showed itself as a patch of dirty and trash-strewn sand. The picnic I had packed was a little too light on the cheese, and a little too heavy on the fizzy water for Abigail's taste. Grace launched herself out to explore the rocks that stretched out into the water. Mom and Dad were awfully good about the whole thing, exclaiming politely about the sailboats and the sausage and the fact that, well, wasn't the rain really holding off quite nicely. We all scanned the horizon hopefully, but there were no starlets to be found.

While they aren't all that common, my sulks aren't pretty. I sulked us back into town, where we found a nice stretch of dockside restaurants we would not, of course, get to enjoy. I sulked us past the shops (also closed) and back to the cars. I probably could have turned things around with a little honest enthusiasm, or even some dishonest enthusiasm, but I was feeling so darn deflated. Where was all that free chocolate mousse? How about a good old sailboat trip? Or, at least, a little sweet sideways glance from good old Jean-Luc? Of course "old" would be the operative word to describe Jean-Luc these days, but can't a girl enjoy a little nostalgia?

We had been outdoors for an awfully long time, so, on the way home, I will admit that I pulled Liesel and the girl car into the previously maligned McDonald's to use their restroom. Perhaps other people have also learned this little trick, but I've always thought of the golden arches as my own personal W.C. for long car trips. Say what you want about the evils of restaurant chains: they do provide the world with some of its more reliably clean toilets.

Mom and I took some pity on the kids (really more on ourselves), and ordered up a few cheeseburgers and some hot salty fries. Abigail had her only fun of the trip, scampering up and down the outdoor slide with a few giggling French kids. And, predictably, the end of my losing chess match with Bill produced a nice warm feeling for us both. I'm sure he was equally glad to be rid of me, speeding back home in the car with Pops, who would probably tell him a few more stories from the European tour of 1959. I bet Polly and Ginger never had a snit.

Mom and Dad were, as usual, stoic, steadfast soldiers in the face of family foolishness. But if we ever return to St. Tropez, we'll know better. Even without our guidebooks, we'll know to head straight for the old waterfront, find a café, eat a snack, and stroll by the enormous yachts. We'll skip the cemetery tour and take a nicer walk up to the old fort. We'll pick a day of glowing blue sky. The roadwork will be done by then, and, in this dream, future scenario, we'll have our own lane (or two) to zip us there and back. No one will even guess what a wreck we were our first time around.

That day we added a corollary to The Rule of We're Here: when something stinks, admit it and move on. Take the loss and learn a lesson for Next Time.

CHAPTER SIX:
If It's Not Good, It's Bad

I T'S ONE THING TO BE LOLLING about in France, age 40. Another to be 10, in school all day long.

In sending the kids off to French school, I managed to find myriad ways to deny this now obvious truth. Conventional wisdom was never our family's strong suit, aside from Abigail, who inherited it in spades from her grandparents. But here I will say it, with awful chagrin: the conventional wisdom turned out to be true, and damn every one of my prescient friends who was right in worrying on our children's behalf.

I loved, adored, cherished, and thrived on the moments, days, and weeks we spent so embedded in the natural world of France that fall — so far from our old home, and sewn so tightly into a new one. But I have to tell the rest of the truth, the unhappier part. The girls often flat-out hated school, in their own individual ways. And while Abigail always seemed that she was going to push through it, I was never sure about Grace.

Just before her grandparents visited, Grace endured several weeks of school-time misery. The best day included the time she played at recess for a half-hour with the popular little girl who also spoke a little English. Grace even gave her a little present that day after lunch. But not all of our days had a high point, and each one started in tears.

Basically, it proved so much harder than we had thought for them to speak French and to break into the tight social world of a small town in a foreign language. We made it harder for the girls by not insisting forcefully enough on their learning French in advance, and by squandering and wasting all the summer time when they could have been doing so. But worst, the children (and parents) of this small rural town wouldn't embrace us, or them, and we didn't exactly figure out how to reach out and improve the situation either. Our usual bag of tricks, honed in Brooklyn, didn't work in Aups.

Things seemed fine at the start. We had one first day of fear at the *portail,* followed by several weeks of relief and ease when Grace was immediately pulled into a little girl clique, despite having no French at her disposal. Two other children in her class spoke English, and the principal pledged that they would help her out; apparently he did so without actually enlisting their assistance, as neither of the two would speak a word to her. Her teacher at first seemed pleasantly aloof, the kind of guy to stand around gazing benevolently while she got into the swing of things.

It took Abigail a few more days to get with the program, but she quickly turned to her strengths (tag, mostly) to engage kids to play with at recess. She employed her practical wisdom in the classroom as well, learning to sit next to Jessica's son and to copy everything he did.

When one boy picked on her, she fretted for a day and a half, then took care of him as swiftly and silently as Tony Soprano; she would never let us in on exactly what she did. Her teacher spoke a little English with her, just enough to help her to figure out what to do, and she took an interest in what Abby was learning. Abigail was starting to be able to pronounce French nicely when she read. Some days she even ran ahead to school to get a chance to be independent and strong.

But in the ensuing weeks, the bloom fell well off the rose, most obviously with Grace. First, her teacher shouted at her because she "forgot" to bring in

15 euros. We missed the grade parent afternoon, our one opportunity to hear directly from her teacher. This was not sloppiness on our part: there was literally no official communication from the school on this one. None. Grace wrote "V" in her book for the date — who schedules a parent meeting for Friday afternoon??? — but since she didn't know what it meant, we didn't either.

We found that we could never understand Grace's homework, once the teacher stopped sending home plain old worksheets. We also didn't understand that the list of art supplies the teacher sent home was what we should buy for her. We thought it was just a vocabulary list of words to learn, so at least she knew the French names for the objects she didn't have on the day her class did artwork. She spent the day she could have been painting sitting still and watching.

Perhaps it was just as well, because that day her teacher ripped up the painting of another child when it displeased him.

Grace's art teachers have long been her gurus; the shock and contrast of somebody ripping up a child's work was a little too much for her. The whole "old school" approach of this rural French school went overnight from being a curiosity to being just plain scary.

Additionally, there was the coughing. Common pet peeves are nails on a chalkboard, or cat posters, or overpowering cologne. For Grace, it's cold season. So once she realized that she not only couldn't understand any French, and no children would be willing to translate it for her or let her even see their work, she spent all of her time in class hearing only the sound of a little boy's hacking bronchitis. Instead of having her sit next to a kid who could speak English and translate for her, they seated her next to some sort of 11-year-old tuberculosis patient.

M. Souris insisted that the girls would learn French quickly with the generous help of the French government providing regular instruction. The French lessons that were promised turned out to be the highlight of their school experience, mostly because their French teacher spoke some English with them, but as the lessons started late and happened only once a week, the girls had had only a total of three 2-hour sessions in the first two months. The magic of foreign language immersion had yet to take hold.

But perhaps the worst thing, the nail in the coffin of Grace's adjustment to school, happened when the one little girl with whom she had played for several weeks, and on whom she had pinned most of her hopes, dropped her, in just the sort of painful way that children (and grownups) across the globe do to one another. She not only cast her off, but did it with that finger waggle followed by arm cross that all four of us had come to dread. Suddenly, there she was sitting alone in the schoolyard, left wholly out of the loop. I can't be sure whether it is a good or a bad thing that she didn't understand enough French ever to have any idea why.

So there we were, the beneficiaries and victims of our grand plan, coming face to face with every single should, could, and would we had heard and managed to ignore.

We should have chosen a bigger town. We should have found a bilingual school. We could have pushed the French so much harder. We would have (if we could have) figured out how to set up opportunities for the girls to play outside of school with other kids in their classes. We should have realized that with all of the pleasures of being together as a little family unit all the time would come the social isolation of being together as a little family unit, all the time. We could have realized that *le portail*, the language barrier, and old-school French formality not only would limit our ability to shape the girls' school experience in any way at all, but also prevent us from really knowing what goes on there for either one of them.

Or, to listen to Abigail, we just never should have gone there at all. Just as I reconciled the losses we forced on ourselves by leaving, and figured out how to stay in touch with my old friends, she was suddenly mourning all of it. Why did we rent out the house? Why did I give up my job? She missed her school, her friends, her favorite teachers. She was *not* learning French, she told us every day. I couldn't tell if it this meant she couldn't, or wouldn't.

For Grace it was even worse. A lot of days she simply did not want to go to school, or couldn't get herself back there in the afternoon at all, despite our forceful and supportive efforts. The boys threw erasers, she said, and maybe even little rocks, when the teachers weren't looking. We never knew what the homework was. She was so busy holding it all together that not a word of French seemed to be getting through all the *blah blah* rip-up-that-painting *blah*. And when you sit alone in the schoolyard all through recess, it becomes a jail.

Before we arrived, we told ourselves that we had just a few goals: the kids would learn French. They would each make just one friend. Their math skills would not dissolve and dissipate, because we would work on that at home. But while Abigail seemed to be on her way with both French and friendship by the second part of fall, we started to think it might be time for a change of direction for Grace.

Whenever we made a wrong turn while driving Diesel Liesel, she wouldn't berate us or point it out rudely. Instead, she would suggest that we head to the next roundabout and take the *quatrième sortie*: the fourth exit, which would take us back from where we had come. While it was not yet time for the *quatrième sortie*, I couldn't see that we'd force ourselves to drive straight ahead either.

Sometimes we had fantastic days. When we complained to the principal about the boys who were throwing erasers and little pebbles at Grace, he briefly convinced everyone to be extra-super nice to her. She cried bitterly one morning, but before Bill and I had walked away from the schoolyard, she was already playing hopscotch. That day, she had all sorts of tales to tell us about the other children, and Abigail pledged to beat the stuffing out of anyone who bothered her big sister.

I tried then to imagine that this was the roadmap for what was to come. But up ahead, I saw a familiar sign, marking a roundabout with roads leading off in different directions. Straight ahead was stay in school, limp along, hope and pray that things stay more comfortable, and help her along the best we can. Appeal to the principal when things get tough, and give her lots of candy and hugs at the end of each day.

There had been years of our own lives, even as adults, when each of us had to do just that, and we did our best to help each other through. I hope I am not the only mother in the world who sometimes wishes a better parent would show up and fix things for us. In France, we were our children's resources, full stop. On the worst days, all I could think was this: our poor, poor girls.

Nona and Pops left on Tuesday. Thursday was the first day back at school for all the children of France after a dozen vacation days off. When Abigail realized

Wednesday morning that she had no more grandparents to cushion her, and would soon be going back to *blah blah* recess *blah* once again, she burst into the angriest and most miserable tears.

I tried to talk her down, but her pathetic wails eventually brought Bill and Grace actually running in alarm. I told them what the matter was, and we all climbed into our big bed together to talk over the problem. Faced with three anxious, loving faces, she started to calm down and tell us why school felt so hard.

She was trying, doing her level best, but was frustrated, not seeing the results of her efforts. She took a big hard test in late October, right before the vacation, and the teacher (sensibly) wouldn't let her copy her answers from the children next to her. She left most of the test blank, reinforcing her own sense that she was not moving forward. And she missed, missed, *missed* everything American. When Abigail repeats words three times, they get louder and more dramatic each time. To Abigail, being in France felt like pointless foolishness.

So we told her, again, our theories of why we were there and why we were so proud of her: she was learning a new language, but more importantly, learning a whole new way of doing things. Knowing the reasons behind something is important to Abigail, and when we told her that the real leaders of the world know how to relate in lots of places, and learn to adapt just like she was doing, that meant something. Grace gave Abigail big-sisterly advice and praised her ability to make new friends at school.

"Even if you don't see yourselves learning, we see it every day," Bill promised her.

"We're even starting to hear it in your accents and your words. Remember yesterday when you said, "*La lune*" on the way home from school?"

She had pointed up at the huge disc of a moon on one side of the sky, then said, "*le soleil*," pointing at the other.

I kept going. "And you, Grace, with all that '*J'ai vachement faim.*'"

Grace giggled. "I have cow-like hunger," she translated. "French is so silly."

We followed up our talk and full-family snuggle with an entire day of things we thought Abigail would like: pancakes with Nona and Pops's gift of real maple syrup, Monopoly at the kitchen table, and even a trip to a street fair that happened to be set up in Draguignan, including bumper cars, midway games, and an AcroBungie trampoline.

But when I asked Abigail at the end of the day what had been the best part of the day, she went back to our talk in the morning. "I liked snuggling with the whole family. You really made me feel better."

This, I was finding, was home: a feeling among the four of us, all together all the time.

But I knew that we all needed to grow, and needed to push ourselves beyond the walls of home. But just how hard should I push Grace to school, I often wondered? Because as sisterly and grownup as she was in the face of Abigail's tears, she herself found it awfully hard to go back the next day. Unlike Abigail, whose teacher and classmates seem to be helping her out, using plenty of English, Grace was on her own in her class. She was sick a lot, and upset some, and missed a lot of school. Nobody helped her out in class. And while she made a new friend after the Principal gave the kids his be-nice-to-the-foreigner and don't-throw-erasers lecture, she accurately recognized that that friendship was not particularly resilient. She was afraid to lean on it too hard, lest it break like the promising early ones all eventually did, dropping her hard to the ground.

Sometimes she seemed just fine in the morning, but when it was time to head back to school for the afternoon, it was usually her turn to be upset and tell me how she was really feeling.

One afternoon, she started out with weepy quiet, then gradually progressed to hard sobs.

"The other kids were kind for a time," she said, "but eventually they turned back to their own language and shut me out of their games. Nobody ever helps me, Mom. Not the teacher, not the children in my class. How can they be so mean?"

I tried the old pat on the head, and a kindly "There, there," but I didn't have the answer she deserved. I never would have tolerated this back home in my school, if I had known a child was suffering as she was, but I was chagrined to realize that perhaps this was the kind of thing kids didn't always tell.

Her confessions came in fits and starts. "I can never, ever, get past 'Salut,'" she choked out. The tears came harder, and she started to struggle a little bit to breathe.

I tried my usual tricks to calm down, but nothing worked. Now she was wailing about missing even more school, knowing that she really really wanted to learn French all of the sudden. As we walked to the school, we were back to the old misery, but somehow another degree worse. She seemed to be dying to go to school — intent on pushing through the uncertainty and anxiety — but truly unable to face *le portail* again.

I wondered then if I was somehow making it worse by listening — somehow giving her fears unnecessary credence. Because once, a few weeks before, I had gotten her to the *portail* and sent her in, where she had quickly been absorbed in a game and had a perfectly nice day.

But the closer we got, the more it became clear that she was not going to be able to stop crying. She started actually to clutch at my down vest, hanging on my side. Bill had walked ahead of us to drop Abigail off, and came back to us, but Grace couldn't calm down. Her chest hurt, she told us. She couldn't breathe, and she was starting to do what I guess people call hyperventilating. I'd never seen it before.

I couldn't think all that clearly, either. Part of me believed that if I could get her into school, she'd adjust. This was what the Principal had insisted we do, and I was trying, awfully hard, to do what he said. I even feared that she was dramatizing for herself and for us, knowing that it would take a larger-than-usual meltdown to keep her out of school.

But then I heard panic, not just upset, creep into her tears. She was talking about wanting to go to school so that she could learn to speak French, but feeling like she couldn't.

I realized that if we were home in Brooklyn, and she were acting like this, I would have had her in the school nurse's office in minutes. Then, as we walked, I recalled that back at work, I had called 911 in similar situations. The more I looked at her little girl face, and felt the fear stirring in my own heart, I realized that this felt less like a mere going-to-school problem, but instead a question of her actually getting enough air. Whether she was hyperventilating from anxiety or for some other reason didn't matter anymore; despite our calm best efforts, she was getting worse.

But we were outside, with no phone, and couldn't walk back home. Bill set out to get the car.

While I sat with her, and she talked about her throat closing up, my mind raced: was it an allergic reaction? I blamed the smell of burning grape vines in the air. Her breathing got more ragged, and she looked at me, not just anxious but truly scared.

When Bill came back, I told him we were going to the doctor's, and right away.

Of course it was by then 14:00. The doctor's, like the bakeries and the stores and the library and the Mayor's office? All *fermé*. Locked and shuttered tight until 15:00. The only direction on the door was to call 15, the benign-sounding teenage number for French 911.

Being a parent to my particular children is by far the hardest thing I have ever done. While on the whole we are awfully happy, so much of who we are feels specific and difficult, and rarely fits a mold I can quickly understand. Maybe we just seem typically bourgeois and whiney from the outside, but to me it was like doing complex multi-variable calculus all day long. To be a good mom to this strange happy family of mine, I weighed impossibly vague and subtle factors all day long. Was I over-reacting? Under-reacting? Giving too many choices, or denying the girls their independence? When should I push? When to pull? When to let it alone and get out of the way?

This particular hopeless circumstance had quickly turned from pushing her into school to getting her to a doctor. Which meant additionally trying to push Bill in one direction — panic — while keeping the calmest possible voice and face for Grace, who was lying prone on the sofa. But as Grace reads me even better than Bill does, I had to resort to French to communicate my distress to him. Which only made Grace ask, in more terrified tones, why I was speaking French.

Whereas I generally worry way too soon and too often, Bill often responds to a crisis by aggressively not worrying, with a kind of forced, slow calm recital of the reasons why things are perfectly fine. When we hit a fight-or-flight situation, we head in opposite directions, our baffled children there in the middle not sure what to think. A lot of times he's right. A lot of times I'm right. Which makes it even harder the next time, and the next time after that.

Plus there is this strange phenomenon, probably also specific to my own otherwise happy family: each of the times we've had to take our kids to an ER I have suffered this same shameful fear: might I be just over-reacting? Shouldn't

I just take them home and try a little Tylenol? No matter that in nearly every single case, this fear has actually produced something a lot more like under-reaction than hypochondria.

Full disclosure: we do not always under-react. For example, during our years in Brooklyn, we went straight to the hospital with the (obviously) broken leg, the (clear) episode of sudden fainting, and the (unmistakable) febrile seizure Abigail once suffered on an airplane jet way. But in a whole bunch of other situations where they've needed care right away, I've always hesitated, unwilling to believe that yes, this is a real crisis.

Like one time, when my kitchen stove was actually on fire, I stood there on the phone, baby Grace perched on my hip, asking the 911 operator for directions how to put out the stupid fire myself. Only after the operator insisted, loudly and forcefully, that it was time to leave this to the professionals, who were on their way, did I realize that the apartment was filling with smoke and I'd better get us both down the five flights of stairs to the street.

So here I was with a wheezy little girl who was quite possibly faking it. Me, Little-Miss-I-Can-Handle-All-This, now just as deluded, but in France, where freaking out, or even my usual forms of worry, seemed so terribly gauche and American.

(I must add that this was *never* true when we called an actual medical professional in France. They all reacted swiftly and carefully, and really, really quickly. If the typical French person was vastly more blasé than I was used to, the typical French doctor was a whole lot more attentive and eager to please and ease human suffering.)

And just then, I also hated that I was unable to handle the situation on my own in the first place. I still couldn't reliably make any sort of phone call in French, as I was not even up to 50% of understanding in face-to-face conversations. I had left it to Bill to deal with the doctors, the insurance, the more complicated practical matters requiring language skill and patience with bureaucrats.

So I wouldn't be able to handle this on my own. I thought with a flash of inadequacy and chagrin just then of my friends who are single parents, and all the times they have had to deal with even worse, without someone else to rely on when things got superbad.

When Bill did eventually call 15, instead of sending an ambulance as they would have in New York, they told us to head for the hospital, which was actually pretty far away. I didn't want to — couldn't really — send Bill alone with Grace in the car the 40-minute drive to Draguignan. We needed to do this together, if only because we still had no idea how even to find the hospital, and no idea what to do if Grace got worse, as they said she might, and was beginning to do just then.

But I had Abigail to pick up in a few hours, and we still had just one friend in town for whom we had a phone number — Jessica, who was also our landlord and chief translator. We were then not unlike Grace, unwilling to put too much strain on the one relationship we had managed to forge. But I didn't have much of a choice.

In the car, Grace was incredibly upset. She wanted to be able to breathe, but going to the hospital sounded like even a worse fate than running out of oxygen. Her face turned from gray to grayer.

So Bill and I started to sing. The call to 15 had turned Bill around to my way of thinking, but also reinforced how important it was for us to keep Grace calm. As I whipped around the corners and barreled down straightaways (other French drivers in their stupid little Cleos were *still* passing us), we sang the lullaby of her childhood, "Sweet Baby James."

I sang as slow and strong as I could, wishing away the ragged edges out of Grace's breathing, trying to wash the dead-looking resignation away from her face. Bill told me much later, after the dull hours in the ER, after the EKG and the chest X-ray and the temperature scan and glucose test all came out perfectly fine, that he had been out of his mind with worry in the car. That as he looked at her, listening to her wheezing, he wondered for a few long minutes if she were going to die.

In each of our non-disaster freakouts earlier in our French misadventures, we had pulled further and further apart, wishing to distance ourselves from each other's bad form. But faced with a real crisis, on the way to the real hospital, we finally pulled ourselves both onto the same page, the same team.

We were singing together, and Bill was holding Grace's hand in the back seat. He was navigating with the iPhone, I was driving like a carefully repressed maniac. When we made the first wrong turn, we worked it out together. He would go in, I would park, we would get there. We would find her the help she needed, that we needed for her to find.

A doctor or a savvier parent might have diagnosed this much more quickly than we did: she was having a serious panic attack. She had been quietly mentioning a tightness in her chest for a few days, particularly after climbing a hill or running too fast. And now, she was having her first full-on attack, brought on by crying and walking in the cold air.

Panic attacks make you feel as though you are going to die. Still, they are never actually life-threatening, as we discovered when we got to the ER. They clipped a little machine on her finger and determined that she was getting enough oxygen and her lungs were working, despite the awful rasp of her breathing. She undressed and sat on a gurney in their pediatric room, which differed from the other rooms mainly because it had colorful posters.

As Bill and I have had many occasions to learn, when you have to wait in an ER, it means that you and your child are stable. Boredom slowly displaces terror, and you spend a lot of time looking at whatever artwork is there. Most of the posters in this ER seemed to be encouraging parents to read with their children, but our eventual favorite, for its sheer gothic inscrutability, was the one right at the end of the hospital bed. It showed a child's drawing of a Mickey Mouse toy being yanked to bits, with an enormous tearful babyhead gazing over the top. Apparently, someone had organized a children's drawing contest on the theme of "*les douleurs de l'enfant*" ("the child's pain"), and this was the winning entry.

Leave it to the French to sponsor a children's art contest on the topic of *suffering*. Next they will make a coloring book of *The Stranger*, or maybe finger puppets that get their top knuckles chopped off in a tiny guillotine.

By the time the ER staff had worked through their usual algorithm, in the usual slow, methodical order, it was late afternoon. Jessica had, of course, been perfectly happy to pick up Abigail, and promised her a pleasant evening.

By then, Grace had been breathing poorly for over three hours, but since the warmth of the hospital had alleviated the wheezing somewhat, and since nothing worse had happened in all that time, and Abigail was with Jessica, we had all calmed ourselves down enough to poke fun at the awful poster.

We were all initially relieved when Dr. Rascasse, the pediatric pulmonologist, walked in the door.

He spoke mostly in French, with a little broken English here and there, but his main diagnostic tool was his cigarette lighter.

"Graaaay-ace, I like for you to blow out this flame, *s'il te plaît*." Grace pursed her lips and blew at it, hard, before bursting back into staccato coughing once again.

Only in France could the pediatric pulmonologist keep his lighter in his doctor-jacket pocket and use it to diagnose children by making them cough.

"*Je suis un* asthmatic," he told us. "It is a very bad case, I have. But of course I smoke." He was a really nice guy, but I had to say that I seriously questioned his judgment when he admitted his habit to us, right in front of Grace, and in English.

"I am thinking perhaps that your breathing (he pronounced this "*breezing*") is bad like mine when I have *une crise* of asthma. I give you *medicaments* in this emergency inhaler."

At the words "emergency" and "asthma," Grace looked stricken. Asthma meant more coughing.

When we asked about possible side effects of the medication, he also told us a sweet story. "In the old days, before we learned about this *medicament,* people used to think that asthma inhalers killed people." He made sort of a "Duh" face as though this were the most foolish idea in the word.

"But you see, that was because they were only giving it to old sick people who were going to die anyway. And they hadn't really perfected it. But now, it is not *dangereuse*, not at all. Sometimes I must take even ten puffs on it at a time! Because, as you know, I smoke."

And then, to prove his point, he gave her a few magic puffs on his own (apparently non-lethal) asthma inhaler, which instantly brought her inhales back to normal and a smile back to her beautiful, beautiful face. Sudden clear skies, angels singing, rays of sunlight filled the darkening room.

It all went very quickly from there: a prescription, some recommendations, a suggestion that she shouldn't worry so much. (As if.) She got dressed, we tried to pay (they would send us the bill later, *ne t'inquiète pas),* and we left to pick up Abby from Jessica's house and figure out what dinner might be hiding in the fridge back home.

Driving in the dark on the way home, I was wholly wrung out. Grace was relieved, and maybe just a little high from the inhaler. Bill finally admitted how afraid he had been. Instead of cranky and tired, we were all a little giddy with relief, glad to be alone together away from the ER, the smoking pulmonologist, and that awful poster.

We turned on the stereo and sang, again, this time belting out harmony to a honky-tonk cover of the Beatles.

When we finally collected Abigail, it was almost 7:00 PM. It hadn't unfolded as we intended, but Abigail had had her very first afterschool play date. She was in great spirits, actually, perhaps grateful to have been with some other more typical family for a while. We chowed down some high-carb comfort food, and put the kids in front of a movie so we could think. Or maybe so we wouldn't have to think anymore, at least for a little while.

"She's going to cry again tomorrow, you know. She's not going quietly to that school," I said.

"Well, lots of kids have to deal with stuff like that. And we promised the French state on our visa application that we would send her to school. We can't just let her bail." Bill had been understandably traumatized by the visa process, and lived in fear of being sent home, or perhaps imprisoned, if he even misplaced one of the stamped documents.

"Can't we? I don't think we even know that. And does she really need an inhaler? How am I supposed to keep her from losing the damn thing once she feels great for a few days and it falls to the bottom of her backpack?"

"Look, Launa, lots of kids are anxious, and lots of kids have asthma. Lots of kids have to fumble with their inhalers, and losing them is as much a part of normal middle school life as retainers and acne."

"And mean text messages from frenemies. I know. Lots of kids get panic attacks, even the kind that take their breath away. That doesn't make it any easier."

Right then, it all seemed a little new, and a lot unfair. "What do we tell her about this new wrinkle in her life?" I asked Bill, as if he could know.

That was the immediate question, but the day in the ER had brought others to a head. What should we do about the girls' feelings of isolation? What about our own? Being in New York meant more demands on our attention, but more margin of error. So was it better, or worse, that we had put ourselves in a place without such a wide safety net, so that we fall back only on ourselves again and again when things get tough?

Should we err on the side of the cliché "it takes a village," or side with the French and stay always *avec toute la famille?* Each solution would lead only to another set of questions.

That weekend, we sought shelter. Paris. Even before our trip to the ER, we had planned the trip there to see friends who had stayed with us in Brooklyn a few years before. They are off-the-charts friendly and generous people, which may be related to the fact that neither was born in France. Hmmm. They had been inviting us to stay with them since they visited us. They also have positively lovely children, whom we knew would be kind to Grace and Abigail. Plus, Jean-Claude was a doctor, and Ruth a teacher. They could give us good advice.

Abigail and Grace went to their special French class in the morning, skipped the afternoon, and we'd all get on the TGV, the Super-Speedy Train that makes Amtrak look like a stone-age relic. This time I knew exactly where we were going. No surprises. Easy trip. I knew how to follow the signs to the station, and I even had 30 centimes in my pocket in case I had to use the bizarro pay-toilet that disinfects its whole self when you are done.

So if we couldn't easily make the small-town school a perfect fit, I knew that we could at least go somewhere else where we would be sure to find friends. If the Mountain would not come to Mohammed, Mohammed would go to the Mountain. At 200 miles an hour. With all of the disappointments of school hanging heavy on us, a change would do us good. Or at least the kids couldn't throw erasers at Grace fast enough to catch up with a TGV.

When we arrived at the TGV station without incident, it was inexplicably crammed – and I mean absolutely crammed – with silent, grouchy-looking travelers.

In the U.S. when there is a minor travel crisis (planes delayed by ground fog, trains cancelled because of a power outage, the café car suddenly runs out of Heineken), Americans tend to talk a lot more than usual to one another. They complain bitterly, or make unfunny camaraderie-building jokes at the expense of the airline or the train line or whoever could possibly be blamed. They break out of their little privacy-bubble to share information or give unasked-for advice. Sometimes they even look sort of happy in the sharing of a little faux-emergency.

But the French people all piled up in the Aix TGV Gare looked even grimmer and more silent than usual. They stood like stones, staring resolutely at the departures board, despite the fact that the trains they had expected to take had been late for at least two solid hours already. Nothing on the boards was changing, no announcements were being made, and nobody was explaining anything. All the typical French staring-through-one-another continued unabated, just with a lot more people to stare through.

We had planned to get a little lunch in the Gare, but every chair in the brasserie was full, as were all the benches and even the little coffee tables that silent waiting people had turned into makeshift seats. So instead, we broke French cultural law and actually stood while munching on our *croque-monsieurs*.

Gradually a few trains started to arrive and sucked a few people off the benches and into fast-moving trains. We still had no idea what was going on to cause the delay, or how long said delay would last. Neither did the one poor employee on duty who was being pelted with questions. I think that they posted a two-hour delay to keep people staring vaguely off into space. But since it seemed that the station was gradually clearing of passengers, we imagined that we would eventually get on our train as well.

Our train did arrive, but our assigned car was not there. There were lots of angry people still grimly and silently bustling around, and lots of contradictory information in French being announced over the loudspeakers. We decided that perhaps the next train would have our car attached, when the beleaguered employee emerged to shoo us all onto the train.

"But what about our seats?" I asked Bill with real alarm. Since Bill was our translator, I expected him to untangle all sorts of impossible mysteries. He tried to ask the person shooing us, but as usual, she knew nothing, and gave a wholly Gallic shrug. Either we would sit or we would stand, but this was the train we were to take. We crowded with all of our bags into car five just as the doors closed, and stood with a lot of other equally bewildered fellow travelers who appeared to have been robbed of their seats as well.

It soon became clear that this train was to travel, high-speed and non-stop, with the passengers of two full trains. Which meant that we four, the last to board the train car, would be sitting on the floor just outside of the chemical toilets for the duration of the trip. This would have been a little funny, I suppose, had Grace not been absolutely petrified of the idea of the train moving 200 miles per hour.

I had tried to reassure her that the train would not be moving *that* fast (this was one of those white lies parents have to tell to get through the day), but she was not to be reassured. As we tend to do in our family, she settled in for a nice long panic attack. She didn't need the inhaler because we started in on the slow breathing, calm-down routine down right away. Her panic lasted until her butt got sore enough to distract her from her fear. It's hard to panic adequately when your butt really hurts.

All along the tracks there were windmills in the hills, each located directly next to the cooling towers of a nuclear power plant. I remember that when I visited France as a teenager, my French father was extremely proud of France's nuclear reactors. But as I was much more used to my own nation's habits of power generation and environmental degradation, I couldn't help but find them creepy.

Sure, back in the U.S. we blow up entire West Virginian hillsides to sift out the coal we burn to generate our electricity. But here, ominous towers sit right within all of this incredible natural beauty, all of these rows of cedars and olives and grapes. They look down on the Mediterranean Sea, and on the beautiful hillside towns and the farmhouses and the fields. It's like leaving a grenade sitting right next to your newborn baby. An incredibly useful grenade, and one that really never blows up because you're so careful with it, of course, but still, a grenade.

As somebody who freaks out in the face of danger, it was getting hard for me to say what was safe, and what should really make me worry. Why are nuclear towers more inherently scary than global warming? Why are cholesterol and alcohol and tobacco so vilified at home, and consumed in mass quantities here? Parts of our lives got safer, while other new dangers emerged.

Similarly, so much ease emerged alongside our brand new piles of difficulty. We had made things much harder for our girls. But everyday life with no jobs, with no schedules, with no social obligations was so much easier for Bill and for me. We had only ourselves and the girls to manage, and drastically fewer responsibilities. I wrote for hours a day, uninterrupted, and Bill was hiking, exploring, and sleeping soundly for the first time in so many years.

In the late spring before our departure for France, seeing this coming, I was a whirlwind of loss, grasping on and mourning all the changes that were coming at me faster than a speeding train. I could barely take them in as they sped past. When people would say, "Oh, you must be so excited!" I would puzzle them with an ungrateful grimace. I couldn't see what was up ahead, only what I was leaving behind. I was afraid, deeply afraid, of losing the world we had put so much into building. I was a petrified ingrate.

I really don't do so well when things are moving too fast. Figuratively or literally. Like Grace, who spent most of the 3-hour trip to Paris clutching her luggage with white knuckles, I'm not exactly a roll-with-the punches kind of gal. Faced with fight or flight, I freeze like a stupid, scared rabbit. (Scientists should study me, and all those deer frozen in headlights, then add "freeze" to the other two f-word options for responding to life's challenges.) When lost, I tend to forge ahead as though the correct road will miraculously appear for me. When I am hungry or cold or tired or grouchy, I tend to go on grimly doing exactly the same thing that got me in that situation in the first place. I try to slow down the very turning of the world.

Bill, on the other hand, finds that high speed induces a sort of nirvana. Nearly the whole trip, he was sitting on our luggage just outside the sickening smell of the train bathroom, just like the rest of us. As the door's air-powered doors opened and closed again and again on my back, he regaled us with stories of his Eurail glory days with Alain, the day-long trip they both slept on the floor of a slow train between Nice and Florence.

During that trip, there was nowhere to sit, and because he was then hung over, Alain really wanted to lie down. So he placed himself in the only available real estate, between the automatic doors, which constantly opened and shut on his head. He did not wake up. Bill passed the long hours in the crowded train watching this happen again and again and again. I guess remembering that trip made it so much more fun for Bill to watch the doors close again and again on little old me.

Bill talks about train trips as though he is a normal person recounting a sojourn to the moon, or at least the World Series. He really really *really* likes trains. France had made Bill positively unsinkable. Neither one of us had any future job prospects to speak of, but to be quite honest, we may never have been happier, aside from the whole miserable child problem.

Happy or unhappy, my bottom was to hurt for the next three days. And we had nothing to eat but a little bag of peanuts during the trip and an old Pago bottle filled with tap water. But there we were, heading for Paris, and friends and the Eiffel Tower and a big old change for the better.

As the train slowed close to Paris, our little cabin near the bathroom (and the door) started to fill up with people who had actually enjoyed seats during the trip, and were now crowding around in hopes to be the first off the train. This struck all four of us as totally unfair. Last on, worst seat, should mean first off. As the doors opened, and a man lunged forward to surge ahead of us, I snapped my arm sharply up in front of his chest.

"You don't understand," he argued. "I have a Eurostar to catch!" Perhaps it was his use of British English, perhaps it was his utter entitlement, perhaps it was just the fact that my poor kids had spent three hours on the floor outside the bathroom. But I snapped rudely, like I don't usually.

"Yes. And I have a few children to care for. We sat on the floor this trip. This time, you wait." As soon as we were all out the door, he rushed around us. But when we got to the end of the platform, there he was, sitting down sending a text. Grace was quick with the joke: "You don't understand," she quipped. "I have a bench to catch!"

We took a bus to Jean-Claude and Ruth's apartment, and they and their three incredibly sweet children welcomed us into their apartment and into their lives. They fed us and gave us soft beds to sleep in. Jean-Claude listened to Grace's lungs and pronounced her to be fine. Ruth, a German ex-pat and also a teacher at a French school, heard out my confusion with perfect poise and total comprehension.

"We walk sixteen times each week to *le portail.* And still, no matter how many times we wait there for the girls, nobody comes over to say hello and talk about the weather. They stare at us, or ignore us completely."

Bill added, "To give the girls courage, sometimes we all walk together, and play tag in the lane on the way to school."

"But on our bad days, nobody has the courage to face all those frowny faces," I admitted. Why are the people in the town so cold to us and our kids? What is this invisible *portail* alongside the real one?

It wasn't just the language I didn't understand. There was a more profound disconnect that I couldn't get my head around; after years of being so fully an insider, I had made myself a complete outsider in a place that has never had a tradition or need to welcome the outsiders. But whether this attitude towards our otherwise perfectly approachable and sweet family was "French" or "rural" or even simply boiled down to the attitude of this particular town, I may never know.

Ruth diagnosed the problem, having experienced this herself when she moved to France from Germany. "I think you are missing the American friendliness. It sounds like the people in your town *sont peu amicaux.* They're not friendly. This is sometimes the attitude of the French. They feel differently than you do, that strangers are not in fact your friends, particularly in a small town. Until somebody they know introduces you to them, you do not exist."

In this context, my desire to have people be friendly to me was of course ridiculous — just not what's done around here. Ruth's perspective helped as the sand shifted once again under my feet.

Of course the people we actually have begun socializing with inside one another's homes — our lasagna party acquaintances, on the way to being friends — were always friendly, even warm. Ruth, Jean-Claude, and their children could not have been kinder. With all of these people, we did the *bisous* and shared our little *ooh la las* and laughter, and we smiled at each other's kids. With them, "*Ça va?*" (How's it going?) was real and open and meant something. Seeing them was like catching hold of a little life raft in an otherwise pitiless sea.

This was Bill's "baguette theory" of French social life — crusty on the outside, soft and mushy within. Which was certainly the case when we were safely ensconced, *en famille,* with Jean-Claude and Ruth.

The next day, we found ourselves overjoyed to be in a city with great public transportation, incredibly beautiful architecture, and a decent number of perfectly serviceable Indian restaurants. There we were in Paris on Saturday morning, wearing our typically Parisian scarves (French people don't wear wool hats), enjoying the typically Parisian gunmetal-gray sky. The girls were pulling out cute little French words and phrases to insert into our conversation as we ambled from our friends' apartment in the 5th *arrondissement* across the Seine to the Louvre.

When we arrived at our destination, both Grace and Abigail were transported and transformed. In Louvre-world, both girls were so engaged and curious and entranced that they actually stopped whining and complaining long enough to truly want to learn something.

They loved the glass pyramid entrance, and the neon-and-stone temporary art installation that served to transport museum visitors from the present into the past. Grace loved the lined-up Sarcophagi, the Egyptian bronzework, the mummy with one hand open and the other hand curled closed. Abigail loved Hammurabi's code, carved into a huge black stone; the Iranian tile lions; and most particularly the enormous grand crystal chandeliers in Napoleon's apartments.

Unprompted, both girls started searching out the little explanatory cards, written in English and several other languages, in the galleries. They asked great questions, totally on point and from the heart. Instead of begging for candy and complaining that their feet hurt too badly to move, they paid attention.

I was thunderstruck: our attention-deficient family had achieved a remarkable milestone: *all four of us were paying attention to the same things at the same time.*

During the summer before we left the States, Bill had a near-religious musical experience. It happened at a street fair his hometown, as he listened to a blues band made up of aging Vermont hippies.

Blues music is one of the truest gifts of American civilization to the rest of our tilted little planet. Just below its apparently simple lyrics is a familiar progression of chords that build expectation and satisfy it, again and again. And underneath that pattern of desire built and fulfilled, a syncopated thump. Blues beats are just bent enough to establish a groove, and just regular enough to be the heartbeat of the world. Blues reminds us we're alive, but that nobody promised that life would be easy.

Bill came back to the house that day literally raving about one of the songs he had heard. Like most blues songs, the song he heard was ostensibly about love, but could be taken to apply to all of our human endeavors. And, like most blues songs, it used the most prosaic language to get to the core of a truth he might have known, but was never able to articulate quite so clearly.

On that August day in New England, these bearded white guys sang out a chorus that Bill brought home for me, and which has become a sort of motto for our family ever since:

If it's not good, it's bad.
If it's not right, it's wrong.

From this song, Bill came to understand a truth that had escaped both of us during our collective 20 years as thirty-somethings: instead of asking us to try to make do, to make it work, to adapt, to convince ourselves of things, this song sought to embolden its listeners to get real.

"It" can be a lot of things – a kiss, a song, a meal, a home, a job, a place. But if it's not good, it probably doesn't deserve all the hijinks I invest into trying to convince myself that it is. Instead, this song tells me to call it what it is: it's bad. Bill and I took this to mean that we should not be spending our precious energy on this planet trying to twist things that are not right into a shape we can live with. If it's not good, grow up. Make a call, and make a change.

At the time of his revelation, Bill took the song as proof that we were doing the right thing by leaving for France for the year. I myself wasn't so sure that France was the answer to whatever Midlife Mystique was ailing us. So I chose to interpret the lyrics as advance reassurance that if France was not good, I could blamelessly bail.

The song rattled around the back corners of my little brain as I tried to figure out how to remake our lives, playing house there in Aups. But I heard it most clearly while trying to figure out what to do about the fact that we kept sending Grace to school in tears, and she kept coming home quietly but unmistakably miserable. The song's chorus was accusing me.

Sunday night we raced back on the train to Aups (this time, with seats!). We fell into bed, the girls still talking about what they had seen and heard and felt in Paris.

And then, the next morning, I heard it again, when I tried to get Grace up for school.

If it's not good, it's bad.

I spent over ten minutes shaking Grace, yelling in her ear, and even dropping her own slack, sleepy hand onto her face in order to wake her up. Although I did my level best not to panic unduly, she seemed hardly alive at all: what people call "dead asleep." Try as I did, I couldn't rouse her. Sure, we had been up a little late, and sure, it was 7:00 AM, and still dark, but I couldn't believe that anybody could truly sleep through my super-cheery "GOOD MORNING" at full volume, nearing panic. How could she sleep so hard?

Once she finally opened her eyes, I force-marched her through the steps of getting ready for school, force-fed her oatmeal and her yummy vegetable and vitamin pep-up juice from the homeopath, and even forced socks on her little feet. But as soon as I turned my back, she was back in bed, burying herself under the covers, and refusing to respond when I called.

This wasn't just your ordinary sleepy, or your ordinary Monday morning brattiness. This was full-on civil disobedience. Thoreau, Gandhi, and King, looking down from heaven on our little girl here below, would have been truly impressed with her sense of commitment. School was too scary, too confusing, too unfriendly. Simply too much. This girl was not going.

And, after two straight months of trying, on a daily basis, I was not going to make her. We had pussyfooted around the idea too damn long, and it was time to change gears, hard and fast.

If it's not good, it's bad.
If it's not right, it's wrong.

But which gear to choose?

After spilling out my indecision to friends and family at home about all of our difficulties with getting our kids to adjust to this little small town French school, I received a lot of intensely felt responses. I expected to be castigated; however, anyone with criticism to offer very nicely kept any I-told-you-so's to themselves, sending us only kind and generous advice as we pondered our options.

I wrote those options down on a piece of paper, just so I could count and weigh them a little better. I organized them into an order of least to most drastic:

Stay put and help the kids deal
Try out homeschooling
Find a new school
Move to Paris
Move to London
Move elsewhere in the U.S.
Move home, evict the tenants, and beg for our old jobs back

It's astonishing how many options there are in life, once you let yourself write them all down.

Some trusted friends wrote that we should have started keeping her home over a month before things got this hard. Others (and here I may or may not be referring to some of her grandparents) advocated the stiff-upper-lip approach — reminding us that things that do not kill her make her stronger. Here I would like to publicly thank the Depression Era, for whatever toughness is still part of the American character.

And several other people wrote to point out that nobody was forcing us to stay: "Just move home, you big whiners, why don't cha?" they said, if not in so many words. In this light, all of the "meaningful challenges" we had set ourselves for the year seemed only pointless wanderings of a foolish family.

Making the list had helped me see that I had options other than forging ahead. The problem became that ALL of these approaches were of course correct, leading us to total indecision. Yes, school had turned out to be essentially intolerable for her. And yes, persisting through difficulty makes you a stronger person. And yes, there was no clear reason for us to be here. All of these things being the case, what were we to do?

Having worked with hundreds of families as a teacher and school principal, it seems clear to me that with the fraying of the social fabric in America, parenting has become a free for all. The problem is not that our generation is worse at it than previous generations, but rather that there are no clear paths for parents to follow anymore. There are certainly no clear guidelines for massively over-thinking parents who find we can never seem to find the conventional way to do anything, and who are doubly blessed with a uniquely unconventional child. (One might say that all children are unique. I say, with good reason, and enormous pride, that mine is just that much more so, bless her awesome and perfect little heart.)

To put it more briefly, whatever is most obvious is least likely to work for our family. If my life were a blues song, I'd sing you this line:

The straight road don't get me there, nohow.

So for us to make a definitive decision among these many options, Bill's and my tolerance for sending Grace to school had to find its end. Parents can make kids do just about anything — as long as they (the parents) are willing to endure the consequences. But that Monday morning at 8:24 AM, the scales tipped — suddenly and definitively. Grace had been exhausted for two months, and asking in a million and one ways for a change. But suddenly I could no longer watch my kid wrung out by school because she "should" go. I was tired of watching her zest for learning crushed. And I was more than ready to take on the bureaucracy and the challenge of keeping Grace home — occupied, and actually learning, rather than suffering through her days.

I changed in part because during the weekend in Paris, I saw the flip side of the failure of French school for her: the success of actual France. Her joy when surrounded by kind faces. Her curiosity and engagement in the museum. Her questions as we walked along the streets, and took in the art, and saw France not as an enemy but as an opportunity.

Perhaps it was this glimpse of good that reminded me that what had been going on at home just hadn't been. Seeing both girls happy and engaged reminded me that there is a different way of learning than we had thus far afforded them. Both of them, when in the right environment, can be spontaneously curious. They pick up the weird small details and the larger esoteric meanings — Abigail specializing in the former, and Grace mystically intuiting the latter. They care. They want to learn. They choose to learn.

And so, back in Aups Monday morning, it was time to go to school, and Grace was once again dragging her feet and dragging my heart. I realized that more than anything, I wanted that little girl in the Louvre to come back to me. To come back to herself.

I am enough of a realist to know that sometimes you just have to make kids do things they don't like. They have eaten their vegetables so many times that they now actually do so on an elective basis. Still, human beings really do learn differently from one another, and all students deserve to be inspired and encouraged and helped to learn, not left to their own devices to sink or swim, to thrive or to fall through the cracks. We had tried that approach: Abigail was swimming hard to stay afloat, while Grace was sinking slowly, day by day.

As a career educator who knows her good from her bad in schools, I know that with a lot of hard work, a good teacher can actually make sure that every single kid learns. I also know how few and far between good teachers are — and what happens to kids whose style of learning doesn't match up with a mediocre teacher's view of What Children Should Do. Because often, those kids start simply to believe that they are in the wrong.

Which means that when it comes to school, if it isn't good, even for one child, it's bad.

In contrast, a good teacher finds ways to see the divine in each child, and to bring forth their best efforts, no matter what they are. But you don't have to be Helen Keller to realize that every minute a teacher spends in a classroom is a minute she is given the honor of being a small-g god to the children in her care. She can withhold the sunshine, or she can let it fill the room. She can make her teaching all about her, or remember it's all about them. She can parse out the worksheets and make the time creep by in nauseating boredom, or give away every moment in the fullest way we puny humans know how.

I have some strong feelings about teaching. And school. And learning. Particularly when it comes to my children. I had spent my entire life in schools, and so had my kids. But it was looking like it might be time to apply my ideas in a different way than I ever had before.

So there we were, just before 8:30 Monday morning. Bill and Abigail left the house. Grace was still curled up on her bed. She must have heard Bill calling to her as he left, but she lay perfectly still, and they left without her. Nobody forced her to make the embarrassing walk to school, crying the whole way. All was quiet and calm as we waited in different rooms of the house.

It was time for a new kind of school to begin.

PART THREE:
IN THE INTERVAL

"The Average French Business man at the end of his life may not have made as much money as the American; but meanwhile he has had, every day, something the American has not had: Time. Time, in the middle of the day, to sit down to an excellent luncheon, to eat it quietly with his family, and to read his paper afterward; time to go off on Sundays and holidays on long pleasant country rambles; time, almost any day, to feel fresh and free enough for an evening at the theatre, after a dinner as good and leisurely as his luncheon. And there is one thing certain: the great mass of men and women grow up and reach real maturity only through their contact with the material realities of living, with business, with industry, with all the great bread-winning activities; but the growth and the maturing take place in the intervals between these activities: and in lives where there are no such intervals there will be no real growth."

— Edith Wharton, *French Ways and Their Meaning*, 1919

CHAPTER SEVEN:

Cooking our Own Goose

I FIND SCHOOL SUPPLIES BOTH THRILLING AND soothing. This unhealthy attachment to paper products is a relatively common affliction among the busybody organized sort of us who so adore school that we go on to become teachers. I hoard paper clips, keep my staplers topped up at all times, and crave the solace I feel when sorting my markers by color and type. New pencils are better than candy. A pile of empty notebooks promises a fresh start and smooth sailing ahead.

So once I flipped the switch in my own head and admitted it to myself — *we just became one of those oddball, insular families who homeschool* — I instantly headed for the stationery aisle at the Intermarché. So what if I had no curriculum, no experience with the fifth grade other than my own? Within half an hour of making my decision, I had a ream of college-ruled notebook paper, a protractor, and a packet of erasers in my cart.

I had worried about this choice to homeschool Grace more than I had thought it through, but suddenly I was sure. As a parent, I was rarely sure of much of anything, but in this case we had made the call, and there was no going back. Certainty is like a very concentrated form of diesel fuel, rather than a GPS: it can take you an awfully long way, but won't necessarily give you any information about where you really are or which way you are tending. Certainty had done both for me in the past: it had propelled me onward, and also snaked me down the worst possible paths towards hell. Time would tell which way things would go with this homeschool business, but after months of indecision I was suddenly zooming forward full speed towards parts unknown.

On my path, I realized, I would eventually arrive at a meeting with the principal. The one who had assured me that my children would have no problem learning French. The one who had told me I must be patient, I must be stern, I must show trust in his teachers and the school by forcing my sniveling child into the building. Having said some of these things myself, to similarly panicky parents, I tried so hard to believe he was right. Damn, does karma sting.

Since regular French people do not homeschool their children any more than they bake their own croissants, I knew that our decision would baffle and disturb M. Souris. This was a problem, because Bill quickly realized, during a marathon internet search into French laws about homeschooling, that our M. Souris was duty-bound to assure the French government that all the children living in his town were being properly educated according to French law. Only he could provide bureaucratic approval. Given what he had said thus far, it might not be easy for us to convince him of the wisdom of our choice. Particularly given the poor state of my French, which he viewed as a moral failing.

While homeschooling is not illegal in France, we had promised France on our visa application that we would send our children to school. Thus we didn't just risk the truancy officer when we decided to keep Grace at home; if we didn't get the proper permissions for this strange act of ours, we risked actual deportation, and the swift end of our magic year.

After an entire lifetime of pleasing authorities, I was about to royally piss off the only man who could sign the bureaucratic paper allowing me to do what I had decided must be done.

During my shopping trip, I mused over this problem, which couldn't be fixed by a pile of notebooks of any size. But then I saw the key to our salvation: a tiny slip of a book. It was a slim volume, no more than an overgrown pamphlet really, filed on the shelf in the grocery store next to the handwriting workbooks and the paperback novels I still couldn't read. It listed the entire curriculum for French elementary and middle schools.

Try, just for a minute, to imagine a similarly slim text listing the K-6 curriculum of every public school in the entire U.S. I know: you can't. But there it was, for sale in the grocery store: the national curriculum. There, in black and white, it listed every goal, every requirement, and every subject to be taught by all the teachers of the Republic, from Nice to Omaha Beach.

There I read that in CE2, French fifth grade, children were to study French for eight hours a week, for a total of 288 hours. They were to memorize particular poems in French, and read novels, and learn to write particular sorts of sentences. *Les Maths* were to be five hours a week, for a total of 180 hours during the year, and classes would cover geometry, arithmetic, fractions, and decimals. There were requirements in art history, in civic and moral instruction, and science and technology. There were requirements for physical education, history, and geography.

Here was the Rosetta Stone to the entire French system: *this* was the kind of guidebook I could use. I would use it to beat M. Souris at his own game. Rather than try to explain to him why French school was stupid and pointless for our child — a clear losing argument in his book — I was going to crib my way into becoming a real French middle school teacher. If I figured out just what notebooks to buy, and then promised M. Souris that we would follow the French system just as assiduously as he was — then perhaps he would sign the paper and send it on to his boss. And we would be free.

Thus, during the first several days of homeschooling, I sent Grace up to her room to read while I created an entire imaginary curriculum. Grace had already missed plenty of school, so we simply called each day and lied that yes, once again she was sick. Terrible cough, I told them — not letting on that it was her classmates' coughing, rather than her own, that was keeping her away.

I was a woman obsessed, creating an entire year's worth of lesson plans in a week. We would memorize poetry, and sing traditional French folksongs. We would learn all of French history from the cavemen to the Revolution, and also cover rudimentary astronomy and chemistry. She would paint and draw from nature, and learn the elements of the water cycle. I would structure her days around the French school schedule, and be certain each day to put in enough classroom minutes to meet all the regulations. We would speak only French in our house for three hours a day.

Grace shuffled around the house in her bunny slippers and bathrobe those first days, happy as a clam. Feeling safely ignored, she pulled out the art supplies and began painting a self-portrait. She opened up the other laptop and started drafting a story about a mysterious letter. She found a children's history of the British Isles and disappeared for hours at a time, emerging at lunch with questions about William the Conqueror. Instead of dissolving in miserable tears every morning, or hiding with the bedcovers over her ears, she got herself out of bed and made breakfast for herself and her sister.

Now and then she'd quietly drift past the desk where Bill and I were frantically translating the educational requirements and dreaming up ways we would meet them right there in the house. I would shoo her away, and she'd go into the kitchen to pick out a recipe to make us all for lunch.

Abigail still went to and from school each day, appearing somewhat relieved not to be dragging a miserably wailing sibling by her side. Freed from that particular ball and chain, she went back to the way she has always done school: showing up on time and doing her best, but never revealing to us anything that happened all day long.

I, however, was creating an entire curriculum from scratch, and was getting excited to show it all off. I stayed up late nights, knowing that Grace's imaginary cold couldn't last forever. I wanted to be more than ready for my date with M. Souris and homeschool destiny. Plus, this was starting to seem like a terrific plan: field trips to the caves of Lascaux! Conjugating -ir verbs every day before déjeuner! We would learn to gavotte!

Why hadn't I thought of this before? I felt like a new convert to a strange religion: homeschool suddenly felt like the answer not just to this problem, but to every problem on earth for all time.

Once I had an entire paper year to convince M. Souris, I had essentially also convinced myself. I would run the world's tiniest French school, with nothing but internet worksheets and sticky tape to hold it all together.

I half-convinced Bill too, realizing that we'd need his French skills if Grace was going to make any progress. I signed him up for French and P.E., and he started calling himself "*Monsieur Guillaume*," and talking about drills for pronoun agreement and *le foot*.

Once we were filled up with our certainty fuel, he called the school to make the appointment.

At first the principal was puzzled, thinking that Grace had been injured in some way and could not make it into the building. When he realized that we truly intended to educate her at home, his voice quieted. This was very unfortunate news, he averred. But he would not be able to meet with us for another week.

We must excuse him, he told us, but he had some regulations to check.

"That's the sound of a bureaucrat talking, Launa," Bill said to me when he got off the phone. "He's got to dot his i's and cross his t's, and since this is France, he won't be persuaded unless that happens."

As a poverty lawyer, Bill had significant experience with American bureaucrats. His multiple visits to the French Office of Immigration had showed him that the French were even less reasonable, and more driven by the forms and the rules.

I put less stock in the bureaucracy angle, never wavering in my faith in the power of lesson plans.

"Just wait until he sees my curriculum," I enthused to Bill's skeptical frown. "I'll win him over."

Once again, there we were facing the same future, but from totally opposing points of view.

Undeterred by the wait of a week, I launched Grace into my wonderful program. In the morning we named things in French. We sorted nouns and affixed the proper endings onto verbs. We wrote little *dialogues*, and translated love songs, just like I did as a teenager. In the afternoons, we gave ourselves a reprieve, and all settled in to read regular old novels in plain old English. Once we were done reading, we multiplied enormous numbers, and divided fractions into parts and back again.

With all that French in the house, and playing from our iPods, I was beginning to feel as though we had enrolled ourselves in the world's tiniest French club. It was time to jettison my mistrust of the townspeople, and my self-consciousness about how uncouth we all were, and just fall head-over-heels in love with all things French. In our little French club, we too would sing *Frère Jacques,* and all buy berets, even though I never saw a single person wear one in Aups.

When I was in first grade, Nathaniel Buck's mother started just such a club in our rural upstate New York elementary school. Nathaniel — we called him Thann —had previously struck me as an occasionally amusing, but somewhat useless little boy. Tiny, blond, and effete, he simply failed to register during the rabid, warlike games of tag-and-kissing on the playground. But he was liable to burst into torrents of complicated and precise vocabulary, reflecting in his wholly original way on the topics at hand in our under-evolved early-1970's classroom.

If I had been a more sophisticated person, I would have immediately seen that he was a funky city boy trapped in a small town, waiting it out until he could somehow get himself to a metropolis, or at least an art school. I could have seen him as a kindred spirit. As it was, he always struck me as bewildered.

But when Than and a few other kids and I started spending Monday afternoons singing "*Alouette*" and making *mousse au chocolat,* out of view of the rough and tumble boys who had previously owned my attentions, he suddenly became a whole lot cooler. Seeing this new side of him was like the moment early on in college when I discovered that the dorky guys were often incredibly sexy. It was the same at age 7 and age 17: instead of chasing the bad boys and trying to get them to want to kiss me, I learned that could stand aloof off on the edge of things and enjoy the company of someone smart and funny who thought I was the bee's knees.

A strange grouping of kids had been signed up for French Club. Membership didn't break down along the lines we knew. But looking back, I can now see what we all had in common: we were the kids with parents who had attended four-year colleges, and who thus knew the cachet of all things French. The parents who signed their kids up for French Club did so at least in part because they knew French to be classy. Life is awfully darned unfair, and it starts early on in subtle ways than we can't understand as they are happening. While the rest of the kids hopped on the buses, back to watch TV in their trailers or in old cow-smelling farmhouses, a bunch of us began to reap the cultural advantages afforded to children with moms who could drive to school later in the afternoon to pick us up.

The French Club met after school. Mrs. Buck's lessons were sophisticated, challenging, and quirky in a way that third grade just wasn't. She was like a bird, but also self-assured and self-contained. She wore much more formal clothing than most other moms, and she seemed a lot older, her skin like beautifully smooth tanned leather. Unlike Annabelle Greenhill's mother, who miraculously retained her British accent for decades, Mrs. Buck spoke English like an American. But she knew her business when it came to French stuff. And for that we all thought she had come from the stars.

Mrs. Buck had a deep familiarity with French language, food, and rituals. Heaven knows what compelled her to share this secret knowledge with our benighted selves, but God bless her. Once I actually moved to France, speaking and eating and trying to figure out the rituals once again, I realized that I owed her a debt I can never repay. She launched me there, somehow, to arrive decades after first grade in a place of marvelous cheese and blue sky, surrounded by a musical but still inscrutable language.

When Mrs. Buck taught us French, she told us that the sweet little vowels and funny words could all be grouped, for no reason I could intuit then or now, into male and female. Apples were girls, but pens and pencils were boys. Flags were boys, and mouths were girls — even if those mouths were on boys. We sang "*Sur Le Pont d'Avignon*," and "*Au Clair de la Lune*." The moon was of course a girl, which made sense, because it was smaller but prettier than the big fat bossy boy of a sun.

But the other words seemed so bizarre as to be surreal. Why would a bridge in Avignon be a boy? Or a table a girl? How could "he" and "she" apply to things so obviously "it"? Mrs. Buck knew all these things, and even how to count to *vingt* and beyond, and she would teach us this secret code all afternoon long over grapes and baguettes.

French struck us all as particularly worth learning: even more so than reading and telling time and speaking the correct words of the Pledge of Allegiance.

When we were in French Club, it was clear that we were involved in something special and important, and Madame Buck was worthy of our greatest respect. Mrs. Buck brought with her the chic of Paris, the soigné of Truffaut, the primal energy of Gauguin, and the whole fabulously snooty attitude of a culture certain of its own enduring superiority.

When Mrs. Buck made crêpes with us, it suddenly mattered how the butter melted and bubbled into froth in the pan on the hotplate. We were careful to say "*S'il vous plaît*" and "*Merci, Madame,*" when she put them on our paper plates, steaming and smelling like heaven. She served them with confectioner's sugar and *confiture de fraise.* Something in her attitude let us know that these were no ordinary pancakes smothered in strawberry jam. These were French, and "French" meant very, very, very good. Crêpes were somehow better than we deserved, but were there, nonetheless, for our taking and cutting up with little plastic knives.

As the year marched on into November, she told us all about a Christmas party we were going to have at her house. There would be French decorations, and French meat, and French desserts. (My adult brain here cues up that John Cusack movie, *Better Off Dead*: "French fries, French dressing, French bread...")

Part of me was excited for *La Fête de Noël,* but an even bigger part of me was nervous. If it was hard to stay obedient and well-behaved for 60 minutes of French Club, how could we all hold it together for a full afternoon of cooking and eating Christmas yummies at her actual house? Also, as we had learned from making those crêpes, French food was nearly impossible to make properly – much more like a magic potion made from sacred ingredients than the actual food we ate in our real American houses: roast beef, boiled potatoes, and white bread with butter. How would we know how to treat the eggs for the mousse? Could we follow a recipe that called the sugar a boy and the measuring cup a girl? How could we possibly behave well enough to continue to earn Mrs. Buck's positive and French regard? Would we have to speak French, *all in italics?*

The party was part disaster, part triumph. We got spoken to a few times for losing our chic, soigné cool, and I think some of the boys got in a tussel over Than's Star Wars figures.

But I can still remember the dark beauty of her house: the candles that she lit for the dinner, the strings of cranberries that we made. The *mousse au chocolat* was rich and creamy, both light and heavy at the same time. The decorations were strange; somehow recognizably Christmas, but yet foreign and inscrutable. The French Santa was skinny, not fat; *Père Noël* eats like a Parisian. At the end, Mrs. Buck brought out a massive *Bûche de Noël* that we were to decorate.

For some reason, which I am sure that Mrs. Buck explained to me over thirty years ago, French people celebrate Christmas with *Bûche de Noël,* a cake that looks like a log. It is chocolate frosted in chocolate, which sounds all well and good, but then it is also decorated with mushrooms made out of sugar. If you're going to make something Christmassy out of chocolate and sugar, I say don't make it look like a log. Chocolate should be melty, small, and perhaps topped with a little salted caramel. Not a fake mushroom. No logs for Christmas.

But then again, the French never asked me how they should celebrate *le Noël.* (While the party, *la fête,* is a girl, Christmas itself is a boy.) They already know damn well how to celebrate Christmas, and they told Mrs. Buck, and Mrs. Buck was there to tell me. This culture has its act together, we were to learn, and we should only be so lucky to get a taste of crêpes and a bite of chocolate log and to know which nouns wore the pants.

For some reason — call it repression, call it forgetfulness, call it better things to do — I hadn't thought about Than and Mrs. Buck for 30 years. How did I forget to tell my girls the French Club stories, while Bill was entrancing them with his tales of Merrie Olde Seconde Grade Englande?

My memories all came back to me the day I decided on the crêpes. I became my own Madame Buck as I suddenly and surprisingly began homeschooling Grace — trying my hardest to teach her *le* from *la* as it applied to the sofa and her shoes.

As soon as I remembered, I stopped worrying about the homeschooling regulations and where to buy the texts and which special notebooks would make M. Souris see how serious we were about our French. Instead of anything quite so scholarly as math and history and grammar, our studies designed to impress the French authorities, that afternoon we took on a most important hands-on project in our world's tiniest French club. Crêpes.

I waited until Abigail returned home. We mixed the batter in the blender and let it sit half an hour. We melted butter in a small, hot pan. I spooned the batter to cover the bottom, then swirled the pan just so. I lifted the edges with a clean silver knife and flipped the crêpe to cook the other side. We ate them first with grated cheese, then with raspberry jam and powdered sugar.

France had schooled us in ways we never had expected. But there, in my past and in my present, was a French lesson we all would remember as warm, and rich, and sweet.

———————

Late that fall, each sunset was more beautifully flaming and camera-worthy than the last. Each evening we were served a brand new combination of reds, oranges, and blues found nowhere else in nature aside from the showiest of tropical flowers. While we were starting to cook dinner, we were drawn outside by a slash of red, fuchsia, or tangerine deep along the western horizon. We walked outside to discover that the quarter sphere of sky we could see from the terrace was spattered in contrasts. One night it was soft sea blue dotted with enormous pink stretchy marshmallows. Another night, the sunset was made of stripes of deepening oranges starting on the hills and fading upwards. The bureaucrats were putting us through our paces, but the sky sought only to seduce.

One evening, we drove again up the bucolic hill above Aups and into the stark and shocking deep bowl of mountains on the other side. Rain was predicted for the next day, and we wanted to use the sunset lightshow to add a little drama to our favorite drive. As we drove up the pastoral Vermonty side of the mountain, the sun was a classic orange flameball sinking down in our back window. We crested the hill towards the stark Colorado side, where the sun painted the hillsides ahead of us in a pinky gold alpenglow.

We drove as far as the bridge over the Gorge du Verdon, and hopped out of the car to look at the deserted lake. But just as we slammed the car doors, a cold wind swept up the beach, informing us in no uncertain terms that our colorful afternoon idyll was over. Time to go stoke up the fire and hunker down.

We headed for home. As we crested the hill to drop back down to town, the sun had sunk behind a miles-high gunmetal wall of cloud. A stark line in the sky marked the edge of the cloud, behind which the whole world disappeared. It advanced on us, and we on it. By the time we got back to the house to finish up the final round of the day's dirty dishes, the stars and the little crescent moon had been blotted out entirely, and fat raindrops started to splatter on the stones tiles of the terrace.

The sky stayed overcast for the whole next day. Then, after that one dreary day of gray, the mistral kicked up in the middle of the night, moaning and banging around in the chimneys of the house, sounding like distant thunder or artillery explosions. There were no flues on the Bastide's chimneys, making for some chilly rooms, high heating bills, and creepy sound effects when the wind blew.

All those noisy sharp gusts of wind blew away the gray shelf of clouds and we woke up to our trusty old color scheme: ochre hills, lush green growing things, and endless blue sky. But the turn towards fall also brought yellow: turning autumn leaves, and soft drippy golden light in the mornings. Even after the wind had done its duty of clearing out the heavy skies, it kept blowing for days and days.

A mistral feels cold and hot at the same time: the wind and the sun battle it out to see which one can rule the day. With the wind blowing like mad and the sun shining so damn hard, you would think that the laundry would have dried on the line. But instead the clothing just whipped itself around damply for a few hours.

It got so windy and sunny that I kept getting extremely confused about whether I was warm or cool or downright cold. I felt lightly baked and air conditioned at the same time. I didn't feel homicidal, thankfully, but certainly unsettled, as this wind was so different from any weather I had ever known before. I hadn't thought that something as simple as weather could be so completely different in different places, as there are really only four factors: temperature, wind speed, humidity, and light. But then I found my whole outlook totally changed by the specifics of the sky.

Jessica had warned us about the high cost of heating a large, drafty stone house, so we decided to see how long we could leave the heat off. Instead, we bought firewood, and wore a few layers of sweaters around the house. But the firewood was wet and dense, and the house turned downright chilly once the sun went down.

The new chill in the air seemed to be changing the way we were being received by our neighbors here in the little town. I had mastered the flat French face and no longer smiled and waved stupidly at total strangers. I even gave up on ever being spoken to at the school *portail*, assuming I would just spend the year enjoying the few people who had already been kind to us.

But then, quite suddenly, we were being greeted by the townspeople who had been so distant at first. One day, as our whole family was walking together down our little walled *chemin*, the lane towards town, a woman driving by in a little gray car *smiled and waved*. Not just a nod or a tidy little perfunctory *"Bonjour, Madame,"* but a true stretch-out-the-sides-of-your-mouth grin and friendly open hand. She did not stop the car or actually speak, but the connection felt like a miracle.

The next day, as Grace was practicing her sprinting on the same little road for homeschool P.E., and I was practicing my own brand-new walking speed — an extremely slow and lazy sort of wander I was aiming to perfect — we greeted an older man with a teeny white dog on a leash. He, too, smiled generously, and even offered a few helpful suggestions on Grace's running form.

He was our neighbor, he told us, and an athlete himself, *un sportif* who enjoyed nearly every form of exercise. When I told him we were from Brooklyn, he excitedly told me all about his very favorite movie — Eddie Murphy's midcareer masterpiece, *The King of New York*. He spoke about its genius the way a freshman undergraduate who has just discovered film studies would talk about Truffaut or Ray or Goddard. Despite the massive southern twang of his dialogue that made it sometimes hard for me to follow him, I found my French skills more than accurate for us to carry on a legitimately enriching and pleasant dialogue for the entire remaining portion of my slow meandering back to our wooden gate.

The following day, yet another neighbor stopped me to comment on how much she liked my shirt, and to question me about where I had gotten it, and perhaps where she could get one herself. I was wearing this crazy swirly print thing from Athleta.com, perfect for the ever-changing weather, and I did a credible job of spelling *ah-tay-ashe-elle-uuh-tay-ah-point-com* for her. We talked some more about our shared affection for one another's earrings. Nothing culturally significant, but no matter: she was seeking me out, unprompted, and we were having a real conversation. I finally had neighbors.

Why was the village suddenly opening up to us, even just the tiniest bit? Was the change in me, or in my steadily developing language skills? Once I learned to say more, I probably became a whole lot less boring and panicked-looking. Certainly my new amble was more welcoming than my rushed New Yorker's stride.

France has lots more reflexive verbs than does English. When speaking French, rather than being bored, one "bores oneself." Rather than being angry, one "angers oneself." I have always liked the way that French puts the onus of these unpleasant feelings on the person having the feelings — rather than implicitly blaming a flawed external environment. Grace agreed, and in honor of the wisdom of the phrase "*s'ennuyer,*" decided to call her homeschool blog "I Do Not Bore Myself."

So perhaps the reflexive verb "*s'approcher,*" (to approach, to come closer) could explain things. Perhaps it is not that I was being isolated, but rather that I needed to bring myself to approach, to find a way to bring myself closer.

Or, perhaps I got so used to being ignored and looked through in this small town, and in France more generally, that my old goofy American standards for what counts as "friendly" were being completely revised. Perhaps instead of seeing Aups as a flawed version of the social world of my old home, I was seeing it more as it saw itself, with its own rules, conventions, and personalities.

As the weather grew colder, and our little family stubbornly refused to disappear from town, we stumbled over the magic invisible line that exists in all of the world's tourist towns between the summer people and the real ones. The villagers long ago decided not to waste their sparse supply of friendliness on the white-sheathed Parisians, Germans, Dutch, and Italians who arrive in August to soak up the sun and be soaked by the high prices at the market. Better to save it up instead for the people you might actually see more than once or twice.

The weather got colder, and the human climate grew warmer. Perhaps the people of Aups remembered some vestige of the primal protectiveness of our deep shared past in the caves. Faced with chilly winds and darkening skies, we pulled a little closer around the shared warmth of the fire.

It was a very chilly morning the day we were to meet with the principal.

On the advice of a good friend from home who had homeschooled for years, convincing her local school board of the wisdom of her choices, I decided not to translate the plans into French. "When you're talking about homeschool, keep things on your own turf," she had counseled me.

"You are not only a mother, Launa: you're the teacher, and you call the shots. Flash your educational credentials and years of experience," she said, "and play like nobody has ever questioned your judgment. Ever."

This would be a challenge, as I frequently questioned myself just getting out of bed in the morning. But knowing the French intolerance for weakness, I would not blink.

Plus, I had this great curriculum to spread out on the principal's desk. And we had sung songs! And taught our girls how to make crêpes! How could he possibly resist?

Bill had other plans. He was glued to his legal regulations rather than wowed by my amazing curriculum. "Things work differently here," he kept saying, as I pressed him to be sure he could cogently articulate the finer points of my science plans. "We'll need to listen more than we'll need to speak."

Our meeting was set for lunchtime on a Thursday. We were prepared for battle, but also confidently, even sweetly, congenial; Bill and I had mastered this art through our years of on-the-job training as middle managers. I had my soft voice and my big stick. Bill had his lawyerly savvy and his cunning, plus his vastly more impressive language skills. Eager to make a good impression, I dug back into the back of my closet and pulled out heels and the only professional wool blazer I had. Bill found a tie wadded up behind his hiking boots.

M. Souris met us at *le portail* and used his special key to let us in. He invited us into his office, where I saw the curriculum guide I knew so well lying on the table between us. If Bill could simply manage to translate to him just how well I had learned his nation's curriculum, Monsieur would *have* to sign the magic paper.

He probably would even congratulate me on my initiative, organization, and penmanship.

Bill spoke his pleasantries as I smiled and sought to give this perfectly kind and generous man my honest reassurance that I knew this entire situation was not his fault or his problem. I proudly spread my documents between us, but M. Souris did not give them a second glance.

His opening gambit set me back on my high heels. "You can not possibly be certain of this choice?" the principal asked, apparently thinking that we were kidding, and had sequestered Grace and set up an appointment with him just for fun.

"We could not be more sure. We will not change our minds," Bill told him.

I added a serious, unnecessary, "*Oui.*"

"Then I have no choice but to demand that you engage in the national program."

But then he gestured not towards the curriculum book and my lovely sheets of paper, but towards a stack of cheery yellow workbooks on the table behind his desk. Each one was marked "CNED," which was not, as far as I knew, a word in any language.

"You see, *our* nation provides for children who can not be properly educated in school." He said this with a tone that suggested that we strange American expat homeschoolers had something to learn from the French.

"We have a national curriculum, designed by educational experts, which prepares all students for full participation as French citizens. With our CNED system, students complete the lessons by correspondence with expert teachers. We use this for invalids, or students studying far away from France, but in this case it can be used as well, I think. Yes. It has been decided. She will complete our program booklets. There is nothing else to be done."

I must have looked awfully upset by this news, because his voice turned even more stern.

"Otherwise I will have to have the academic inspector come to your home. If he does not like what he sees, you will have to return Grace to school."

I started to redden, and clutched Bill's hand perhaps a little too hard. Grace couldn't possibly complete workbooks designed for a French fifth grader. And I would be damned if she'd be forced back to a place where things had become so awful. I almost opened my mouth to argue precisely this point. Bill squeezed back and leapt into the breach before I could speak.

"What a wonderful idea!" Bill exclaimed, in a tone of false, winning enthusiasm. "The French nation cares so much about children, and we are so lucky to have your expert guidance. We are so grateful for this program and your booklets."

I was confused. What about *my* amazing homeschool plans? The gavottes? The crêpes? He expected Grace to fill out workbooks all year long, all in French at the level of a fifth-grade French speaker? I thought I was going to cry.

But Bill was acting as though this were terrific news. "These workbooks will be exactly what we need."

"I am so pleased to have your understanding," M. Souris nearly purred, clearly relieved.

"We are so grateful for your assistance in this matter." Bill said, reaching over to shake his hand.

Sensing the change in the emotional weather of the room, it dawned on me. My lovely scheming bureaucrat-whisperer Bill had a plan. M. Souris was grateful. And I should probably just shut up.

Poor M. Souris. Like us, he had been stuck between the rock of laws and the hard place of humanity. He was trapped in a system he hadn't invented. Once the workbooks had settled the matter, he looked much more sympathetic to me, and I saw the roles we all must play. We would be grateful. He would be victorious. And then, we would go away. Having properly discharged his duties in this ridiculous matter with the picky Americans, and having won our assent, he could go back to class and stop worrying that his boss would get on his case.

Bill grabbed the workbooks in one hand, and my elbow in the other, and pulled me up to stand.

"I assure you, M. Souris, we are all in accord. Thank you so much. We'll be going now."

Obedient for once, I shuffled my papers into a pile and shoved them into my bag. I wasn't sure who exactly would be filling out all those workbooks designed for hospitalized French fifth graders, but my imaginary curriculum wouldn't be needed here anymore.

As is the case in every other marriage I have ever known, no matter how deep the love that binds the parties together, each person is locked in his or her own perspective. Perhaps the most perfect of partners learn eventually to read one another's minds, and never suffer the inevitable disappointments and misunderstandings to which the rest of us fall prey. But I am quite certain that we are not the only couple who — while still remaining deeply in love — also remain completely opaque to one another on at least a few key issues.

We were both utterly silent as we left the school, the tall green *portail* clanging shut behind our heels. This silence required more self-control than I thought I had. We were halfway home before I burst out with my questions.

"What exactly was that all about? How is Grace ever going to understand those workbooks? Chemistry in French? History in French? *French* in French?"

Bill was smiling, relishing his success and his secrets. He put his arm around my shoulder and let me in on his conspiracy.

"Well, this might not be ethical, and it certainly won't be easy, but while you teach Grace what she needs to learn this year, I'm going to do my best to pass the French fifth grade."

I looked up at him, along that familiar angle between my eyes and his.

And you know how sometimes people say, "I was so grateful I could have kissed him?" Right there, in the middle of the road, that's exactly what I did.

———

The next day was Friday the 13th, which should have presaged all sorts of awful happenings: broken mirrors, unfriendly natives, trips to the ER, or even just being embarrassed at the grocery store. But I had already had all those things happen, and it seemed as though we had run through our spate of bad luck and into a vein of pure gold.

Over the next few weeks, I knocked on wood whenever I noticed myself feeling at home rather than worried, but damn did it feel good to feel good, even if it required me to lie to the principal. After all those years of striving so diligently to be happy, willing the world into a shape that would somehow suit me, how strange it was to find myself fit the world instead. We would teach Grace plenty, I knew, but with Bill's new entirely unethical plan, we'd keep the world out of our family for just this little while.

Since our arrival, I had been turning the tumblers of a very complicated lock, waiting for it all to snap into place. And there in mid-November I found myself, simply happy, shoulders down where shoulders belong rather than lodged in my ears.

It gradually became clear that moving Grace's school home was better for all of us than I could have known. I don't know why I had been sending her off to a school that was clearly making her miserable, but there were several top contenders, all of them mortal sins. I was slothfully loath to give up my free time, and more than a little pridefully anxious about becoming one of "those" homeschoolers.

Homeschoolers were religious nuts, I had thought, seeking to escape the evils of sex-ed and pesky theories like evolution. Or they hated school. I had spent my entire life in school, and the idea of floating free of one made me feel naked.

But once we started following a few of my elaborate plans and feeding Grace's old-fashioned curiosity, homeschool revealed itself to be more straightforward and a lot more engaging than any of us had thought. There are any number of incredibly useful ways for a smart, introverted kid to spend her days, and we just picked the most likely ones at hand. She learned a lot of stuff online, as a computer program proved much better at generating appropriately difficult math problems and foreign language challenges than was I.

She was learning a ton about reading, writing, and research in English. We did in fact continue to speak French in the house at least three hours a day, and always during lunch. But she was also learning so much more in terms of the practical realities of life, which we decided to make a real subject. One afternoon she spent an hour or so picking olives with Jessica and Gerard, learning both that olive picking is hard work and that a fresh olive tastes simply awful. I was impressed that she stuck with it for so long, with so little input from me. She also learned to do the dishes, set the table, and make both sweet and a savory crêpes all by herself.

When I stopped rushing around like a lunatic to try to get her to school against her will, I discovered a lot more time for finding the pace Grace actually needed in order to learn things. In homeschool, Grace learned the relatively complicated skill of using parallel structure with a list of serial clauses in almost no time flat. "I gave my dog a nice warm bath, he ate my only clean socks, and it all gave me a big fat headache," she wrote. Math was easy-peasy, even hard formulas like one-half base times height. But to learn to do hard things like open the door, turn on the shower to the right temperature, and fold and put away laundry took a lot more time than I would have thought. Bucketsful of time, really, which we all so suddenly and gratefully discovered we had.

We memorized songs in French. We used poetry magnets to learn the gender of nouns. We found videos on YouTube to research various European cultures. Our favorite was footage of some extremely Tyrolean people yodeling and doing a strange sort of series of knee-slapping moves called *Schuhplattler*, the world's whitest step dance. We watched that one every few days, just for fun. We visited the towns nearby, stopping at every war memorial and public fountain to piece together local history from the cavemen to the war with Algeria. Grace started reading her way through the library at the Bastide, taking in Jessica's British kids' novels, guides to astronomy, and introductions to prehistory.

And then one day Grace asked us, out of the blue, "What is philosophy?" Bill started in on the difference between ontology and phenomenology, but I had a different plan. I printed out Plato's Allegory of the Cave, and early the next morning we stood in a real prehistoric grotto just up the street to read it and figure out what it meant.

The cave was littered with candy wrappers and smelled like urine, but we three stood there, facing the dark, with the morning sun behind our heads. We read Plato together, imaginatively projecting an image of the truth onto the wall of the cave in front of us.

In the Allegory of the Cave, Socrates explains that for most people, life is akin to being chained in a cave, facing the wall. We humans watch the shadows that reality throws on the wall, and imagine that we are seeing the world as it is. One of the goals of philosophy is to reveal the truth of things. Through thinking, we learn to break free and go out into the light to truly see. When the seeking of philosophy suddenly frees us from the chains holding us in place, we are at first dazzled and confused by the light of the real world. As Socrates says, any human seeker

"will require to grow accustomed to the sight of the upper world. And first he will see the shadows best, next the reflections of men and other objects in the water, and then the objects themselves; then he will gaze upon the light of the moon and the stars and the spangled heaven; and he will see the sky and the stars by night better than the sun or the light of the sun by day... Last off he will be able to see the sun, and not mere reflections of him in the water, but he will see him in his own proper place, and not in another; and he will contemplate him as he is."

Grace listened carefully to the words of Socrates's metaphor, turning back and forth from the dark of the cave to the light of the sun.

"So when you stop thinking the easy, obvious way, the same way everybody else does, you can experience the truth of the real way things are?"

"That's what he's saying, Grace. And philosophers have agreed with him for thousands and thousands of years."

She turned her head back over her shoulder and smiled at us, squinting into the light of the sun at our backs.

"Oh, so the truth is the light on the real world. But it's just so hard to really see."

She paused for a minute, then looked thoughtful and happy. "I get it Mom. I really do."

During the fall, Jessica and Gerard were often busy on their farm gathering honey, fattening up the geese, and getting ready for the winter. Farms are like that, requiring periods of frantic activity. Bill had fantasies of acting as a volunteer farmhand, but after the rabbit died, he was never bold enough to offer his services. Our families gathered every few weeks for dinner, and gradually we met the rest of their friends. When it was my turn to cook, I'd try out some new recipe a day or two in advance, to be sure it would be edible. We were still awfully tentative, as we couldn't afford for this friendship to fail.

But just when we had totally resigned ourselves to complete social reliance on Jessica and Gerard, we met Dermot and Anna-Maria. One day Abigail and I went to the Intermarché at an uncommon time for us, and overheard a young couple speaking British to one another and to their adorable blonde 3-year-old daughter.

In shameless social desperation, I threw myself into conversation. They too had been living in Aups since the summer, and we had certainly passed one another on the street without realizing that we were all adrift in the same sea. Abigail started playing with little Lajla in the olive oil aisle, while I nearly fell over myself trying to invite them to our house. Equally quickly, they extended an invitation to Anna-Maria's birthday party, which was to be the next night. I didn't try at all to hide my excitement, and Abigail was positively ecstatic about this invitation, jonesing as she had been for people who speak English.

Dermot and Anna-Maria's rented house in the center of town was tall, warm, and welcoming. They had lit candles all over the place, and had plates of speck and little crackers with salmon on them, and lots of tiny German beers. The guests were a motley mix of artists, travelers, chefs, and people who spoke more than one language. Apparently Anna-Maria and Dermot had been much more successful in making friends. The party felt not unlike ones in Brooklyn, minus the stockbrokers and lawyers, so we felt right at home.

Nobody knew anybody else very well, so we were all on our best and most openhearted behavior. The little boys from Lajla's preschool spent the night pleasantly marauding around, while our girls sculpted playdough and drew pictures and spoke English to people. There was funk and soul on the stereo, and my French had become perfectly serviceable — particularly with the certainty fuel of a few beers behind it. At least it had become adequate for me to express a variety of pet theories and little stories, and to understand the ones I was hearing.

At one point in the evening, Bill and I looked at one another across the room, with the same revelation: we wouldn't have to spend the year all alone saying curt hellos to the woman at the cheese shop and sending lachrymose emails to our friends back home. At that point, I would have made friends with a particularly interesting rock, so to meet some people who were truly engaging and funny and had great stories to tell was more than I could have hoped for.

A charming sculptor flounced over to flirt with Bill, doing this funny thing French people sometimes do of holding up a fake microphone to interview him. Her name was Vava, and she had beautiful apple cheeks and soft brown curls, and appeared fascinated by Bill. She and her boyfriend Jona lived ten paces away across the street, but for some reason he had arrived to the party on a motorcycle.

Jona leaned in to tell Bill and me about his Russian father and his American mom. His English was drastically better than my French. "I was born on a table in the kitchen of our commune in 1968, and lived in France since I was 3," he told us, his blonde curls drooping down into his eyes. "In all that time, I've never followed the rules of this world."

He had enormous hands. I learned later that he was a tree surgeon — French people don't talk much about their jobs on the first few meetings, unless of course they are charming sculptors. I don't think I had ever noticed a man's hands before, but somehow Jona's rough-skinned ones were more alluring than the other hands I'd been ignoring all that time.

He dropped his voice to a low growl, as though he were letting us all in on a secret of great import to us all. "Here is my motto: I do what I want, when I want, how I want it."

Despite his left-leaning politics, Bill has always hated selfish hippies. "So how does that work when what you want, when you want, conflicts with what I want? Who then gets to decide that particular question?"

"That's what the squares always say," he remarked, winking at his sculptor and at me, before strutting off to get all four of us more wine.

The candles were burning low. The earthy woman who worked at the agricultural cooperative was deep in conversation with a chef and a guy who made his living selling tractor parts on eBay. She was there with her British boyfriend, and I couldn't tell whether he was a brilliant aristocrat dropout, or a straight-up pothead. Dermot and Anna-Maria were dancing with Lajla and Abigail, and Grace was walking someone's tow-headed toddler up and down the hall.

When it was time to go, I'm quite sure the *bisous* we received from the sculptor and the motorcycle man were significantly longer than was strictly polite, but I had to assume that this was what happened when you met real French people at a party. Both Bill and I blushed bright red. We kissed Dermot and Anna-Maria and Lajla, and then our family spilled out into the starry night to walk home on our tiny pitch black lane. We all held hands to keep safe in the dark, and Bill once again told us his Yaroslavl story to distract the girls from being afraid.

So this is what it was like to be an ex-pat, to be finding oneself at home so very far away, with strange new companions. Our cheeks still burned where those kisses had been. They certainly weren't bad, but did that make them good? We had somehow lucked into a merry band of people from the town to hang out with during the long dark nights of winter. I'd been wrong, I'd been right, and then wrong and right so many times that it made my head spin.

———————

Thanksgiving — and my in-laws — came just at a moment when I was finding all of these new things to be thankful for. Bill's parents Gus and Linda, his sister Laura, and our nephew Finn were flying in for a visit, and our family would be the only people in the whole town celebrating a Pilgrim feast.

Flushed with my new confidence in the kitchen, and wanting to make my in-laws feel at home, I planned to cook the whole meal from scratch — my own very first holiday dinner. It seemed like a great idea in theory, but as the day approached I realized that this endeavor was scary, in the way that a colossal flop in front of one's in-laws can be.

Bill's family tends to sit firmly on the mild, generous, and sweet side of humanity, but what if things went suddenly and horribly awry with dinner? What if, disappointed by the meal I imagined I might flub, the whole family turned on me, turned on France, or turned on one another? We had already forced them to fly thousands of miles to see us.

My first Thanksgiving dinner had better be good.

I had all the ingredients on hand, except for the last few that we could get at the Saturday market in town. Still, that morning when I woke up, I had made precisely one dish: a somewhat burned and poorly-mixed pumpkin pie. I suppose I could have counted the can of organic cranberry relish Gus had brought, as well as the sausages and cheeses (*Epoisse, St. Nectare, Beaufort Comté*) that some earthy artisan had spent hours crafting on a farm nearby.

Oh, and most importantly, the goose. Jessica and Gerard – purveyors of the big fat goose, so enormous that it could no longer fly — had killed and plucked and cured and stuffed it with chestnuts, truffles, and pancetta. Thus the centerpiece of the meal had arrived ready-to-cook the day before and was hogging the top-shelf real estate in the refrigerator.

That morning, before any of our jetlagged guests could get out of bed, I addressed my worries in a very predictable way: by making a detailed list. First I listed all the dishes, and then put in time order all the tasks and dishes and steps. "Set the table" came right after "wash the celery" and before "mash the roast squash with maple syrup and orange juice." Bill's name for this approach is a "uni-recipe," and as much as I laughed at the concept when he first employed it, I found that reminding myself of the actual steps involved tended to alleviate the worst of my anxieties. Uni-recipe in hand, I could reason with myself: generations of pioneer mommas have made Thanksgiving. If they could do it, I could, too.

With a uni-recipe, I could construct the entire meal as though it were a single dish. First I read all the individual recipes closely to insert all the steps of the shorter recipes into the open spaces in the longest recipe. When I first read about goose in the *Joy of Cooking* I bought in an American bookstore in Paris, I caught the first hour-and-a-half roasting period, but somehow missed the second one.

Luckily, I caught my error before I ended up serving Grandpa Gus — a biochemist with a serious appreciation of the destructive power of all things germy — a raw and bloody mess of fatty goose skin and flesh. Once I charted out all the basting, flipping, resting, and carving the goose would require, I could fit in the rest of the steps, including an apple pie made with Pink Ladies and sweetened with an intensely flavored forest-flower honey.

Over the course of a few lovely hours, it all came into being. The crust, the pie, the squash, the goose, the celery, the salad, the potatoes, the beans, and the nibbles were readied and heated and mixed and basted and coated with the big three of *provençal* cooking: wine, olive oil, and honey. Since it wasn't just the usual French meal, but also Thanksgiving, there was also a fair amount of butter lubricating things: a full-butter pie crust made in the food processor, plus butter in the squash and the potatoes and slathered all over the green beans.

The kitchen had only the smallest amount of counter space, but was dominated by an enormous square table that served dinner to eight just as well as it served as headquarters for any major cooking project. I rolled out the dough there, and stacked up the ingredients. I used at least eight of the thirty knives lying around, including the enormous murder-weapon-sized ones. I used the ceramic baking dishes, the whisks, the wooden spoons, and even the baster.

(I lacked only a meat thermometer, which really would have made Gus's day.) And as I cooked, Bill used the two deep sinks to stay a half step ahead of the most serious pre-dinner washing up.

I begged Bill to chop off the grotesque long neck of the goose with the homicide knife, then we made a broth for the gravy out of the horrible long neck boiled in water with celery leaves, onions, a bay leaf, red wine, thyme, and a lot of carrot chunks. I loved smelling it, boiling there on the stove for hours. Soon the potatoes and garlic cloves were sitting in water, ready to go. The green beans were snapped and lined up in a pretty blue pan, ready to be steamed in broth in the last few minutes. The kitchen was starting to fill up with the smells of goose, squash, and maple syrup, layered over the scent of the broth, the apple and cinnamon, and all that dairy and olive fat.

While I was cooking, I felt as though I were channeling every adult woman in my life, as well as my Dad and my father-in-law, as I had the dubious fatherly honor of taking responsibility for cooking a large hunk of stuffed poultry as well as all the sides. Although I have always been a reasonably responsible and effective adult, I was still trying to find my domestic groove. It helped to imagine all of my culinary mentors dancing around with me to the R&B CD playing in the kitchen.

When you work full time and raise kids, you have to let a few things go. Our year away became a way for me to grab one or two of those things back. Watching myself juggle all the dishes and sieves and oils and vegetables of all colors and sizes felt a little like the first day I drove my car alone. I felt like a kid just pretending to be a grownup, but somehow pulling it all off.

Of course, it didn't hurt that Bill, Gus, Linda and Laura were on hand to slice and dice things and to cook the parts that I wasn't so sure about. They all kept up a steady stream of encouragement and advice, and kept the pesky kids out of my hair. Bill got the last minute groceries and picked up our mess of a house, then swept the terrace, set the long stone table outside with two yellow cloths, and put out the good dishes and silverware.

We ate outside, in the sunny warm November afternoon. Bill parked a big blue glass vase of irises at the end of the table, past which we could see the orange, green, and blue layers of the hillside, the trees, and the sky far beyond. It was a beautiful day.

It turned out that I had plenty of time, help, and clear *Joy of Cooking* recipes all meshed together to get it all done, without ever breaking much of a sweat. I even got to sit outside and eat cheese, watching Grace and Finn place the last pieces in the jigsaw puzzle they had been doing all afternoon, and to take the time to hear Abigail outside with Grandpa on the driveway, zooming up and down the hill on her little pink bike.

I used to think that cooking was magic, or impossible, or otherwise somehow beyond me. Now I saw that it is all about ingredients, and attention, and time. Since I had all three that day it really wasn't as hard or scary as I had predicted.

I cooked the goose until I was sure that it was good and done, and then loudly announced that I was giving it 15 minutes more, "just to be safe." I was weighing the value of easing Gus's mind about potential microbes against the possibility of overcooking the meat, but I was confident that it would still be good, as I had basted the skin all afternoon with molten fat.

Once carved, the goose itself was a total revelation. "That goose isn't happy," Finn remarked upon seeing it pulled from the oven, all dark and hot and bursting with little bits of bread and chestnut and pancetta. We all laughed at his unintended joke, then Gus carved it apart into slices and drumsticks and crispy brown skin. With no disrespect to all the turkeys I've loved before, I must say that Jess and Gerard's goose was just the tiniest bit better.

Maybe that was just the rush of pride (and wine) to my head, but it seemed perfect. Bill's kind and gentle and generous family praised my efforts, ate seconds, and savored every morsel. The sun moved around in the sky to shine on our table as dinner unfolded.

So unless you are looking at our Thanksgiving dinner meal from the perspective of the goose, our Franco-American Thanksgiving was a slam dunk.

It dawned on me one day as I stood in line at the grocery store and pulled out my *carte de fidélité* when the clerk asked for it, that I was no longer a stranger in town.

I loved the fancy French name for a plain old frequent shopper card — card of fidelity — as it evokes the sort of relationship one has with the love of one's life, or perhaps one's dog. If I were a different kind of person (say the kind who actually can read in French) I could have achieved this realization with a library card. Instead, it happened — like all my big moments — in the grocery store.

It's not like Max the cashier knew my name, but since he wore his nametag faithfully, I knew his. And it's not like I knew what to do with an enormous can of duck confit, but I knew exactly where to find it in the store, along with the frozen puff pastry, the almond paste, the *pastis*, and the *M. Propre* (Mr. Clean). It had been a while since I was a tourist, and eventually I was no longer even a traveler. I just lived there.

When December blew angrily into town, a solid 10 Celsius degrees colder than I wanted it to be, it brought with it our fifth French full moon. The chill made sightseeing and picnics a lot less pleasant, just as our decision to keep Grace home for school made life a lot more. We hunkered down in the house with our books and our new recipes, working with various degrees of diligence on our French. Abby was toiling away at her math homework. Bill was inching his way through the CNED workbooks, while I was carefully documenting our actual homeschool adventures in preparation for the day when some unidentified school authority might want us to account for ourselves and our culturally bizarre decision. I was also trying to get comfortable with the fact that we were doing something so out of step: in France, nobody homeschools a kid unless that kid is physically ill.

We were in an interval, the friendly open space between the chaos of getting somewhere and the eventual confusion-and-relief of the time to go back.

We built a lot of fires and played Monopoly in the evenings. We traveled less, cooked more. Five months out of my old job, I was a full-on *femme de foyer*, one of the Real Housewives of Aups. I did the grocery shopping and the laundry, and cooked breakfast, lunch, and dinner, in between teaching math, picking Abigail up at the *portail*, and helping Grace write a research paper on children's rights, the topic she had chosen for herself. None of this would help me professionally, or create new and exciting drama in my life. Yet there it was: the comfort of home. My home.

Things were finally coming together, there in the last months of my 30's.

Edith Wharton, seeking to explain the essence of *French Ways and Their Meaning*, returns again and again to the assertion that the French are more "grown-up" than Americans. According to Wharton, this maturity is a result of hard and industrious work, but actually happens only "*in the intervals*" (italics hers) between periods of intense effort. We mature, she tells her readers, not while winning the bread, but while eating it, slowly, with our families over lunch.

A New Yorker who relocated to Paris and Provence at the end of her life to write and enjoy a passionate love affair, Wharton had plenty of time to reflect on the differences between the bourgeois classes in both nations. She begins her book with the usual caveats (comparisons are odious, most books like this are wrong) and then tucks into a series of fairly vague but undeniably accurate observations. As I was reading a reprint of her book, I kept having that pleasurable "Ah! Yes!" feeling you get when somebody says something you have thought before, only more clearly than you could have said it yourself.

According to Wharton, Americans have a lot to learn from the French. The French are less superstitious, less prudish, and much more aware of the value of history and manners. Cognizant of the real threats to their culture and way of life, they have the good sense to preserve, rather than constantly to jettison and reinvent. They live more fully grounded in their five finely-honed senses, and have oodles more natural taste than do most Americans. Wharton deftly excludes herself from this group of "most Americans," as she has the taste to notice that the French do too.

All of these factors are among the reasons she finds the French to be "grown-up" in comparison to the more childishly optimistic and okey-dokey folkies she remembers back home.

I found her to be pretty much right on target with nearly all of her observations, despite their sweeping nature and superior tone. And it's possible that France, as a nation, *is* much more grown-up. (Those flirtatious *bisous* at the party seemed awfully grown-up to me.) But I had to wonder whether she noticed so much growth and maturity because of where she herself was in her life. Or, more likely, whether she noticed real differences between French people and Americans, but named the French qualities "grown-up" because she became a grownup herself while she was living there.

This was what we found ourselves up to in our own French interval: growing, and growing up. Instead of grabbing a cereal bar as we ran out the door, then eating our sad little sandwiches at our desks at work, we ate three meals a day together around a sturdy oak table. We taught the girls to clean up the kitchen with us — a more challenging task than you might imagine, and certainly more challenging than just doing it ourselves. We worked towards the goal of letting them walk into town independently of us, although I took this project awfully slowly and cautiously, realizing just how hard it is for either of them to look both ways at street corners.

I had found the middle. Not just of our time away, but also, quite undeniably, of my life — if I continued to be lucky. And at the same moment that it occurred to me that I really lived there, I recognized with equal clarity that I really wouldn't forever.

We hadn't yet learned how to live like the French as much as we might have liked. But instead of playing house, we were at home. We had cooked our own goose. Our growing sense of comfort was only one sign of the growth that was unfolding in this interval, as the four of us were learning to take our time, and then give it back to one another.

CHAPTER EIGHT

This World Is Weird

I HAVE SPARED FEW EMBARRASSING TRUTHS ABOUT Bill and myself in these pages. I suppose this could be seen as being in service to this, ultimate, admission: one of our shared favorite movies is a Jackie Chan and Owen Wilson flick called *Shanghai Noon*.

In the film, Wilson plays an inept Wild West outlaw who gets himself into scrapes from which Chan must rescue him with kung fu acrobatics.

In one such moment, Wilson finds himself cornered and outnumbered by lawmen, and pulls out both of his guns to shoot his way out of the situation. Every single one of his several dozen bullets hits wild, causing him to comment, quietly and to nobody in particular: "These guns are *weird*."

Bill and I have always loved the subtle, throwaway nature of the line, indicating just how deeply the character misunderstands his own role in the whole business of aiming and missing his intended targets.

We love how unaware Wilson's character is that blaming his tools brands him as a poor workman. We often quote this line to one another to signal moments when we suddenly recognize ourselves or one another being pathetic or lacking perspective. Which, because we are who we are, is just about all the time.

There in France we noticed,

"These measuring cups are weird," (when we measured weight as volume, and the pancake batter came out like cement).

"These maps are weird," (when we misunderstood Liesel's directions and lost ourselves in Nice).

"This car is weird," (when we repeatedly stalled the Renault hairdryer-mobile on hills).

"The route to the hospital is weird," (when we set out to the Draguignan ER in a panic with no idea how to get there).

"This *bisous* thing is weird," (when we couldn't remember how many kisses to give people, or when we weren't sure which side of the face to aim for first. We also said this when the men in town kissed each other, sometimes three times, and sometimes four).

And then, again and again, "These children are weird," (which, I have to admit, they sort of are, although since we are fully responsible for both their nature and their nurture, their weirdness is clearly our fault).

The food got weird now and again, but really, whose idea was it to order stockfish soup? Stockfish soup smells weirder than you could possibly imagine.

And while some of the French people we met were perfectly normal, sometimes they were inexplicably weird, particularly when they (weirdly) did not understand our French.

French itself? Also weird, with all those reflexive verbs, adjectives following the nouns, and the whole business of assigning gender to things so obviously without any.

The whole world felt weird to us because we had chosen to live on the edge of someone else's universe, rather than in the heart of what we knew and understood. Because this new world was weird, we made mistakes all the time, from little *faux-pas* in the grocery store to life-threatening errors like forgetting to let the cars turn in from the right before zipping blithely past. We *tutoyer*-ed when we should have *vouvoyer*-ed, and vice versa. We put the em-PHA-sis on the wrong syl-LA-ble, and then wondered why nobody brought us the nice *rosé* we imagined we ordered. We just never could get the guns to shoot straight.

France's history goes back thousands of years, building towards what it was when we encountered it. Yet we could never quite tell: what parts of the place were characteristically French? What were just random moments in time? What events expressed a deep and lasting tradition and *comme il faut*, and which moments were aberrations we happened to stumble across because somebody was having a bad day?

France kept smacking us with its strangeness, its variability, its specific and compelling differences. The weather, the buildings, the politics, the food — it was all just similar enough that we assumed it would not be different, and then suddenly it was all so, well, *foreign.*

From our limited perspective, sometimes this felt as though the nation had neglected to ask our opinion about how things should be. But then, eventually, we remembered that neither Sarkozy nor anybody else had invited us as guests of the Republic.

So if anything or anybody was weird, it was the four of us. And that didn't start when we got on the plane in August. (Of course, if you ask Bill, he was still more likely than I was to think that our family's guns really *were* weird.)

I have always wondered about what it would feel like to be a true denizen of a place: someone who really lives somewhere, has always lived there, with their families who have always lived there, never intending to move. They fully understand the places they live, and rarely see their worlds as weird. They understand the reasons behind its customs, its habits, its specific ways of being. They either fit (and know why and how) or do not (and know it's their own fault for being out of step.)

Since leaving the tiny towns in which we grew up and where everything made perfect sense, Bill and I have always lived somewhat on the edge of worlds, not fully enmeshed in the history or culture or attitudes of any one in particular. Even in Park Slope, where we lived the longest before moving to France, we never felt particularly like insiders, always noticing that for some reason or another, *this borough is weird.*

Brooklyn is in fact weird, and Aups even weirder. Still, the longer we perched there, the more things did make their own sense. When I wasn't flat-out baffled and lost, I enjoyed watching this slow evolution of our perspective, particularly as we saw how being somewhere so foreign was shaping our girls as they grew.

"I like *Comté* better than *St André*," Grace would opine at the cheese counter.

"The cavemen of France had it great, with all these fresh herbs growing everywhere," Abigail would say. "I bet they just invented herbed roast chicken when they dropped some meat on the ground."

"People in France are, like, *addicted* to boring historical presentations," Grace would observe at a museum. "That must be what makes them so much smarter and their schools so hard." She was in awe of the fifth graders who could fill out the workbooks that were so thwarting her own dad.

But being in this weird world also focused the girls in a new way on America. Once as we walked together around Fréjus, a not-at-all weird coastal town, Abigail spoke up, having finally decided something that she needed to explain to us all.

"I know you guys really like France," she said. "But America is the best place for me. We all like different things. And I think I'm going to live in America when I grow up. And run a hotel for people and dogs. And be the President and also an acrobat."

You would think our goal was for the girls to really love France, to imbibe its air, its vowels, and its cheeses so fully and happily that they become lifelong Francophiles, or at least French majors in college. But really, our time shaped them into citizens of the world, and more-informed citizens of the United States, rather than turning them into permanent expats.

Because how sad would we be if, exactly as we have done to our own parents, our children grew up and moved thousands of miles away?

If we gave our children any particular gift with this weird stick-out of a year, I hope that it was this: that they see that living in America (or wherever they end up in the long term) is not a given, but a conscious choice, one among all of the other ways and places to spend one's days and months and years on this planet.

We were trying to get them to experience the fact that when their guns feel weird, there are many possible explanations why. To see that while the world was not designed for their convenience, it is often wide open for them to learn endless new ways to drive, to hear, to smell, to eat, to see. To live this remarkable gift of life.

The long nights of that winter meant I could read all the books I should have read before I arrived. The best was Julia Child's luminous autobiography, but once I read it, I began envying her at deadly-sin levels. Julia threw herself at France with her enormous besotted enthusiasm, charming everyone by being herself so completely charmed. I asked myself, again and again that year, What Would Julia Do? If I had been able to answer that question, we would have had a better time. I would have become a 6-foot-tall television sensation with my own exhibit at the Smithsonian Museum of American history. Bill would have been employed by the State Department. But the girls would not exist.

Of course, some days I could follow Julia's lead and simply love France, despite and because of its weirdness. By the middle of the year, I had overcome my fear of shopping. When faced with a *marché*, I knew just what Julia would do: buy all the freshest things, and ask how to cook them. So that's exactly what I did.

The *marché* took place on Wednesday and Saturday mornings, when sleepy little Aups woke from its off-season doze. The stores that had been shuttered all opened wide, suddenly and with lots of extra merchandise set out for sale. The olive-wood carver put out a bin of newly-fashioned walking sticks; the slipper store spilled booties and socks out onto the street; and the olive oil, spice, and *fleur-de-sel* store stacked intensely flavored gift-sized bottles and tins in front of the shop. It was time to buy some of the best and freshest food in the world.

When we first got to town, the butcher and the fishmonger appeared to keep hopelessly random hours that baffled the tourists. But as residents, we learned to read the telltale signs. The butcher set out a giant pig-headed chalkboard when meat was for sale. We could see from the top of the hill that the fish store was open when the fishmonger's socially desperate black-and-white dog sat outside, ready to snare anybody who would play fetch with him for a minute or two.

On market days, beyond the town's one-lane thoroughfare, vendors parked their little tables and awnings along the main road into town in front of the *Mairie*. Tables outside the café closest to the market suddenly filled up with families enjoying their few dozen cups of *café crème* and some breakfast beers.

It was though the tired little *ville* suddenly recalled her summertime glory days, and put on her fanciest dress, setting up a pink parasol for the gentlemen who might come calling.

At the market in Aups, there was an invariably delicious selection of local produce and specialties of the region. Honey that Gerard and his family gathered near the Gorges du Verdon. Beautiful orange-colored *girolle* mushrooms. Walnuts. Garlic. Jams, olives, breads and clementines from Corsica. The rotisserie chicken man, my hero of dinner, roasted an array of birds, potatoes, and sausages on a ladder of turning spits. The juice dripped down from all the birds into a meat juice trough at the bottom. On Saturdays, he also sold couscous and paella; but our favorite treat was to buy one of his roasted turkey legs, which looked like props from a Renaissance Faire.

The market was as full of smells as tastes. We bought soaps in just about any *parfum* we could imagine: strawberry, raspberry, lemon verbena. Cinnamon, vanilla, coconut, chocolate. Ocean, persimmon, olive oil, pine. And the queen of all the Provence smells: lavender. The soap-and-perfume tables were Abigail's favorite spots, as she is an olfactory aficionado. She hovered there nearly every week, slowly making her choices, trying to get the most scent for her euros, and breathing in as much free lavender as she could hold.

The variety of things on sale was tremendous, should one want or need any of the particular and strange things for sale. Rainbows of pashminas. Huge racks of gray and black acrylic sweaters, replaced by similarly huge bundles of white cotton shirts and dresses come summer. We could (but did not) buy a wide-array of trashy-looking Stevie Nicks style suede boots, off-brand tennis shoes, and zip-up jackets made of polar fleece.

There were 20-kilo wheels of cheese covered in black and brown mold. Tables of cheap made-in-Taiwan jewelry. A woman selling paper puppets that appear to dance in midair. Strange little towels intended exclusively for wet hair after a shower. Dead, plucked ducks, geese, quail, and chickens. A glittery silver top made of mirrored sequins. Bins upon bins of outdated mascara, too-shiny blush, and concealer in colors nature never knew.

There were bouquets of flowers too beautiful to be believed, and bouquets so garish that that even the skankiest city corner stores wouldn't dream of selling them. Tools for removing unwanted hair. Double beds. Knock-off watches. Single naked legs of mannequins with tube socks pulled half way up their suggestively shapely shins. All of this mixed in with raspberries, avocados, and zucchini in unfamiliar shapes.

It was as if the Dollar Store exploded inside the Greenmarket, raining down its wares in and amongst food so delicious it sometimes made me want to cry.

But here is the strange thing — strange to me as an American and a New Yorker, at least. It was all temporary. Predictable, certainly, but temporary. The market arrived at its appointed time on Wednesday and Saturday mornings, then was gone hours later. If we wanted what was for sale, we had to get it then or wait until the next *marché*.

There was no bodega in Aups, or anywhere near Aups. No all-night anything whatsoever except the moon, and even she came and went as she pleased. There was no Wal-Mart, lurking all sterile and reliable on the edge of every town in America, seven days a week. No Cumberland Farms.

Not in France, and certainly not in Aups. *Le marché* followed the rhythm of the life of its place, and we bought things when the market was open.

Inconvenient, certainly, but there was the flipside, the magic of this old-fashioned use of time: we stopped buying things — *and did something else entirely* — when the stores closed.

While the times of the market were entirely predictable, what was for sale was not. Aside from the ever-present lavender, honey, vegetables, *chèvre,* and soaps, we could not quite count on a particular thing, or even a particular merchant, being there from one time to the next. So, on any given Wednesday, there were always surprises for us at the market. One day there was clothing for dogs, advertised by a small stuffed pup, missing one ear, wearing what looked like a leather jacket and zipped-up black leather boots. In his outfit, the little dog looked out of place in our market, and more like he belonged at a motorcycle rally, or perhaps in a bar in the meatpacking district of Manhattan.

But if we wanted a turkey leg some time other than market hours, or if the chicken guy ran out, or if he didn't feel like roasting turkey that day, we were ducks out of luck. Sometimes the friendly smiling woman with the nose ring was there, making potato *galettes,* and sometimes she simply was not. We might get the guy with rows upon rows of spices one week, and then not again for weeks. Sometimes we could buy a double bed, a Moroccan leather bag, or a great Corsican *manchego* we sometimes bought from the guy who also sold donkey sausages. Other times, we had to do without, because they were not to be had for love or money.

One such market day, Bill and I lay in bed, talking and enjoying a wholly undeserved break from our usual weekday routine. It was *Mercredi Libre,* our delicious mid-week weekend and, while Abigail and Grace had both gotten up earlier than they ever did on school days, they were leaving us alone to do our usual grown-up craziness of musing over the errors of the past and worrying pointlessly about the future.

On that morning before *le marché,* on a Wednesday in the middle of December, I was in a self-critical mood. Despite our few successes, I was regretting all the things we hadn't yet accomplished during our time in France.

"We haven't found a bosom friend in town for Abigail and Grace, at least not the sort of friend who would invite them over to play," I complained, as though they were entitled to such a thing.

Bill was more focused on his own sense of entitlement. "I know! And when the poor kids are stuck with us 24/7, we're constantly stuck with them as well!" With a few vitally important and wonderfully kind exceptions, we hadn't yet established the kinds of connections with people in town we had imagined we might. Or even met a likely babysitter.

"And French," I added. "None of us are even close to where we thought we'd be by now." I realized, with great chagrin, that I had learned more in five weeks when I was 15 than I had learned in four months at the Bastide. I still got flustered anytime I had to use a tense more complex than "I will (someday)" or "I have (already)."

"Grace is doing pretty well, even though she's learning my terrible accent. But I don't think Abigail understands more than a few scattered words after all this time."

"And yoga!" I hadn't done more than a few dozen sorry little downward dogs in four months.

That fine morning, regrets piled on anxieties, one on top of the other and then set themselves aflame. Christmas was coming, and then my birthday would, and these dates on the calendar shifted my attention to the passing of time. We had used up four of the nine months we planned to stay.

It's sort of incredible the number of ways I can make myself really super cranky, even lying in a bath of sunshine in a beautiful bedroom in Provence. Just as I was thinking myself to be an awful failure of a world traveler for not having achieved these particular milestones by this time in my life/this trip, Bill again came to my rescue.

"But you know, sweetheart, this time is not like *any* other time in our lives. This is the year we eat real meals together three times a day. This is the year we make friends with a handful of warm, funny, generous French and British people and drink Rhône wine together until late at night."

I crinkled up my nose, and then breathed out, acknowledging just how right he was. "This is the year when I discover just how much I love to write, and to see what emerges when I give myself time to do so. This is the year when I have just *two* students to care about, rather than a few hundred."

This was the year that Abigail started riding her bike and Grace started writing her novel. It was also the year we let the kids learn to navigate the town and the market on their own. While I still could not read *Le Monde*, I suddenly had enough open time that I could plow through a dozen or so of the books in English stocked at Amazon.fr. It was not the year of yoga, but it was the year of lots of slow wandering in and around small walled roads next to olive groves. There were no skyscrapers, just the inevitable stripes of ochre earth, green olive trees, and a huge blue sky.

Their Eyes Were Watching God had given me those distant ships to ponder. Lying there in bed that morning, I thought of another line from Hurston's book:

"There are years that ask questions and years that answer."

For most of our lives, Bill and I had asked and answered two questions, over and over again: Can We Do It All? And, if so, How? We answered the first question in the affirmative. The second, we answered in every possible gory, exhausting, and wonderful detail.

But then another question appeared, during one lazy morning a little like this one, a year and a half before we left for France:

What might happen — to all of us — if we did something else entirely? Something weird, somewhere weirder?

This became the year that answered. And then, with those answers, the seeds of new questions floated in on the wind through the doors and windows we opened in ourselves. This was the year when new things were born deep within us all, although they started out tiny and might not show themselves for years and years.

For example, this was the year that laughter came into our family. We took the best two-or-so minutes of each of our Brooklyn full-time-employed days — the time at dinner each night when we would burst into shared laughter — and let it become long passages of leisurely time together as a family.

This was the year of us. It was the year of France, *bien sûr*. But it was also the year when a world grew up in the tight square among us four.

Sure, we had our tantrums, disagreements, and spats over whose turn it was to do what chore. These have always been a part of our family life, and will likely be a fixture forever. But that year we laughed every single day. Where once we had an inconsistent and always surprising trickle of giggles, never sustainable or sustaining, in France we had laughter pouring forth, from all of us, all the time. Stupid laughter. The laughter of our foolish mistakes, of our surprising revelations, but also of our moments of pure joy.

It was a year of time. Time enough for lying in bed and having remarkable revelations about the world that had been hiding in plain sight. Time to reflect on our lives, what we had made of them, and what we might make in the future.

It was also, at that particular moment of that particular day, time for getting our arses out of said bed and hightailing it down to the market before all the rotisserie chicken and baguettes would disappear. For to shop like Julia in France, one must market during market time.

At first, the limited hours of all the businesses made us totally irascible, but then we came to prefer having times clearly set aside for particular purposes. We could not get any food in small French towns between 13:45 and 19:00; but the fact that there were specific hours for eating and hours for not eating tended to remind us to eat a great big slow *déjeuner*, with cheese and baguettes and slices of pear afterwards. We could not work, shop, or go to school during those hours, anyway, so we decided we might as well focus on and enjoy our meal and those with whom we ate. (And after a meal like that, we were not particularly hungry again until the national cafeteria opened once again. Dieting advice like, "Don't snack between meals," works so much better when you actually *eat* meals.)

We got ourselves downtown and into the market in time for our own café crèmes and breakfast beers, served just at the hour that brunch would be in full swing on a lazy Saturday back home. (But today was our lazy *Wednesday*! Just think about it! God, I still miss France.)

At the market, we ran into Dermot, Anna-Maria, and Lajla. We pulled up chairs around a table at the café and joked about applying for government funding to start a new club in Aups. We could tap into France's socialist munificence to fund an Association of Strangers for all of us foreigners who had purposefully marooned ourselves there.

We watched our girls dart back and forth among the aisles of the market with their little purses full of euros, looking for just the right Christmas presents. The market was just big enough for them to get the tiniest bit lost, and just small enough for them easily to find their way back to us to show us the magical things that they found. On this day, it was soap (as usual), but also two giant hunks of cheese.

Four months earlier, I could hardly buy a box of cereal at the grocery store without a frantic meltdown. Yet on this other continent, our kids gained the independence, the language skills, and adequate knowledge of French cheeses to be able to choose, purchase, and savor relatively obscure varieties entirely on their own. So much for my morning's regrets. This was success of a very different sort, and I'm sure even Julia would have approved.

The sun shone through empty branches of the plane trees over the sandy *boules* court. It wasn't the beauty of a summer sky, or the intense color of autumn. It was gloriously, astonishingly, winter-y beautiful. I looked up at the lacy skeleton the pruned branches of the plane trees made against the blue. And, for just a moment, the past and the future both faded away.

France was teaching us a new way of experiencing time. In this new daily rhythm, when one thing was happening, the others actually, and entirely, stopped. On this free Wednesday, we found ourselves in the middle of the week, in the middle of the year, and in the middle of our lives. And somehow, we made time stand still for just a little bit to take a look around. And for this minute, because it was time to be in the market, I could set aside all that we had done and all that we left undone.

Whenever we went, then we were.

Sometimes when I woke up feeling all diffident and rootless, I just took a few huffs of one of Abigail's soaps or pillows to remind myself to chill out. For almost as powerful as its visual and gustatory delights, the scents of Provence really kicked us in our pants. Most of the smells were so good and so French that we really could not believe our luck to smell them. Like the endlessly varied and gorgeous sunsets, and the overwhelming flavors, the smells of the herbs and the flowers turned our sense organs up a notch.

But then there were the equally astonishing funky, off, weird and horrific smells as well, just as pungent and just as much a necessary part of the place. In case you think we became hopelessly hoity-toity, arty-farty, and airy-fairy living in the lap of *provençal* luxury, let me break it down for you into first grade potty language: sometimes the airy actually smells neither hoity nor arty, but more toity and farty. Just as bad, and worse, as the bottom of the Brooklyn garbage can after the Fourth of July. As rank as the pee smell in the subway. But different, and specific: even the bad smells are somehow specifically French, and more stinkily personal.

For example, the smell we once smelled at the Aix-en-Provence train station. The train station is open and glassy, with doors everywhere open to the outside. While we were standing in line, waiting for our tickets, we were gradually aware of a powerfully awful stench, the likes of which I had never experienced before. I couldn't get it out of my head that the man behind us had committed some awful crime against nature and had come to the station without having had the decency to shower. But as we moved away from him and the stink only intensified, I realized I had been unfair to blame this perfectly hygienic young man.

Then a worse thought occurred to me: what if he had thought that awful smell was coming from *me*? He could not possibly know that I am famous in our house for smelling good. Great even. Abigail, Grace, and Bill routinely nestle a head into my neck, take a deep inhale, and breathe out, happy, telling me, "Ahh. You smell so good." Please pardon my hubris: there is no polite way to communicate such things in any language.

I had to assume that it was animal waste being spread as fertilizer on a field somewhere nearby, because it was impossible to imagine any other reasonably wholesome source for a smell as rank, deadly, and bodily as that one was. The hundreds of people on the TGV platform just stood, breathing calmly as though it were the most natural thing in the world for one's life to be suddenly coated in stink. It was all Bill and I could do not to gag and make childish faces at one another, but for some reason the French people were a lot more blasé. Perhaps Edith Wharton is right, and the whole French nation is simply more mature. About manure.

There was also a rank stench just outside of Sillans-la-Cascade, the town where we lived for before moving into Bastide de la Loge. During the very short week or so that Bill and I went on sporty little runs together (before I gave up), we would always argue over whether we would take the high road (and nearly be killed by some Italian tourist's speeding Mercedes) or take the low road (and be blasted with foul-smelling air as we ran by the sewage treatment plant). When it's hard to decide between an oncoming car and a stink, that's some powerful stink.

Most often, of course, France lives up to its pleasantly fragrant reputation. Once we were driving on a high plain from Riez to Quinson, and the kids were in a full-on riot in the car. In a fit of inspiration/desperation, I pulled over in a lavender field, got out to steal a few stray flowers off one of the bajillions of plants there, and thrust them towards their noses.

I know, I know. It wasn't my lavender. But you'd steal a loaf of bread if your kids were starving, and you'd steal lavender if you thought it might shut them up for a few minutes, too.

And yes, more reasons to throw us in the parenting clink and throw away the key. But it was worth my descent into petty crime. The girls spent the rest of the trip home in a sort of beatific silence, just inhaling and grinning. After that, I tried to spritz a little lavender water around when the girls were getting too cranky. Worked every time.

Our path to school, the most prosaic of little country roads, burst with smell as well. As we left the door, we were sometimes greeted by the random blooms of a plant on the terrace. When it flowered, it was as though the whole world had been doused with overwhelming, cloying perfume. Walking up the path, we passed a plant that smelled like Mr. Clean, and emerged onto the road to be met by the dusty dry smell of the red rock cliff covered with thyme.

Further down were two-story high juniper plants, whose fresh gin mint mingled with the unmistakable smell of fresh dog doo. I learned when to inhale, and when to hold my breath.

As we continued past the diesel smells of the idling Mercedes school buses, and walked down into town on the medieval *ruelles*, a damp, moldy ancient smell emerged by the foundations of the castle where all the dirty feral cats live. No matter how hot the sun on a summer's day, the narrow streets never really got the light, holding tight to the musty air of the thirteenth century.

Going back even further in time, there was the smell of the caves up the hill. They smell, as you might imagine, of moldy rot, of bats, of dank and must. We dared Bill once to walk deep into the one that smelled the most like a dead animal. Because he is Bill, he did it, but the rest of us couldn't quite get past our fear of whatever was so stinkily rotting in that dark place.

La Bastide was a sort of cave as well. It was built deep into the hillside, so that cars driving past the living room sounded as though they were driving just over our heads. The entire East wall was a windowless fortress against the tiny juniper-and-dog-doo *Chemin*. So when we opened up the cabinet in the back wall to pull out the house's 1970's British version of Monopoly, it smelled like the friendly musty scent of somebody's grandmother's house. Because it was. Grandma's cave, with its regal broad back to the hill and its grand open face smiling wide to the Western horizon.

Southern France is to caves as New York is to tall buildings: you would think that nobody would like being in a cave, or living a dozen or more floors in the sky, but they do. There are varieties of caves, like there are different kinds of tall buildings in cities. Wine tasting caves were Bill's favorite discovery, scented with old wood and spilled wine. These were not musty caves, but rather smelled as though for years people have spilled a lot of wine on oak, and left it there to dry in the sunshine. Bill brought all of our visitors to his very favorite cave, at the Vineyard *St. Jean de Villecroze*, where he sat indoors and lapped up wine as well as the attention of a particularly beautiful *caviste*.

Abigail is the smellingest member of our family. One day she skipped into the room and had this to say: "Hey, Mom. Can I tell you something? Let's talk soaps. France really likes mixing their smells and their flavors. Like they even have OLIVE smelling soap!" And then she skipped right back out. France really does mix soapy floral non-foody smelling smells with their food. And vice versa. Like olive soap, and olive oil ice cream, and the violet or orange blossom syrup they put in champagne.

More disturbingly, sometimes there were intensely animal — or even vaguely human — smells in the food or the flowers as well. The floral scents and the food scents and the biological scents got all up in each other's business, with some of the cheeses smelling like feet (and tasting like heaven) and others smelling like cheese, but tasting like pineapple. Soap was cinnamon just as easily as desserts were flavored with rose. I never ate something floral, food-al, and physical all at once, but quite frequently two of the three were mixed together.

The market thoroughly jumbled scents, just as Abby described. Next to the meat smell was the sharp citrus of clementines, and little bundles of sage. The olives sat between the soaps and the wooly lanolin smell of the Nepalese sweaters, a few stalls down from the fish, the ewe's milk cheese, and the frying potato pancakes.

But the strongest smell of the town was just outside of the church, in the center square. At first I could not figure out whether the scent was the residue of a pungent plant, or the lingering smell of the herb merchant, who usually sets up his dozens of enormous burlap sacks just there. It's a powerful and earthy smell, but floral at the same time. It's one of those sledgehammer smells that you can't ignore unless you've got an awfully bad cold.

Gerard finally cleared this up for us. "It's the incense from the church," he said. "They've burned it every Sunday for hundreds of years."

When I walked through that part of town, I looked up at the entryway to the church and saw the watchwords of the republic rather than "Our Lady of the Miracle of Thus-And-Such." Whenever I smelled that strong incense, to me it was the smell of Liberty, Equality, and Fraternity.

But an equally powerful contender for the Smell of France was a much more earthy, sexy, homely little entity: the homely black *tuber melanosporum* fungus that Gerard and Jessica brought to a dinner party so we could all eat it, thinly shaved, on toasted baguette.

According to Gerard, there are three ways to find truffles. You can train a pig, and follow the pig around the bases of oak trees, *les chênes*. In the old days, you would have to be sure to get to the truffles before the pigs did, but now they just put little muzzles on their snouts. You can also find a smart, even-tempered dog and teach him to do the same thing.

But the magical huge one he brought us to sniff and to savor, he found with the most challenging method of all: *à la mouche*, by following a specific sort of fly. Being a true son of the *provençal* soil, he pretty much knows where to look, and when he is near the right kind of tree, he looks for a special fly to alight in just the right place. Once he saw the right fly alight twice in the same place, he dug down and pulled out the mammoth one he brought our way. Gerard is totally cool.

The truffle's smell, way more than its taste, was magical. It was distinct, and unsubtle and right on the correct side of the border between awesome and way too intensely scented to tolerate.

Bill had his own way of describing the smell of a really great black truffle, sliced thin and set on a homely piece of toast. According to Bill, it smells "like making out with your girlfriend. After you've both been running around playing flashlight tag until you're sweaty. On the first day of November. And it's after all the leaves are off the trees, and they're all wet on the ground. Like kissing the girl you really love, in the damp woods, while night is falling."

Like all that, and more.

Once we had been introduced to the remarkable smell of truffles that winter, Aups — and Jessica and Gerard — had another trick up their sleeves for us: the *Fête des Truffes.*

I assumed that this would be the usual smalltown Var event: a few scattered card tables, lavender soap for sale, and all the town characters meandering around the town square, frowning at one another. Thus, I was pleasantly surprised to see a crowd that nearly rivaled the throngs of midsummer. There were little knots of tourists for the first time in months. The crazy Varois accordion-playing cat man even showed up. His cat sat perched on his neck as he played, attached to him by a leash connected to his own neck: a bizarre and unpleasant situation masquerading as entertainment.

For the *Fête*, the central square in front of the *Mairie* was full of local truffle farmers, wine merchants, and jam ladies hawking their wares. There were card tables, covered with lots and lots of little stacked piles of black truffles, and truffles boxed up with eggs so that the eggs could soak up their scent through their shells. The air smelled like a mushroomy version of heaven. Every time the air wafted his way, Bill would inhale obscenely deeply and sort of groan.

Also on sale were scrawny-looking oak trees — *chênes* — which under the right (or perhaps wrong) conditions become the unhappy hosts for the fungal malady that results in truffles. Apparently, when you are looking for truffles — with your dog or your pig or your close attention to particular sorts of flies — the best place to look is under the scrawniest and most pathetic looking oaks. Truffles are a sort of athlete's foot for the roots of trees, but with more dire effects for the trees. Apparently, you can buy scrawny oaks at this festival, plant them, dig up a fortune years later, and sell them at your own fabric-covered card table.

When we first were researching where we should live in France, I came across a photo of "villagers" in Aups wearing "traditional dress," doing a sort of square dance sort of thing. The women had white caps and mismatched floral dresses with long aprons. The men were bareheaded, with white shirts open at the neck. They looked very picturesque, and should have been my first clue that I was actually moving to a foreign country, not just to the part of Cobble Hill, Brooklyn, with all the bistros.

No such "villagers" presented themselves to us when we arrived. Native dress patterns had shifted away from peasant chic, I assumed. Instead, the women wore boots, skin-tight leggings and butt-hugger sweaters with a fussy jacket and a sour frown. The men tended to look a little more jovial, but significantly less fashionable — usually sporting an enormous and bright-colored wool sweater tucked into filthy cargo pants.

But there they suddenly were at the Truffle Fest: those traditional villagers from the photo. By now I recognized them all: the women who buy their bread and meat early, and the men who sit by the church. The boy who comes tearing out of school at 11:30, heading at a full run into town, and the girl who befriended then dumped Grace. But because it was the *Fête des Truffes*, they were looking all 19th-century French. And weird as hell.

The whole group was led by an older gentleman playing a penny whistle with one hand and beating a somber tattoo on a drum with the other. The "villagers" moved slowly, marching in gendered pairs, with the kids up in front and the grandparents in back. My generation was entirely absent from the procession, which was probably a good idea. Nothing says "I'm 40 and miserable about it" like a headscarf and a full-length calico skirt.

After a while, the kids in the group started to dance, a joyless shuffle with no discernible rhythm. How weird that those "traditional" villagers in the photo were these people I sort of knew. I liked the dancing villagers a lot less once I actually knew who they were. They had looked nice enough in the photos, but now we saw them every day. My poor children and I had been regularly stared down by them on our little lonely ambles through the town.

I hope that the other tourists in town that day enjoyed the dance more than I did. But as somebody who lived there, I had seen just how little fun the more upstanding, traditionally-dressing citizens of the town allowed themselves — or the rest of us.

Which was why, once we had had our fill of all that nice truffle-y air and the traditional frowny dance, I was so excited to get in the car and drive up to Jess and Gerard's mountaintop. I had finally learned where the fun was had, and it was rarely at the *Mairie*.

This time, Gerard made us lots and lots of truffles. Truffles in scrambled eggs, and shaved on toast, and then more scrambled eggs on top of that. Truffles on top of rabbit, cooked in a rich and heavy cream sauce. Even truffles layered into a melty, creamy round of cheese. There were no truffles in the dessert, thankfully, just almond flour and lots of oranges.

After lunch, Gerard took us out to show us where all this bounty came from. Goya, the retriever, loped along close by his side, encouraged by the smell of sausage in his right-hand pocket. She knew her job, and knew she would be rewarded for doing it well. She sniffed along the ground, encouraged by his gentle tone. "*Cherche. Cherche, Goya*," he intoned, serious and certain, in a voice more quiet and calm than usual. We walked around by the scrubby, rattier-looking oaks with their tiny leaves.

It was cold outside, and the air was clear and sweet. After not too long, Goya stopped and pawed the ground. Gerard knelt down with a pickaxe and dug up some earth so that she could root around a little more. She stuck her nose deep in the ground, snorting and snuffling against the red dirt. She pawed a little more, then Gerard pulled up a handful of dirt for us to smell, too. It was redolent of the truffle buried just six inches or so under the surface. He found the truffle, about the size of a horse chestnut, and tossed it up to Bill. Goya got a bite of sausage.

The sky filled up with the puffy clouds that foretell snow. Goya kept going, even once she had had her fill of sausage. She found truffle after truffle buried in the earth, even under rocks sometimes. It might take Gerard some time to dig it out, but there was a soft black gem there, every time.

I'm embarrassed to admit this, almost more embarrassed than I was about how little French I learned. But now, with the distance of time, I can admit yet another weird thing about France:

French women loved my husband, and made their approval as clear as day. But to put it mildly, I didn't get nearly the same amount of attention. To put it more frankly, I was roundly ignored.

I soon learned that my sultry-hunky tree surgeon flirted with nearly everyone he met, so his fleeting interest at Anna-Maria's party didn't count. Aside from that, I got no male interest whatsoever. Nada. Zip, all year long. I was nearing 40, sure, but I wasn't dead. In America, a head or two still turns my way when I'm on my game and remember to comb my hair. But not so in France.

Bill, on the other hand, was on fire all year, and not just with the charming sculptor Vava. He was flirted with at dinner parties, while walking Abigail to school, at the grocery store along with his change. The woman at the cash register would hold his hand in her two, for just an extra moment or so, and deliver her, "*Merci, Monsieur*" in her most suggestive tones. (I know this only because it's one of his favorite stories. When I was standing next to him, she was perfectly discreet.)

His favorite vineyard was the one with the beautiful and attentive *caviste*, a snazzy dresser who was apparently put on this planet to stand in a damp underground space and pour glass after glass for her male patrons. She gazed lovingly into each man's eyes and complimented his excellent taste in reds and *rosés*. He brought all of our male visitors there, and they invariably returned with a half-dozen bottles of wine and a dreamy expression on their faces not solely attributable to the effect of their *dégustations.*

I can joke about this because Bill has never been the flirty type. (And I'm sure I'm joking. Really.) Back in Brooklyn, he certainly never invited aggressive female attention, but in France he had to fight them off with a stick.

And I might as well have been wearing a fanny pack, a brown paper bag, or a nun's habit. I rocked my jeans and high-heeled boots, sporting a little extra lip gloss, just like the rest of the women. Now and then Jona might stop his motorcycle to chat with me about what trees he was about to wrestle into submission, and I would feel all schoolgirlish for a minute, thinking perhaps I'd get another lingering *bisou.* But other than that, the most action I saw was some old guy with his sweater tucked into his pants glancing at me in an avuncular way. The rest of the time I might as well not have existed. In France I was not even qualified to be a cougar.

One (large) part of me wanted to greet this particular lesson with some sort of horrible freakout about the sharp waning of my formerly powerful charisma. It's not like I intended to use it for anything in particular, or wished to be led into temptation; I just wanted my mojo not to have dried up entirely.

But instead of accepting the demise of my powers of attraction, I chose to attribute this sharp decline in the strength of my man-magnetism to cultural differences, my theory being that the mechanisms of attraction work differently in different places. I elected to believe that lust — just like everything else — was culturally determined.

For example, to make one massive overgeneralization, the women in France were drastically more attractive than the men.

This is of course a matter of taste, and you are free to disagree as strenuously as you'd like. Plenty will. But when we first arrived, Bill and I would regularly see French couples walking together and then quietly sing to one another a few lines of the Joe Jackson classic, "Is She Really Going Out with Him?" Soon, we just got used to it. No offense, French guys; but from where I sat, they were just not all that in the way the ladies tended to be. My jaw dropped upon seeing a French guy precisely three times all year long. Of the three, probably only one was straight, and the other two were in Paris.

You would think this disparity between French and American men would mean I would have earned more attention, rather than less. That the not-so-hot men would be grateful to encounter a friendly blonde like myself. But in a nation that uses the same word for "smile" and "mouse," my friendliness did not make me more attractive.

The hard truth was that the attractiveness ratio between Bill and me had been redrawn. Bill, who started out plenty hot, became a whole lot more attractive, relatively speaking, than he was back home in the States, and this threw things off between the two of us.

Add to that the fact that French women really put in serious effort. They don't tend to go all droopy and soft in the middle, or turn all skeletally exercise-obsessed. Instead, they hold onto their tidy little shapes. Then, they extend whatever they've got by tarting up whatever God gave them. They don't wear exercise pants in public. They don't slouch around in sweatshirts or wear anything functional like backpacks, hiking boots, or warm wool hats. I'm quite certain that French women are issued a set of beautiful flimsy silk scarves by the national government and never leave the house without one knotted smartly around their necks. The scarf phenomenon is also the law for Parisian men — both straight and gay — but not of the men out where we were in the countryside.

French women work the makeup and tight pants pretty hard, and they have really terrific hair. Beauty products are serious business, sold in medicinal-looking packages by fully-qualified pharmacists, rather than stacked offhand in bins in a grocery aisle. Women have either a bold cascade of hair in a messy-sexy "I just copulated" sort of up-do, or a super-chic short crop that says, "I am the gamine of your *Breathless* dreams." They throw on a leather jacket and lace up boots with their long, tight sweaters. Very infrequently they choose an unfortunately oversized blouse and some strange Ali Baba pants with an oddly distended crotch. But, usually, it's tarty-sexy all the way.

There was simply no way I could keep up.

So we had a definite shift in the attractiveness ratio in our marriage. But, also, if our limited frame of reference was any indication, it was the women in France who tend to do the flirting, rather than the men, or rather than the mutual way we're used to back home. French women initiated most of the *bisous*. Their eyes did much of the lingering, and it is they who stoked the little fires of minor social dramas.

The men, on the other hand, seemed to hang back, cool, detached, and barely breathing. Perhaps they were just used to being wooed, or desired, or getting to date women drastically more attractive than themselves. *'Cause if my eyes don't deceive me, there's something going wrong around here.*

Of course, the more likely interpretation is not so much that this world was weird, but that we — the newcomers and outsiders — had no idea how to read the cultural signals. Perhaps in France, female coquettishness is simply required. Or perhaps it means much less than it does back home. Perhaps, like *bisous*, when women flirt with my husband they mean nothing more than, "Hey, nice to see ya!" Perhaps that *caviste* is just looking to increase her commission on all the wine she sells. Perhaps I was on the receiving end of so little interest because I just was not feeling the lust myself (except for that terrifically popular American man who lived in my house).

To understand what was really going on, I turned again to Edith Wharton. She served again and again as my guide to France, despite the fact that she's been dead for decades. Wharton had a number of fascinating things to say about France (including the caution that one should not leap to off-the-cuff overly-generalizing armchair anthropology, which is pretty much my go-to mode).

Wharton appears to have traveled to Paris in the first place mostly to have the first sexually satisfying relationship of her entire life. Her hot stuff went down with an American businessman, not a French guy, but they seemed to use perceived French morality as a convenient excuse.

For example, in *French Ways and Their Meaning*, Wharton told her American readership that French marriages are made for stabilizing families, rather than for love. According to Edith, French husbands and wives assume they will find their life-sustaining passions in affairs, rather than in one another. When I first read this, I assumed that she was looking to explain away her own shady behavior. But then, all those cute scarves and longing looks and messy up-dos got me wondering whether she was more right than I first wanted to admit.

Some aspects of France we took in as fully as we were able: the visual beauty, the remarkable smells, sights, sounds and foods.

But parts of the French experience we left unexplored. Certain items stayed off the menu. Like steaks made of horse meat, lust *à la française* was one mystery we remained happy not to plumb. Bill innocently soaked up the attention he got, and I just tried to remember that in some other country, maybe Lichtenstein, I'd still be all that.

———————

Abigail's school? Also, and still, weird. Parents in rural France did not put bumper stickers on their cars advertising their children's scholastic progress. There was no Aups PTA — at least not one that was made known to me. No weekly parent bulletin, and no individual parent-teacher conferences. No "volunteer opportunities." The *portail* held firm. This tall green mechanized gate that swung open and shut twice a day was a clear dividing line: school on one side, and family on the other. There was also no discernible "crisis" in public education, as we are fond of finding here. By and large, parents trusted the schools to educate their children. Everybody liked things just the way they were.

Two teachers did stand outside the *portail* to have a cigarette with a select few parents they deemed worthy. This also felt weird to me, because even in the 70's, when the teacher's lounge was so smoky, my teachers never would have lit up in front of my parents.

For a while in the fall, I tried engaging my fellow parents in conversation, and tried saying *bonjour*-s to the smoking teachers. But when the gathered adults started up with just a tiny hint of gossipy complaining about one of the students in the school, I saw the group for what it was. I have an almost allergic reaction to hearing any adult demonize another person's child. So I quickly gave up on becoming one of the ones lucky enough to be gossiped with over a Marlboro light. I chose a place to wait far away from *le portail*, just near enough so that Abigail could find me when she walked out onto the street.

I struck out in my attempts to try to learn about the school by talking to Abigail herself. As she has never shared details of her school day under normal circumstances, she was not about to start in France. And since Abigail never fully comprehended the language, even after almost an entire school year, she herself had hardly any idea what was going on in class. The entire enterprise was doubly opaque.

When we arrived, planning to send our kids to a small rural public school, I knew full well that school would be very different from what we had left behind. I knew that nobody would speak English — with the kids or with me. I knew French families were tight-knit, and therefore often closed to outsiders; and I recognized full well that we had compounded the effect of that insularity by choosing to live in a tiny town without any other Americans. We knew that — unlike in America — parents in France have not battered down the schoolyard gates, expecting and even demanding access and information about every aspect of their children's school lives. We knew all this, and chose this life for our kids and ourselves: both despite and because.

I knew all the risks, but also imagined that there would be a good side to all of this distance between home and school. Part of me had been utterly exhausted by having my professional and personal lives so deeply intertwined, and I fantasized about a return to the Bad Old Good Old Days of Yore, when parents knew zippo about school. Bill and I imagined we wanted the benefit of being in a place where we couldn't easily escape into English all the time. We wanted to be thrown together as a family. We wanted a different kind of challenge for our kids and for ourselves. (And we wanted it all with good weather and even better food.)

But when we actually had to drop Abigail off at school every day, I found myself just so much more upset about the difficult parts than I had hoped I would be. Bill and the kids should have worn t-shirts reading, "I'm with Conflicted."

Back home, the girls attended a school I knew inside and out, believed in, and even loved. They didn't always have an easy time there, but at least I could figure out why. Although neither of them was ever particularly forthcoming about the details of their days, as the head of their school, I had plenty of ways of knowing how things were going. For one thing, if I wanted to know what they had done on a given day, I could just reach in my desk and read their classroom schedule — but really I already had a pretty good sense of it in my head, as I had created the darn thing myself.

Even had I not been there at school all the time, with such extraordinary access, I would have had plenty of ways to know what was what. There were classroom newsletters a few times a month, regular notices home from the main office, plenty of paper and electronic communications from and meetings with the parents' association. There were formal school social events, concerts, and curriculum nights. There was also a circuit of kids' birthday parties just about once a week, at which the parents would all stand around and talk (usually about school) for two hours while the kids bowled, painted overpriced pottery, or ran around Chuck E. Cheese.

In addition to all of this hefty communication, every single family in the school was asked to sit down at least twice a year with their children's teachers for half-hour formal conferences, and then were mailed reports detailing every aspect of their children's academic, social, and emotional development. And believe me, they were detailed. Because I read every page for every kid, three times a year.

But in France? Abigail was invited to precisely one other child's birthday party. We heard about it from the boy's mother, our neighbor, late in the week, but it happened to be on the only Sunday in September we had planned to be out of town. After then, nothing. I never enjoyed the privilege of hearing a full sentence spoken by her teacher, or of seeing her classroom. We never learned her teacher's name, and neither did Abigail. "She doesn't tell us," Abigail would explain, her voice flat with acceptance. So much for "*Je m'appelle.*"

There was no school website to check, nothing beyond a tiny bulletin board at *le portail* that reminded us when school vacations would start and end. By way of paper communications, I received one Xeroxed notice — on the topic of how to treat head lice. We were happily nit-free all year, but I saved it as a souvenir.

On the day before winter break, the school sent home a lengthy government-printed report card, a list of all of the skills that Abigail was to have acquired during her hours at school. The teacher had left the entire document blank, aside from two sentences in a tiny comment window. She wrote only that it was not possible to evaluate Abigail, as she remained silent in class and had not "integrated herself" into the classroom community.

That particular day I was not conflicted. Instead, I was so angry I cried. After how hard this all was for my kid, after how hard she had tried, she got two paltry sentences? She did her best, and her best was not good enough for Madame Whatsername.

When it felt too weird, I tried to remember we were guests, the beneficiaries of someone else's school system, someone else's educational philosophy. French schools are not set up to reach out to foreigners, even in the ham-handed ways American schools sometimes do. Instead, French schools make children into French citizens, a task they take seriously and accomplish effectively. It was certainly not set up for me or for my benefit, or to earn my approval.

There would be no bumper stickers, no warm fuzzy conversations with the teachers, and no PTA. Hell, there wasn't even heat in the bathroom. Get used to it, *Maman*.

Thus, rather than having things be great, I settled for things being pretty much fine, and for noticing the ways in which Abigail grew, because of and despite how different things were for her.

She kicked and screamed on Monday mornings, angry and miserable that she had to go to school. On those occasions I reminded her, and reminded myself, that she was not the only child who disliked Mondays. She pulled herself together to walk out the door, and by lunchtime she had regained her usual equilibrium, skipping down the lane and back.

She copied all her answers from whatever child was seated next to her. The teacher must have picked a smart child to sit by the American kid, as Abigail's answers on the worksheets and in her *cahiers* were pretty consistently correct. Plus, since she was in class all year with students learning to read aloud, she learned to pronounce just about any French word more perfectly than I ever will. While she remained mystified by almost any spoken French she heard, it was a cool party trick for her to roll those r's and correct her parents' pronunciation.

All year, we took her to French classes once a week a half hour away in Lorgues, at the behest of the French educational authorities. We assumed that this was a useful activity. But since she refused to tell us anything she did there (aside from drawing flowers on the blackboard with Fatima, the girl from Spain), I never knew for sure.

Once we drove the half hour to Lorgues and dropped her off, having stupidly missed a telephone message from her French teacher that she would not be able to teach the class that day. The French don't really go in for substitute teachers, at least not in our small town; when the teacher wasn't around on a given day, parents just took their kids home. Any students who remained were farmed out to other teachers, and spent the day doing elaborate coloring projects.

The day we missed her teacher's call, Abigail stood there in the schoolyard in Lorgues until she realized that her teacher was not coming to retrieve her. In a panic entirely uncharacteristic of her, she burst into hard sobs. This drew the attention of another teacher, who also made the uncharacteristic move of asking her if she were okay, and then inviting her into her classroom for the morning.

The school didn't call us. Either they assumed we didn't care that Abigail had been abandoned, or figured we just didn't need to know that she was spending the morning coloring with a teacher she did not know. After those few awful moments, I think she had a day that was slightly better than usual. "The teacher there spoke English," she told me, pleased and gratified. "She was nice to me," she added. Encountering a nice teacher had been a welcome surprise.

Abigail deals with the troubles of the world, and of the schoolyard, with a steely sort of privacy and unshakability, flashing a little anger now and then, but only showing any trace of the intensity of her emotions when safely home with us. But the traces are rare and oblique indeed. Once, when she was barely three years old, she fell off the jungle gym at school and broke both of the bones in her right shin. She cried like crazy just until I got her in the car, at which point she fell sound asleep. She woke up at the hospital completely silent.

After that point, she treated her broken leg as though it were a regrettable inconvenience. If somebody asked her about it, she was liable just to turn her head away, as though she were a queen being asked about something distasteful and beneath her notice, like flatulence or warts. She preferred to pretend that the large purple cast, immobilizing her from ankle to hip, did not exist.

For a while, it seemed that Abigail would spend the year treating all of France as though it were that large purple cast. She wasn't going to kick and scream about her distress in public, she had no interest in being homeschooled, and she wouldn't be caught dead misbehaving in class, but she was not about to let herself make the number of mistakes she would need to make in order to learn to speak.

It's clear to me what I could have, should have, and would have done had I known earlier what I have learned now. First, I would never have told her how quickly she would learn French. Pretty much every adult (including her parents) who had talked to her before our trip had promised her that it would come so easily to her, that she would start to understand and speak almost effortlessly. When this didn't happen as quickly or as magically as she had been promised, when she went months in the schoolyard without making a single friend, she decided to hunker down to wait it all out. As a self-protective gesture, perhaps to be sure that eventually we'd take her home, she refused to let us believe she was learning any French at all.

In the meantime, almost despite how hard school felt to her, she was learning. But she was just too darn ornery to admit it to herself. Or perhaps she's too much of a perfectionist. She learned the names of the numbers almost immediately, and while she could never fathom "the weird way they add and subtract here," she came home and asked us to show her how to regroup tens and ones so that she could do the harder math problems of second grade.

One afternoon I was shocked to overhear her singing a little tune in French, and asked her about whether she had had an actual music class, like the national curriculum guide had promised. No such luck — aside from a video about jazz that the class watched once, the teacher stuck tight to reading, writing, verb conjugation and mathematics. Her French teacher in Lorgues had taught her the song.

And what of French, which so bedeviled us both? Well, despite her protests, despite the way she still frowned and cringed when I spoke to her in French, she occasionally could catch what I said. She tried her best to keep this hidden from us, but when I was adequately crafty, and talked about items of interest to her, like candy, croissants, smells, or euros, I caught her understanding more than she would let on.

And then there was The Great Week. The week when I would have gotten my bumper sticker, if the school had had one to give. Abigail, having been bribed by Bill, had just started in on a binge of serious hand-raising in class. We don't usually motivate with bribes, but with parenting, particularly when you've got kids as stubborn and unique as ours, you've got to go with whatever works. She was still only willing to say numbers, but that gave her plenty of opportunities to rack up coins to spend on soap and Haribo gummy worms.

She had also seemed that week to have made a real friend. She and a classmate named Claire had started playing during recess a few weeks before, little pretend games that did not require much speech. Abigail had initially won her over when she started to bring a shiny purse to school each day full of markers and coins and little plastic toys from her room. Sometimes she brought the catalogue from the American Girl Store, which drew the other little girls like honey. These were dangerous gambits, for sure, as she had to weigh the social clout she could gain with her little trinkets against the likelihood that they would be broken or end up in someone else's pocket. It took me rather longer than it should have to allow her to take anything at all, but once I realized that all her tchotchkes were helping her connect to the girls in her class, I almost packed the bag for her.

All fall we asked if she would like to have a classmate come over and play. The answer, week after week, was no. She really enjoyed playing with Jessica and Gerard's kids, and with the sweet boy who lived next door, but she couldn't make a new girl friend in school. Maybe she had a clear and realistic sense of her social position, and thus knew better than to be rejected. Perhaps she had simply had enough of being yammered at in words she couldn't understand, and didn't want that to continue at home.

So when she mentioned Claire, several times over two weeks, saying that she was "fun, and wild, and crazy, just like me," Bill and I asked her if she would like Claire to come and play. She did, and so Bill wrote a note for Claire to give to her mom. She would come over after school for an hour and a half on Friday.

That was The Great Week. All week, we all looked forward to Friday. Emboldened by her success, Abigail even played with the boy next door a few times, asking if they could go ride bikes together.

On Friday, when she came over to play, little girl Claire turned out to be sweet, and clearly really smart. She — like all the French kids I have met — was incredibly polite with Bill and me, and seemed to enjoy talking to us as much as she enjoyed playing with Abigail. The girls played dress up, and carted around the American Girl dolls. Abigail took her up to her room, and they played some tinny-sounding music on the iPod.

And then, as the girls were sharing an afternoon snack in the kitchen, Claire proudly told us that Abigail had — just that day — received the class's weekly honor of *Félicitations* (Congratulations).

Jessica had told me about this tradition of weekly *Félicitations* — essentially, one child per week in this class was singled out and congratulated for some sort of meritorious conduct or academic achievement. There was of course the opposite possibility as well — kids could be called out in front of the class for doing something bad. This child was called "*Le Pire,*" which literally means "The Worst." It struck me as stingy just to congratulate only one kid per week, and downright mean to call out a little kid so blatantly in front of his or her whole class. But there I go again with my weird American expectations about the educational process.

You would think that Abigail might have mentioned the *Félicitations* herself, not waited for Claire to tell us that she had been publicly congratulated for her progress in school. That, in essence, she was that week's honor student in the Aups Elementary School's second grade.

But when you're as self-contained as my little girl, it's not just the bad stuff that stays locked down tight. Apparently, the good stuff is also a big fat secret. As Claire filled us in, Abigail just looked down, and off to the side, as though averting her eyes from the large purple cast of her own achievement. But I could see a tiny smile playing at the side of her mouth. While she was not about to admit it, she was proud underneath her embarrassment.

That was the best moment ever of The Great Week.

Monday came, and Bill teased Abigail sweetly that maybe she would be the first student ever to get *Félicitations* twice in a row. Claire's mom had been super friendly when Bill dropped Claire off at the end of their playtime, and she promised us that she'd call and have Abigail over.

But something must have gone wrong, something none of us could see or understand. Abigail didn't mention it at first, but when we asked how things were with Claire, she told us that Claire had started spending recess playing with her other friends. This was fine with her, she said. She might have been let down, but said that she understood. She returned to her former habit of privacy and containment within herself.

As did I.

The easiest way to look at this whole thing would be to tell myself a simple story: that the French are insular, or just inexcusably rude. But really what I had to understand was the fact that it was just *so astonishingly different.* It wasn't about better and worse, but about a lifetime of cultural expectations so ingrained that I could only see them in retrospect — raised in the harsh relief of having myself and my kids feel so very out of place for so long. In *school*, the place I've always felt so at home.

That *portail* was not just out there, green and forbidding. There was also a *portail* in my mind, dividing me from the France outside of our immediate family home. To say that it was in my own mind is not to say that it was imaginary or unimportant, but rather to recognize that part of what makes travel and transformation so hard is a lifetime of ingrained experience.

When we moved there, we moved with deep and powerful cultural expectations about how people behave. About schools. About friendships. About how and when to smile, and who gets kissed and when. Even if the language barrier were to have fallen — magically and fast — the cultural ones would remain, ones it could take a lifetime for us really to comprehend.

We did not have a lifetime. The question, "What Would Julia Do?" continued to haunt me. I still wish I could have better used her example to figure out in the short time we had just how to embrace a place that so resolutely resisted my acquaintance. Perhaps if I had ever answered that question in relationship to anything but shopping, I would have figured out how to help Abigail be successful, even popular. I would have liked her to like it there.

What would it have taken for me to overcome my own confusion in order to be more usefully intrusive on Abigail's behalf? Once I had learned to hold my face stern and unsmiling, what would it have taken to loosen it back up, to call Claire's mom and see if we all might try again? Even as I asked these questions, I realized that the only sane response was to fall in with the French parents, and stop worrying so much about what happened behind the green gate. In that way of seeing things, it was none of my damn business who befriended my child, or whether she was named the best or the worst.

I cursed my own hungry need to know, my insatiable curiosity/anxiety. It was always too much; it was never enough. I tried my best, but I could not let go. This world was still so weird.

By the middle of winter, we had spent so much time together in many enclosed places. Grace was loving school, Abigail generally hating it, but resigned. And we were *still* that damn shopping cart. On a typical day, three of the four of us were heading in the same direction, with just one of the four dragging behind, slowing down the team's forward progress.

However, when we traveled to a new place, we were more challenged than usual to get on the same track. Without a habitrail to follow, we sputtered off in all directions, often working ourselves into a serious fuss. We were no longer a shopping cart, but a small and deeply unhappy group of people drawing and quartering itself.

Our fusses took many forms. Bill was the most likely to lead us into a blind alley, a raging stream, or a perilous ascent, but the least likely of us to be a pain in the neck.

Abigail was the likeliest to pass out, to pitch a screeching fit, or to suddenly find herself in desperate need of candy; however, she was also the most likely to lead by skipping ahead joyfully, high ponytails flopping in the air.

Grace was the most likely to suddenly need a bathroom at a highly inopportune moment, to find a snail trail that needed following, or to wander into oncoming traffic; but she was equally likely to find the coolest piece of art in any museum.

I'm not sure whether traveling with me averaged out to be in the plus or the minus column. If you polled my family, they would tell you even more than I have about my short temper, deficient spirit of adventure, and excessive concern with safety. But since I have always been the one who drives, navigates, cooks, shops, packs, and unpacks, they let me stick around.

Our specific and craggy personalities make us the family that we are, but sometimes we four contorted ourselves into the most ridiculous, awful, and uncomfortable configurations and conflagrations.

But then a table — really almost any table we met — somehow solved all that. During our year of accidental adventures, we found ourselves, at least once every single day, sitting in a square, facing one another and sharing a meal. And very often, it was three times a day we called out "*À table*" ("to the table"), then met each other there.

Sitting down together acted as a family life reset button: each time we sat down, our diffused, often deeply contradictory impulses came back into alignment. We stopped looking out at everything else, and saw only one another. We sometimes brought our foul moods with us to the table, but they were very hard to sustain for long when we found ourselves face to face to face to face.

We four, sitting foursquare, were home.

I'm giving credit to the table and our position facing one another, but it was also the food that made us feel the love. Whether it was the chicken or the egg in this case doesn't matter: we had a little of both, please, with salt.

We all really liked to eat, and shared a relatively healthy and adventurous palate. Happy omnivores, we did our best to try and enjoy new things as often as we could, without becoming hopeless food snobs, addicted to constant servings of fancy novelty foods. It was pleasure, rather than gourmet excellence, that we valued. The highest praise in our family was reserved for he or she who could say "Wow, that's delicious" the most times in any given day, about the widest variety of vittles. "I don't like that" was for babies. Even "No, thank you" got you a bite-sized portion, and everybody tried everything.

When we showed up *au restaurant* and said *"Nous sommes quatre"* ("Table for four"), the kids never ordered off the *carte d'enfant* kids' menu. No burgers and fries, and no nuggets of not-really chicken.

I loved having children who ask to eat things like frog's legs and sushi, not to mention broccoli, carrots, and big glasses of milk. Like all kids, they ate candy until it was all gone, then immediately asked to go get more. Sometimes they were hard pressed to finish things they found unfamiliar. But they also took pride in the health and variety of their diet, just like the French.

Before moving to France, our Brooklyn dinners at home together formed the core of our lives. Bill and I were well aware of just how lucky we were to have jobs that would allow us to be home in time for us all to sit down, to tell one another what we were thankful for, and eat healthy good food in one another's warm presence.

But our dinners there were often the very first moment of the day that any of us had been granted a reprieve from the pressures of the outside world. (In France, without jobs, the world had zero interest in us, so there were fewer pressures from which to take shelter.) In Brooklyn, just as we sat down to eat, Bill and I would try, desperately, to talk with one another, nearly famished with the desire to share our daily woes with the only person who would really understand. At the very same moment, both girls would compete tooth and nail for both parents' undivided attention. Eventually one or both of them would get furious with us, or with the other kid.

We ate way too fast in Brooklyn. By the time we sat down to eat, we would all be ravenous, gulping down spaghetti and store-bought meatballs, sometimes without even really tasting them. We also felt pressured to move things along — if not by Samson nudging us to set our leftovers in his food bowl, then by the knowledge that we still had to clean up, make the lunches, and get the kids in bed before we'd have five minutes to ourselves to think.

But in France, we ate French food in French time: slowly, deliberately, in several distinct courses. We laughed. In fact, we told the same jokes night after night, and still laughed. We talked about the family and friends we missed from back home, conjuring them into the two empty seats at the table. We tried new things, and shared bites off of one another's plates. Usually we ate together in the kitchen, with all the food spread out on the wide oak table between us. The table was so big that we had to lean forward to hold hands for our ritual of saying what made us feel thankful.

In a restaurant, we usually skipped our Thankfuls, as Abigail found the idea of holding hands in public utterly mortifying. But we shared food rather than gratitude, and always shuffled our plates around at least once. Abigail rarely finished what she ordered, but always liked what I chose.

We found tables in all sorts of places. Once we ate lunch in an Indian Restaurant near the *Gobelins* Metro stop in Paris, just before we had to get on our return train to Aix. The restaurant had lost electricity, but the waiter invited us in, lit a candle on our table and brought us great korma and biryani. At a ski resort we ate at a white plastic table set outside in the sunshine, ski goggles pushed up on the girls' heads as they tried (and loved) mayo on their fries. We loved tables in French brasseries, with their red-checkered tablecloths, fussy little glasses, and standard-issue menus of pizza, salad with goat cheese, and steak slathered in Roquefort, with *frites*.

On rare occasions, we ate sitting on cushions on the floor around the wide, low Moroccan table in the living room. One night Bill built a roaring fire and we stuck hotdogs on a sharp stick to roast in the flames. We heated up the leftover pasta that wasn't a bit better the second time around. We shared the joys of clearing off the table and washing the dishes, then we set up Monopoly. I got the stuffing beaten out of me, but loved watching Grace giggle hysterically as I gradually bit the dust. I landed first on the British Version of Park Place (on which she held three houses) then Boardwalk (four), and had to hand over first all my cash, then my deeply mortgaged assets. I do like to win at Monopoly, but if I can't, there's nobody to whom I would rather lose.

We spent my 40th birthday at just such a table. After a lot of build-up, a lot of dread, a lot of what-ifs and would-haves and wondering what would be, there we were. I was 40, with the people I loved the most in this whole wide world.

So here is my toast is to the humble table: wooden or metal, square or round, large or small. Any table will do, as long as it pulls the four of us together with its gravity. Eating, playing, talking. Adrift in a weird world, yet right where we belonged.

CHAPTER NINE:
That Which Endures

THE WINTER WEEKS FOLLOWING MY BIRTHDAY were quiet. The moon rose and set, shining full into our west-facing windows. It was cold that winter in the south of France. According to several of our trusted local sources, the winter we happened to choose was the worst one that anyone could remember.

Apparently they meant by this we had to wear our coats most days, that the blue *provençal* sky was gray three out of four days, and that there was way more rain than usual, like maybe once a week. There was also an eight-minute hailstorm once, just after several glorious hours of sunshine during the market.

Our local sources even went so far as to apologize for the low mood of the place and its people; apparently the frowns during our winter were more dismal than usual, not how things usually are. I found this admission touching in a way, as I had been so accustomed to the general French indifference to my presence.

That winter, I read novel after novel while Grace wrote page after page. Abigail pushed her way through the bleaker days in class, then came home and took solace in her own school for dolls. Bill became even braver. He picked up his bass guitar and joined a musical association, with the twee name "The Merry Little Notes of Les Salles."

French towns provide funds for groups of people who wish to pursue hobbies together. When we first arrived in Aups, we attended a town-wide "Activities Fair" for adults. There was a booth for the Lion's Club that also somehow overlapped with the booth for the veterans of the wars in North Africa. There was a Judo club, and a group whose name translated as "the Association for the Socialization of the Old People." At another booth they were making anchovy paste by hand, and invited us to join in this *grand patrimoine* (big heritage) of our new home.

Some French towns have dance associations, mushroom-categorizing associations, or groups for people who love to drive Fiats. Aups had five dance schools, which included ballroom, hip-hop, ballet, "Sarabande," and just plain scary. But in Les Salles, two towns over, the mayor was a tuba player, and also a communist, so he wisely commandeered adequate funds to build a town music center to feed his habit.

Bill drove over the mountains every Wednesday night to play American blues with a group of people who could not pronounce English unless they were singing. He tried to get them to teach him some French folk tunes, but the Merry Little Notes had developed an odd attachment to Doc Watson and a group that they called "Cree-denss Clear-wasser Revivalle." They rolled all the r's whenever they pronounced the name of this, their favorite American group.

His new band friends took on this marginally important American music in a classically French way: with the highly serious intensity of purists.

"*Non, non, non,*" they would argue amongst themselves. "The chord does not resolve to *sol* before the fourth beat of the measure."

"I am in accord with you relative to the Cree-denss version, but in the original recordings by Monsieur Lead Belly, the chord resolves on the downbeat!"

It was nerdy in the extreme. During jam sessions, children, grandparents, and passers-by would arrive at the communal band room and sit quietly. There was not a whole lot else to do in town aside from watching their comrades play "Down On the Corner" for tuba, mandolin, and electric bass.

The group squarely emphasized the 1 and the 3 of each measure, in the European fashion. They clapped ONE two THREE four, instead of the cooler American other way around, one TWO three FOUR. Put on some hip hop and try the square way for yourself; unless you are yourself hopelessly European in your sense of rhythm, you should hear the problem.

As the foreign exchange student from the land of the hip, Bill tried to teach them the trickier loose rhythms that we Americans learn so early in our lives. His goal was to make their American blues sound less bland, but their focused approach and impassive audience left little room for things to swing.

While he played funk that winter, I just stayed in one. I have always had to grit my teeth just to get through the drawn-out misery of the long nights and cold days of winter. I have long wished to be a different sort of person, but there at 40 it became clear that for better or worse, this was all the me I am ever going to be. A winter grump.

Acknowledging that I live in the grip of my moods doesn't make it easier to gain perspective. I bob up and down, in and out of the light, within and at the mercy of the movements of the spheres. You'd think after all this time, my conscious brain would overcome the lizard one underneath, and I could realize that the world does not in fact change itself rapidly from lovely to awful depending on the day, the month, the weather, the moon.

But no. The spring comes, and I can't imagine why anybody would ever have wanted to wear that awful scratchy turtleneck sweater for four months straight. A raincloud crosses my path, and suddenly any hope of hope is snuffed straight out. Bill had good reason to escape my dark moods for the pleasures of the Merry Little Notes.

It was not until the start of March we had the first *vrai beau jour*: warm and beautiful all day. The extra minutes of sunshine each day were gradually shoving the chill out the door; but it was a particularly stubborn guest who had nowhere else to go. I still wore a coat to cut the wind, but the thermometer had no trouble climbing up into the high teens. In Celsius, fifteen degrees is the sweet spot that jostles your tired winter bones, telling them to wake up, dammit; you've made it to spring.

One week when I went out to pick thyme to grind up and smear on the pork chops, the plants were there all right, all along the road, but scrubby and dried-up from the long winter. But then the next time I made the same dish, each tiny woody branch of thyme had sprung tender new leaves. When I crushed them between my fingers, they released a smell that put the dried, bottled herb in our kitchen to deep shame. One or two flowers in the garden started doing their thing, just two and a half months after the last roses of late winter had given up the ghost. Down the lane towards school, the junipers from which I picked berries for beef stew were pushing new growth right out on top of the old, turning the big trees an impossibly beautiful blue-green. Big black bumblebees were once again drunk with desire and nectar on the fragrant white blossoms outside our door.

Those days, we perched on the cusp of change, driven by the slow turning of our part of the sky towards the sun, and the growing plants all around. Even our appetites changed with the seasons. We did not stuff ourselves with heavy dishes anymore, and I kept finding myself pulled into the fish market for something light and salty. Grace continued working her way through the dessert section of the French cookbook Jessica gave us for Christmas. In the cold months, Grace had mastered a heavy, sticky, gooey *crème brûlée*. But the first week of spring weather it was cream puffs to die for.

The weather forecast that spring often called for rain. The sky fell in heavy gray sheets. On rainy days we moped through the sodden day, drinking tea and playing Monopoly to wait out the rain.

But the sunny days were glorious. A long walk along the terraces of olives. A few hours spent reading in the sun. Cream puffs and cheese soufflé, both light and full of air. A full moon setting and a golden sun rising.

Just as spring sprang, it was time for yet another school vacation. France grants four two-week long breaks, not including the long summer vacation and all those free Wednesdays. For our last enormous break of the French school year, we drove Diesel Liesel to Florence, renting an apartment overlooking the Duomo from friends.

Vacationing in Italy is really not such a big deal when you're just driving over from the South of France. We didn't even need passports; it was a little like driving from Brooklyn to Virginia Beach. As we crossed over the Italian border, Liesel's GPS instructions suddenly changed. She still provided driving directions in her crisply Germanic French, but whenever she had to pronounce the name of an Italian locale, her sexy Italian cousin under the hood would step in and speak for her. We took to hitting the "replay" button on the console just to hear her say "*Mee-LAH-no*" again and again.

It was a glorious ten days, full of long walks, hot pasta lunches and big jugs of Chianti. We made a homeschool project of seeing as much art as the kids could take in any given day, then went back to the apartment each night to make dinner and laugh together. Through all those months of practice, our little American girls had actually become skilled travelers, and the four of us moved as a tight little unit through the city streets. No more wonky wheels on our shopping cart. After all of our practice in France, in Italy we finally found a groove.

We walked all over town, discovering as many landmarks and museums as we could find. But the week was almost over before we stumbled upon our favorite spot. High on a hillside overlooking the entire city of Florence stands the church of San Miniato al Monte. Legend has it that in the third century after Christ, the devout man who would become Saint Minias was living as a hermit on this hillside, near a pagan temple. When he was beheaded by the Romans for his Christian beliefs, he was said to have picked up his own head and carried it back to the hill. Christians built a shrine to him there in the ninth century, and then began building a church there in 1013.

That's a thousand years ago. Which sounds big when you think about it in one long swath, but smaller when you think of it thus: 1,000 is 25 times 40. If you add up the life experiences of the kids in my kindergarten class, we have lived a collective thousand years: every one of them since the man walked on the moon.

But still, relative to the age of everything else I knew, San Miniato was old. The church is significantly bigger now, having been added to during the 11th, 12th, and 16th centuries. Large portions of the interior were built of re-purposed Roman and Byzantine materials, and many of the geometric designs inside the church look Greek or Arabic rather than Italian. Cultures, forces, and histories swept in and out, and still it stands.

We loved San Miniato, and its view of the entire city of Florence. Some monks were singing as we walked in the ocean-green doors, and the sound drew us down towards the crypt at the heart of the church. The monks were standing in a semi-circle around the tomb that is said to hold the remains of Saint Minias himself. Their notes ballooned outwards from the crypt, filling the huge space and bouncing back into layers of sound. When the monks were done singing, they just shut off the electric lights and walked out in that awkward and official way priests sometimes do when they are finished with religious rituals. I guess any ritual, even a sacred one, eventually becomes rote. The music was like silk, but the monks' departure from the crypt made them look like insurance salesmen leaving the office.

After we listened, we read the ground below us. The floor tiles of San Miniato were entirely engraved with names and Latin words. There was nowhere to walk without stepping on the words of the past. San Miniato was all geometry and fresco. It was dark and beautiful, and made me want to stay there and be silent all day.

But when you travel with kids, there is no such thing as silence (only loud whispering, if you're lucky), and no such thing as staying anywhere very long. I felt an insistent breath in my ear, tried to ignore a few impatient tugs on my sleeve, and then walked out into the sunshine. We followed a path off to the side of the church, which led into a warren of crypts and gravestones. Elaborate half-size houses marked the avenues, each decorated with a family name and a particular style. Between and among the rows of houses, there were huge marble stones on the ground, marked with the names and dates of people long since dead. There were stone and concrete busts everywhere, as though the dead had been frozen by the people who loved them, only to moulder slowly into mossy-soft versions of themselves.

Lots of the gravestones looked recently tended, with fresh flowers, or at least not-so-beat-up fabric ones. But other stones were cracking into shards under the weight of weather and time. Some of the little houses had glass windows, but the glass had been smashed and never repaired. It was a lot like the rest of Italy — not overly tended, and full of a design mishmash: lots of serene lines and colors, spattered here and there with gaudy excess. For a graveyard, it was an awfully lively place.

The girls found the children first. A headstone, with a cameo picture of a baby, a terrible story told in numbers: 5-4-35 to 10-6-36. Here was a teenager, grinning wildly and holding an ice cream cone. Or a 10-year-old, or a toddler. One gravestone featured the bronzed bust of a 6-year-old girl. The stone spoke of the joy she had brought her parents in life, and the pain they suffered once she was gone. The little girl had died in the 1930s. Her parents are gone themselves now, but the little statue and the Italian words I could barely make out brought my fresh tears.

And then, further into the stones, we saw two life-size marble statues. One was a young man in an officer's jacket. The other, facing him, was a young woman in a long flowing dress. At first I imagined that these were statues placed by somebody's children to commemorate a long and loving marriage. Looking at them standing there, staring at one another with such longing and affection, I fell in love with them myself. While I have never really thought of life-size realistic marble statues of dead people as anything but weird, these two people standing on Saint Minias's hillside were the very picture of an enduring love.

But then I got up close and read the dates. The man had died at 25, in 1944. The woman was born in 1922, and died early in 1945. I realized with a shock that these long-ago lovers had never been parents, and had barely been adults. They were children in comparison to Bill and me.

Bill came up by my side. "They both died in the war."

For some reason, I had thought that about the soldier, but it hadn't occurred to me that his young bride would have been a casualty as well. If his military uniform was Italian, that made it even more complicated. Hard to know whether he was on the side of the right and the good. He might even have had a hard time with that question himself.

I don't know why our strange family loves graveyards so much. Perhaps because they are quiet. Perhaps it's the stones. Perhaps because we love the stories that emerge. They are of course creepy places to take our kids, and this reality only worsened once they started searching the stones for stories of more and more dead children.

But despite all the children, or perhaps because of their photographs, this lively graveyard held memories full of clear, obvious joy. There were the marble statues, so in love they were nearly dancing. There were the smiling babies and the happy *Nonnas* and plenty of flowers — fake and real. If you've gotta be dead, this would be an awfully sociable place to end up.

But perhaps we also like graveyards because they remind us, without any shadow of a doubt just how alive we are ourselves right now. We are reminded that we will not always be, which makes our living all the more remarkable.

We took the bus back down the hill. The streets were crowded with tourists, with businesspeople, with buskers, gypsies, and West African guys selling Fendi knockoffs. They were all alive, barely conscious of the miracle of their own existence, thronging the living streets below the city of the dead. How many of us ever remember how shocking and strange and wonderful this all is? Even the awful parts, the disasters, the tears, the wars?

While none of us would walk that day carrying our own heads up a hill, the very fact that we were all living struck me as its own kind of miracle. And then we did what any sane living person does in Florence, again and again and again. We stopped in at Festival di Gelato. We chose the freshest and strongest flavors we could find, and savored them, bite by bite. We shared, passing four cones around. Peach. Coffee. Hazelnut. Lemon.

All of this reminded me of perhaps the best reason we took this year away: all the time we get in our lives is borrowed time. I saw it in the contrast between the pulsing life on the streets and the lives memorialized in stone high on the hill. I had climbed the hill of 40. I could only hope there would be plenty more surprises on the way back down.

And while there would likely be plenty of time to taste everything I hoped still to try, why shouldn't I prioritize love, beauty and dessert?

Back in Aups after our spring break in Florence, we settled back into our homeschool routine, and kept sending Abby off to school.

She was our gyroscope, spinning powerful energy inward rather than dispersing it out into the world, maintaining her balance despite constant dipping and weaving. This furious spinning kept her upright and steady in the face of all sorts of difficulties. But during our year in France, she spun mostly to duck and deflect the lightning bolts we kept hurling at her.

Of the four of us, Abigail had lost the most and gained the least with our move. Grace had homeschool, a haven of quiet and books and long stretches of open time, a mode of learning that just then suited her to a T. With our move, Bill and I gained the freedom to become the parents we'd always wanted to be, with all of France spread out at our doorstep. We taught Grace about prehistory while standing in real caves. We taught her to juggle a soccer ball, to conjugate verbs, and to calculate the area of geometric figures. And even if we left her to her own devices, and hid all the remote controls, she would pluck some amazing book off of the shelf and settle down in her room for a few solid hours of reading.

Abigail became the only one of the four of us who craved America nonstop. And she was also the only one who spent significant chunks of time each day interacting with people who spoke only French. Despite her incredible accent, she had a difficult time comprehending much of anything at all. Rather than giving in and trying to speak, she held on, spinning inward, white-knuckling it, just waiting for it all to be over.

At first we thought of pulling Abigail into our homeschool. We tried folding her into the routine of reading, writing, math and hikes, but each day was more disastrous than the last, full of arguments and begging for more TV. We were fine as parents, she seemed to think, but she simply couldn't learn from us when it came to school. After several days of our best efforts, she was ready to go back to the devil she preferred. "I guess home school isn't for everybody," she noted diplomatically, and never considered it again.

Not all of her year was misery. She could multiply faster than the other kids — even up to the big numbers that required her to say things like "four twenties ten nine" when multiplying eleven and nine. And now and then she would make a new friend. She might learn the name of a little girl, share her *American Girl* catalogue with her, and find herself the happy recipient of a real French smile for three days in a row.

These breakthroughs were promising indeed, but then the week after we returned from vacation, she came down with a rotten cold. It made her throat creaky, then stole all her energy before packing her head with green snot. It slowed down her spinning and she started to list, tumble, and fall.

As the default small-g gods of our children's worlds, we don't just hand out umbrellas to keep their heads dry on their dark days; we make the weather. We build them a world, hoping that it gives them joy, but we also must take our places as the authors of their misery.

This is the case from their perspective, but it's also true in an absolute sense as well. We, Abigail's ostensibly loving parents, ripped her away from everything she knew, and promised her she would understand the language a lot sooner than this. And we found ourselves to be wrong.

When the cold knocked her feet out from under her, it no longer mattered that she had raised her hand in class and made a friend. Once *la rhume* took away all her little girl fighting energy, she felt beaten down by all those incomprehensible words at school. The kids who *might* be talking to her might also be teasing her. The adults — being French — never ever seemed to smile, and never threw her a bone. She once again hated school, and despite the chocolate, cheese, bread, and terrific health care, France became the worst place on this big blue marble.

Raising kids is like that. One step forward, two steps back, until it seems they've lost every hard-won thing. They slip into the depths of a rising current. You plunge in after them, swimming hard against the cold to catch them before they sink into something even worse.

And then they're suddenly out of the water, sprinting out and away, faster than you could ever run. And you're the one feeling lost, and soaked to the bone. Proud, of course — because whose kids are as tough as yours? — but lost just the same.

I should have known that Abigail wasn't feeling well when she started to be afraid of the dark again. Nearly every night, she'd sneak into our room, and tell me, in her quiet night-mouse voice, "Mommy. I'm afraid again." She might spend her days independent and resourceful, but she needed me close at night to ward away the intolerable uncertainty that lurks in all of our darkened corners.

After a few nights of fighting the cold and the monsters in her bedroom, one morning she faded — hard and fast. She got up quickly enough, but balked at every step of getting-ready-for-school. Suddenly we were back at square one from the fall, hardly able to get her to put one foot in front of the other. When she stared with dread and hatred at her breakfast cereal, burst into snot-dripping tears, and crawled into a ball on my lap, it was clear that she was in no shape for school.

She was sick enough to stay home, well enough to learn. With a few French Tylenols in her system she could read *Farmer Boy* and add big numbers together. She got double doses of chicken broth and multiplication.

Still, despite the TLC, that afternoon she really broke down, crying in a torrent of feeling, anger, and distress. She was hating France, hating school. She missed her friends. She didn't want home*school*: she wanted home.

But mostly — it came out after a time — she wanted a bagel. Even more than her friends and her grandparents, she needed American food. Demanded it. Craved it, even angrily so. She missed burgers, with ketchup for her fries, and bright orange macaroni and cheese, from a box.

But mostly, bagels. Of all the differences between the U.S. and rural France, it was the bagels she missed most loudly and frequently. She had pointed out on perhaps a thousand occasions that the French were exceptionally deprived in the bagel department.

Bill and I, actually frightened by this dervish of sadness, promised we would somehow get her bagels. This seemed to calm the worst of her distress, but left us in an awkward place: having promised we would give her what she had asked for, how would we get it?

Necessity being invention's mama, this upstate New York recovering-non-cook found herself in a Provence supermarket using pantomime and pidgin French to learn from the courtesy clerk the French word for "yeast." I first tried the *Joy of Cooking* recipe for bagels, and way overcooked the first batch, earning only Abigail's most grudging thanks for the effort. With the second batch — not overcooked, but sadly unseasoned — she tried one, and while she said it was "good enough," she really wanted her usual. An Everything.

Let it not be said that Abigail sets her sights low. When it comes to my little girl, it is Everything or Nothing. But here is where I wish I had access to a little divine wisdom to go along with my power over my children: what does God say when someone gets down on her knees and asks, pretty please, could she have Everything? Particularly when that someone really does appear to deserve it all?

Lacking total control of the Universe, I made recourse to my usual tactic: more internet searching, followed by a trip to the Intermarché. I found a recipe for Montreal bagels, and then I went back to the store, and found *grains de pavot* (poppy seeds) and *sesame* (duh, sesame) as well as some powdered *ail* and *oignon.* I threw on a little celery salt as my own little addition to the mix, since my family would probably eat dirt if I put enough salt on it. Once the dough had been kneaded and left to rise, I shaped it, let it rise again, shaped the mush into eighteen little Saturn-rings, then boiled them in water and honey. I dried them off for a minute, dumped them in the pile of Everything, then put them on the metal sheet to bake.

I will spare you any false modesty and just tell you, straight up, I could do this for a living. My Montreal-style bagels were just this side of the border with amazing.

If you are as lucky as I am, you should be careful what you wish for, as often you will get it. Because then, just as I was pulling our Everythings out of the oven, what showed up in a care package from back home from my mom? Bagels. Also baking powder, so we could make pancakes as well as crêpes, and New York State Maple Syrup to put on the top.

And, miracle of miracles, five boxes (two of them family-sized) of bright orange macaroni and cheese. This felt a whole lot like divine intervention, if not on a holy, then on a wholly human scale. My own mother has practiced her parenting a lot longer than I have, and has learned that for homesickness, the only cure is starch — and lots of it.

Each April day brought a new kind of tiny flower growing in the grass along the side of the roads, or a new tree in blossom, in a color I hadn't anticipated. First the soft yellow Mimosa emerged, like fuzzy muppets populating the hills above Nice. Then cherry and apple blossoms burst forth gorgeous on trees that I had never really noticed before. Suddenly a willow tree announced its existence to me, covering itself in just two days with that first fleeting green that Robert Frost calls gold.

I fell hard for one sort of tree that probably had a nice French name, but might have been an old familiar redbud. Its thin branches looked as though they had been encrusted overnight with small blooms, or maybe bright white mollusks. These trees had never flowered for me before, and perhaps they never would again.

Before I landed in France, I never knew that rosemary plants bloomed. That spring I discovered their blue-purple flowers, which smelled incredible when crushed between my fingers. But the next time the rosemary plants would be ready to show off, I wouldn't be living there anymore.

Just a few days before the Equinox, we bought tickets for the trip home, planning to leave a few days before the summer solstice. We had reached the last season of a "someday" we dreamed about for 20 years. We had actively planned the trip for more than 18 months. The someday was for a time our today. But soon it would become our yesterday.

Right around the time that Provence was bursting into bloom, I got an email from a friend back home in Brooklyn. He took a picture of the tree growing in front of our house, an awkward little star magnolia with all kinds of unruly watershoots growing up around. "You know it's spring," he wrote, "when your tree starts blooming." The tree is no great shakes, really — other than being the first one in our neighborhood to bloom every year — but for the few weeks it announces spring, it is worth its weight in just about anything I can imagine.

More to the point, it's the tree that marks the moment of each year when I stop white-knuckling my way through my life and re-emerge as a tolerable person. I looked at that digital image of white blossoms beginning to unfold, and I started to cry. I had been missing home so much — yet I had pushed that homesickness down so deep that I had managed to forget. I was taken by surprise by how my throat tightened and my eyes filled up just seeing the tree — and thinking of the friend who had sent the photo. The tears hurt, like they sometimes can when they've been held back way too long. I felt at home and homesick at the same time.

Spring changes my entire outlook on life. As I start to feel the sun warming things up enough so that I can drive with the windows down, I relax and start to breathe again. The muscles in the back of my neck start to untie themselves. The sunshine starts to win its battle with the chill in the air, and suddenly I want to move my limbs around. After a few months of being frozen into myself, I want to feel.

Unlike a the winters of my childhood, which could start in late October and occasionally stretch straight through to May, that winter in the Var hewed quite strictly to its proper boundaries. It was still plenty beautiful and warm right up until December 21, with a last few roses blooming in the garden and the herbs pushing up out of their pots. By early January, the ground was covered with the lightest coating of snow, and the trees and shrubs looked deeply chastened by a few weeks of deep cold.

The living landscape never really died back fully, and the walls, lanes and fields stayed green all winter, even if they didn't add on any new leaves. I learned that olive trees in the Var do not lose their foliage. The leaves stayed silvery green, clinging to their branches all winter. I fell deep in love with these olive trees, with the way the tops and the bottoms of the leaves created a texture that looks like soft velvet.

One day I saw a farmer out by the trellised hills of olive trees I walked past every few days. He was hacking away at an olive tree, doing such violence to the limbs of the trees I almost wanted to call the *gendarmerie*. It looked as though the olive trees (his of course, but somehow mine) were being massacred.

The farmer was clearly out of his mind with his chopping. How could the trees possibly withstand so much cutting back, with so much dead wood and silvery leaves strewn around the base of each tree?

The ground was covered with branches, but as I looked more closely, I saw that his method was even-handed and perfectly sane. He had chopped expertly and sensibly, opening up the very center of each tree to make way for more growth. He hadn't just given it a trim, cutting off its edges and leaving it bushy inside. He had made space right at the core, right where the tree had gotten crowded, and where room to grow was needed the most.

I also noticed, at the very base some of the trees, that their trunks were actually relatively tiny branches growing out of the edges of much wider, rounder stumps. The trees I had been walking past for months, the trees I had taken for old and wizened – they were all brand new growth springing out of an ancient source.

In contrast, my blooming magnolia back home is in its infancy. Imagining it to be the voice of the seasons, the wisdom of the years, I have organized my life around its rhythms, allowing it to remind me to emerge back into life every year. I've been looking for life advice from a newborn.

A tree grows in Brooklyn, in fact lots and lots of trees. My magnolia, and all the others, stood guard there for me while I was gone. My friend who took the picture was there too. The broad, wide tree trunk of my life so far did not disappear. Good thing, as it was the only base from which new growth would emerge.

The spring before we left, I had more second thoughts about our trip than any sane person could imagine. I imagined at moments that I was chopping my life to bits. I panicked, even though Bill and I had both so freely chosen this — had elected to carve away our jobs and peel ourselves away from our friends and our hobbies and everything we loved. That spring, even when the dogwood bloomed and urged me to get on with living my life, I stayed pretty much frozen up inside. Bill rushed around hiring the movers, opening up foreign bank accounts, arranging for a rental car, planning the year to the last detail. But I dragged myself to work, I stumbled home, and then I sat on a doggy-smelling brown chair and played Sudoku online for hours at a time.

You could say that we weren't exactly on the same page, but it was worse than that. Neither one of us had left home, but we were nearly in different countries, just a room away from one another in the same house.

I knew I would eventually go to France, but I got awfully cold feet. It got to the point that Bill had to promise me that if things didn't work out, we could fly straight home. I can't believe, in retrospect, how patient and kind he remained in the face of all my foolish fear of change.

Pretty much as soon as we landed in August, touching down in Nice then driving to the Var, I saw what a ridiculous and short-sighted idiot I had been. This overwhelming new world opened itself wide to each of us, giving us a place to empty out the old stale air and fill up with something fresh.

Clearly, my life was just overdue for a massive pruning, which we accomplished by cutting out of Brooklyn. While we were gone, our old life went dormant, but somewhere deep inside all of us, we were gathering strength, getting ready for the next phase.

There in Aups, my trees were blooming. Flowers were growing out of every nook they could find. On the lane between our house and the school, an entire apple tree grew out of the long stone wall. It began its uninhibited show, and then dropped its petal confetti on the lane. The stones of the wall, loosened by a winter of freezing and thawing, were pushed aside by the tree trunk, and fell down on the ground in a little pile. The tree burst forth, knocking the wall down around it. It's not just the little baby flowers, but also us big old trees, that can push time aside and find a new way towards the sky.

It was time to thaw. Time to stretch. And, ready or not, time to grow.

Back in the fall, just after we moved to Aups, I held that first real dinner party. I was nervous as heck trying to throw a real party in a foreign place. But while I barely knew any of the people at that table, I was comfortable in their collective presence almost immediately. So what if I couldn't speak their language, or serve cheese with the appropriate utensils. I really liked them.

As it turns out, the people who came to that party became our real friends. After all my complaining about how unfriendly French people were in general, we made actual friendships, a loose web of French parents and some of the coolest Brits you will ever wish to meet.

It happens slowly, this building of friendships in adulthood. You have to suss people out, and you see only gradually what they're really like. When you're in the eighth grade, you can make a new friend almost instantly — or at least by enduring a 45-minute study hall together on three or four consecutive days. But with grownups, particularly with other families, it's more complicated. Some people you might like immediately, and then find that your spouse finds them insufferable. Or others you might think were a lot of fun, and later discover that they don't return your emails. The good news is that friendship drama doesn't sting nearly so much in adulthood; there are just too many other things going on.

Gradually, the lasagna party strangers became close friends. The kind of people to whom you tell the truth when they ask you how your week has been. The kind of people who really understand when your kids are having a rough day. The kind of people I was starting to realize that I was going to miss like crazy.

In April, Jessica also turned 40. Since I was the elder stateswoman of our little clique in Aups, I invited nearly everybody we knew in common over to celebrate her. The crowd of our shared friends was about half French, half British; half kids and half adults. Her Mom, the decorating whiz behind the terrific house we lived in all year, was visiting from London, and we got to ask her a million and one questions – about Jess, and about the house itself. She told us that the bronze bust that had watched over us all year was a cast of the first president of Sri Lanka, and the crown he wore was the prize for several dozen years' worth of costume parties she held in another small French town nearby. We learned who painted which portraits, and where she had met them all.

The rest of us at Jessica's party were a motley crew of parents speaking English and French with varying degrees of skill. Jessica, so exceptionally capable in both, had become the point around which the rest of us could balance. So the most important thing that we all had in common was that we all loved her. She was the first friend that most of us had made in town.

I never counted how many people showed up to celebrate (a fact that had some bearing on my failure during the evening to provide the appropriate numbers of spoons, bowls, plates, and slices of cake) but all the chairs in the house filled a few times over during the course of dinner.

Taking my cues from the happier lessons of our year, I let things spiral out of control. The kids went completely wild. After about a half hour of balls flying everywhere, of little girls rummaging through the dress-up basket, and all of the kids running in and out of our house, our neighbors' house, and the shared courtyard, one little boy came running inside, blood streaming from the top of his head down onto his white shirt.

He had tripped and somehow gashed his head. But he was neither crying nor particularly upset about the fact that his head had been gouged open. His parents, showing a calm equanimity that seems characteristically French, first did this sort of parental neurological exam, asking him to follow their finger with his eyes back and forth. I wasn't sure if they were kidding, but he must have passed their test, because they asked for a little antibiotic cream to daub on him, then sent him back out to do more crazed running around.

Our girls, as is their wont, slipped in and out of the action. True introverts, they always stayed on the sidelines of any truly wild party, despite my deep wish that they would sometimes simply let themselves play with greater abandon.

When it finally came time to serve dinner, everybody wanted Bill's Moroccan *Harira* soup. I had a vague idea of setting up the kitchen table as a buffet, but when the kids all installed themselves there instead, I let the chips (and the quiches, and the salad, and the bread) fall where they may. I even took the bold American move of putting cheese out *before* dinner, which seemed to the

French kids like I was serving ice-cream sundaes as appetizers. Everybody pulled up a chair and tucked in.

Despite the fact that I spent a whole year shooting holes in my professional resume, the year was not without accomplishments in the domestic realm. For example, I discovered my own personal style of entertaining. I call it ramshackle chaotic mishmash: good food, and even better company.

After dinner, once the kids had all settled down and most of the grownups were smoking on the terrace, Dermot and Anna-Maria somehow cornered Bill and me in the same place at the same time.

"We have something to tell you," Dermot announced. "And we've been dying to get you alone."

For the briefest moment I was afraid we were in for Jonas-and-Vava style *bisous.* But their news was much more welcome than a kiss, and much more wonderful.

"We're having another baby," Dermot announced.

"We've known since before you left for vacation, and we kept running into you now and then. But we wanted to tell you when we were all together." Anna-Maria was grinning from ear to ear, and Dermot looked, as the British say, nothing less than chuffed. We hugged them hard, American-style.

Before their baby arrived, both of our families would move back home. They'd be in London, and we'd be in Brooklyn. It might be years before we met their second child, but I felt like a proud aunt nonetheless.

There were other changes on the horizon for our little club, the Strangers of Aups. Most importantly, we'd all been invited to Jessica and Gerard's wedding at the start of the summer. All spring they had been preparing, renting an enormous red-and-white circus tent, planning the menu, and figuring out where they would move the beehives, the donkeys, and the goats so that they could use the pastures as parking. While Bill and I were thinking about endings, new lives were springing up all around us.

Our friendships were the best bittersweet surprise of a year away. We expected to learn about France, about the language, about the landscape, and about ourselves. We expected to become attached to the Var, and I certainly fell in love with the remarkable house the second I saw it. But I don't know if we anticipated the real joys of new friendships.

Or the way that we would miss our friends, when it was time to go.

PART FOUR:
LEAVING SO SOON?

CHAPTER TEN:

Bon Voyage

MY COLLEGE FRIEND ĐAVE LIVED IN France after college as an *au pair*, mastering not only the French language, but also the technique for making a really killer *tarte tatin*. He married Megan, one of Bill's classmates, an American who was brought up in Paris. Back when we were in the idle chatter phase of planning our trip, we did a lot of our musing in their direction. Dave gave us great advice because his brother, a world traveler like himself, had just finished his own family sabbatical. Dave's brother kept a blog about their adventures, in which he explained the joys and the reality of relocating one's children to a foreign country.

At the end of his time away, he wrote this about his experiences overseas supporting and nurturing his children: "My pom-poms are tired."

Dave, wise man that he is, passed this comment along to us — in part because it was so funny, but also by way of a gentle warning: it might not be so easy to uproot our kids and hope they would grow easily where they landed.

Dave had lived in France and married an ex-pat. His brother had clearly lived through exactly what we were setting out to do. But, true to form, Bill and I didn't really listen to him. Or if we did, we didn't believe that we'd have the same problem, and so we failed to take some of the precautions we might otherwise have taken.

You know, like being a little more systematic about teaching our kids French, or finding them a decent bilingual school, or living somewhere that felt a little less rurally woebegone in the middle of winter. Or airlifts of bagels.

For so long, Bill's and my decisions were driven by our theories about things, rather than by actual evidence or learning from the smart things that other people told us. Which is why Dave's brother's strange condition — Tired Pom-Poms, or TPP — struck us only as strange at the time.

Or perhaps it struck us as something that a different sort of parent might say, as we simply couldn't imagine it could be all that tiring to take care of our own two kids. Back in Brooklyn, when we both worked full-time, we both got awfully tired. Bill sometimes got so tired, in fact, that he would spend an entire weekend lying on the sofa to recuperate. We gradually learned that this had a name but not a cure. For some reason, calling his exhaustion *Chronic Fatigue Syndrome* made it easier for him, and me, to let him rest when he needed it.

Compared to that, how hard could it be to help our kids through a single year away? Neither one of us would have a job. We'd scale down our expenses, and live on savings and rent. We would have acres of time to share with one another.

We set what we thought would be entirely reasonable goals. Each child would learn French. Their math skills wouldn't atrophy. They would each make a friend. When we put it that way, it seemed nearly impossible that we couldn't achieve what we set out to do.

And what did we discover?

Well, eventually we discovered that our pom-poms got so tired that they felt like barbells. So tired that we determined that we would need to leave a month before we had planned.

Because of our initial lack of understanding of Dave's brother's malady, TPP, it took us an awfully long time to admit it. As stubborn as our children are, we are more so, and we had to come up with a whole bunch of ways to justify that the challenges we had set for our kids were not beyond them — or beyond us.

But in the late spring, our kids started driving us nuts. Although we had both gotten much better at tuning into their needs over the course of the year, their new levels of neediness caused us to temporarily lose patience with them. To some extent we even lost sight of the reasons we had come in the first place.

I realize now that we had committed the common sin of letting ourselves get frustrated by who our children really *are*, emphasizing only the negatives. Rather than "persistent," Abigail was "stubborn." Rather than "creative," Grace was unfocused and impossible, unable to finish anything useful. And, as awful as this sounds, we were both angry at them — so unfairly so — for not having made close friends their own age in the village.

As the date of our departure approached, we had to face a number of unpleasant minor realizations, including the fact that not *everything* we thought would happen did. My French never got fluid. The girls never really got comfortable socially. Bill had to recognize that several mountains in the Var would go unclimbed, and admit to himself that he could not learn to play the bass guitar like John Entwhistle in one year. At the start of things, a year felt like forever. By the first of May, our year was a memory and a month.

On good days, we really liked it there. Bill wasn't able to play the bass line to "My Generation," but he loved playing with the dorky Merry Notes, hiking all over the landscape, and becoming a full-fledged expert in Côte de Varois wines. (Do not be too impressed with my Bill. Saying this to a real French wine snob is sort of like bragging about being an expert in the wines of Western Pennsylvania.)

I learned to cook, learned to love homeschool, and despite all those frowny faces at the *portail,* created the comfortable domestic cocoon I had dreamed of for all those years when our jobs overtook our lives. We missed Brooklyn like crazy, and France was nothing like we thought it would be. But we made real friends, and just as the girls were letting us know how much they needed to leave, Bill and I began to feel we'd only started to explore everything we could learn.

We were better than fine, but the girls needed things that neither France, nor we, could provide, unless we planned to stay forever.

Grace was happy enough, but had begun to miss her friends something fierce. Even a seriously introverted kid eventually notices that she has been trapped with her parents 24/7 for three seasons in a row.

And for Abigail, France never was home, and she insisted that it never would be. From her perspective, we took away her house, her friends, her language, and her dog for selfish reasons of our own. We hadn't realized this when we up and quit, but she had been deeply attached to our jobs, seeing them as status and stability. While during the year she learned, and grew, and experienced remarkable things, she stubbornly clung to a spar called "America."

"It's hard to be in another culture where nobody cares about you," she told me one day, during the usual Monday morning school-induced misery. "I won't live anywhere but America for the rest of my life."

Whenever they drooped and sagged, we propped them up. We said yes to bon-bons and scented soap and bits of cheese at every market we found. We let them watch lots of TV. We took them on trips to the beach, or hikes up the mountains, and ate croissants nearly every day. But America called, louder than ever. As much as we loved watching the girls grow and change from little into big, from monolingual to bilingual-ish, at times it all seemed way too hard.

The more we thought about it, the clearer it became that "family" meant "we do things together." Our home could be just about anywhere, as long as it was where we all could all thrive, where we all could get what we needed.

So we made the call. Tickets changed, airplane booked. Our year away had been for so long that ship in the distance. When it came into port, it changed us all. Now the ship was leaving once more, and I hadn't mastered France. Not even close.

The Var did its best that spring to distract me from my regret, and the girls from their homesickness. The plants bloomed, the sun shone, and a series of festivals unfolded through the longer days and warmer afternoons.

First there was Carnival. A local chorale performed — badly — over the town's loudspeaker system around noon, after which Abigail and her classmates were walked into town for a puppet show she did not understand. Later that afternoon, the kids in town dressed up like it was Halloween, and marched through the streets, their parents dutifully supervising, but still not smiling awfully much. They stood off to the side and smoked while the kids sprayed one another with silly string. As we walked along, the people in charge of the event threw confetti, which littered the ground for weeks.

Somebody in town had made a papier-mâché king's head, probably years ago by the looks of it, and it was dug out and stuck on a long pole to be raised over our heads on the parade. The French kids all ignored Abigail and Grace, so they goofed around with Lajla and her friends from preschool.

At the end of the parade, we marched down into a part of town we'd never visited, and were surprised to find ourselves and our costumed children parading through the hall of an old folks' home. Some of the faces were cheerfully grateful we had come, and clapped along with the strange music they had chosen to play for our indoor parade. But many of the faces were hauntingly blank.

A few weeks later was Easter, which in nearby Tourtour was the *Fête des Oeufs*: the Festival of the Eggs. We drove over for a picnic with Jess and Gerard, Dermot and Anna-Maria. Eggs were decorated, hung in trees, tossed exceptionally long distances by young men, then caught by other young men. Huge decorative nests had been built in the plane trees over the sand of the boules court, and eggs bigger around than a bike tire set in place in them, as though the dinosaurs had never left France, and had just stepped out of their nests for a minute.

One even more enormous egg sat in a nest of hay bales strung up in effigy next to the church. I kept thinking that an army would pop out of it, like the Trojan Bunny in *Monty Python and the Holy Grail.* But, of course, this being France, it is the *cloche* (the church bell) who delivers and hides the eggs, not a bunny of any size.

Eggs were also being thrown about among wandering hordes of middle-schoolers, smushed on the heads of young and crushworthy girls by the boys who fancied them, and slopped along the roadways, left to bake in the sun. I loved being around all that outrageous spring fecundity, particularly with Dermot and Anna-Maria, so fully thrilled with her pregnancy. We'd heard that Vava and Jona were expecting a baby as well. She was due just a day after Anna-Maria. Something was clearly in the water on their street.

The friendly, bohemian mood of the *Fête des Oeufs* was a significant departure from the festivals we'd seen in Aups. It was rather light on the sale of agricultural products, and heavy on the whimsy and children's entertainment. There was an entire section dedicated to kids' games, where Abigail played with, or at least near, the other kids. Two friendly grownups were doing *maquillage* (face-painting), for some reason dressed up as Native Americans. Thousands of tourists had come from somewhere to fill the town with sound, life, and euros they could spend at every overflowing café.

And all up and down the hill between town and the church were parked giant musical instruments made out of wood, toys, old bicycle parts, and rubber gloves. They were made of wheels, of old saucepans, and of hula-hoops. One instrument was made out of recorders with some of the holes wrapped with tape, and connected to rubber boots so that when you smushed a boot, the boot would force air into the recorder and it would play. Some mad genius had made them all, for reasons I couldn't understand even if I had lived there forever. Sometimes, this weird world is delightful.

The day was sunny and warm and beautiful. The town was crowded with people who looked eager for the summer season to begin after their long hibernation. It made me sad to think that once the season had begun, we would be gone. We wouldn't get to steal fronds of fresh lavender in blossom, as it would not flower until after we had left. We would have to make do with as many bars of purple soap as we could take in our bags.

A few weeks later, just as we were starting to pack up, Aups celebrated the festival of its patron saint. Apparently they needed a weirdly-named saint to protect our weirdly-named town, so they chose St. Pancras, the patron saint of teenagers. That day, all the men in town behaved exactly like depraved adolescents. They shut down business at the butcher's, the agricultural collective, and the bakery — all the businesses, really, aside from the bar. They donned wild costumes — cowboys and Indians were popular, but there were also plenty of guys in drag.

And then these otherwise upstanding men of our town, some wearing tutus and wigs, proceeded to get exceptionally drunk. Falling down drunk. Throw-your-buddy-in-the fountain drunk.

Bill, having heard about the St. Pancras Day tradition in advance, fished around with Gerard for an invitation. He had heard that after all the drinking, the townsmen would walk up into the hills with their hunting rifles and shoot at things, and he wanted to join in. It's unclear to me why he would have found this enticing, but you never know what's going to float Bill's boat. Gerard wisely warned him off of the drinking, and the guns.

"It's a foolish afternoon," he told Bill, forgetting that foolish is one of Bill's favorite modes. "I used to go when I was a young man," he told us, "But not any longer." Presumably Jess had a few things to say about it, and was aiming to protect both Bill and Gerard from unnecessary harm. As it was, Bill spent the afternoon walking down to the post office to mail a few boxes back home. One of the drunker celebrants, dressed as a cowpoke, grabbed one of our boxes out of Bill's hands and threw it to a temporary Indian.

"Take this back to America, for the American," he yelled out. It was the first time either of the men, whom we had seen all year long, acknowledged they knew we were there.

I found myself walking through the house, running a finger along all the surfaces that had held our family all year. I told myself that I would not forget this. And this, and this, and then, oh, also this. I would not forget the way Abigail's hair smelled when she crushed in for a hug. I would not forget the shine of Grace's face as she drove the electric boat that day in May, fishtailing back and forth through the Gorge de Verdon.

I would never forget the way that millions of wild poppies started to bloom all along the roadsides, on top of stone walls, and interspersed with the grasses of the fields. They grew at random everywhere that May, apparently unplanted, so astonishing in their color and in the fragility of their papery petals.

By writing each moment, or taking its photograph, I somehow reassured myself that I had preserved it for some imaginary someday. For some version of myself yet to be, somewhere else. So stunned by the fact that we were leaving, Bill and I sorted through our belongings and scraps of paper, looking for what to save and what to cull. Which old ticket, or to-do list, or tiny shell from the beach would help us to remember how we lived there, what we did, how we felt? What could possibly remind us just how sweet the air smelled in Aups, when it didn't smell like poo?

I did not hang on to everything, of course, because those who live too powerfully in memory can't truly live in the present. If everything becomes a souvenir the moment we experience it, we merely curate our lives, rather than living them.

And, more importantly, the biggest memories, the ones that endure, are rarely the ones we stow away so consciously. Who knows, from day to day, which chance encounter or bold move will grow into our defining legend, shaping all the living we have yet to do?

As Bill and I packed, we talked about what our girls would remember from this deeply different year. What would they tell their friends about this experience — so separate and so distinct from their tiny pasts and their vast futures? What smells would they remember? What tastes would they crave? What would become their Proustian *madeleine* and bring their France spilling back?

The very first day I woke up in Provence, I had an impulse that I hadn't had in over 20 years. For some reason I can't explain, I knew exactly what to make for breakfast. I heated up a pan of milk, mixed in chocolate, and poured it in bowls. I cut baguettes lengthwise, and set out two different kinds of jam. I hadn't eaten *tartines* and *chocolat* for breakfast since I was 15.

When the girls are grown, what will the word "Provence" signify? When I first saw the orange, green, and blue landscape, I felt that I had escaped to the moon. I wonder if they were young enough during that year that the sounds, smells, snails, language, and sensory life will become a part of them. I wonder if *tartines* and a bowl of hot chocolate will someday become a breakfast that makes them sigh and feel the cozy crush of childhood memory. Will they taste crêpes with raspberry jam when somebody says "Provence"? Or will they always crave eggs and toast from the diner?

Memories accrue in the strangest of ways. Driving in and out of Aups all year, we often rolled down the windows and put all of our gusto into a heartfelt rendition of our favorite John Denver song:

Country road, take me home
to the place where I belong

At first, we were singing wistfully about the America we had left behind. But when we started to sing the same song each time we traveled that stretch of French road, that became the country road taking us home, back to the little house in the olive trees with windows open to the sky.

Before we arrived, we had only ideas. We talked about France *ad nauseam* with everyone we met. We served as the repository for other people's dreams as well as our own unfounded fears. Upon our arrival, all those ideas receded in the overpowering realness of the place. We lived the color of the stones and the sky, the feel of the dust, the smell of cheese and spices at the market, the sound of the bats flying and the cats calling in the night. Our senses trumped our ideas, and the real muscled aside the merely theoretical, carving new grooves in our brains.

We parents are in the memory business, but we have no idea which ones will stick. We provide the stage for our children's experiences, we tell them their own stories, and then have to spend the rest of our lives living down our inevitable mistakes. But although we live in the same houses, share the same days with one another, our children's memories are *only* their own, vastly more unpredictable than the ones we stash away for ourselves.

Once Grace left school, she blossomed, and truly relished the rest of the year. Abigail resisted France every step of the way, even as its challenges and sensations seeped in to become a part of her. She insisted that she understood nothing, and would only look blank and terrorized if some adult tried to speak to her in French. Still, by the late spring, when she played with her American Girl dolls, she was likely to be speaking to them entirely in French, as long as she thought we were not listening.

When I asked them one day at breakfast what they would remember from the year, that was pretty much how they called it.

"This is the year I became amazing," Grace told me. She was thinking of how she acquired a new language, a new way of learning, and a new sense of her own bravery, intelligence, and self-reliance.

"This is the year to which I will *never* return," countered Abigail.

But I'm not so sure that these are the stories that will endure.

I say this because memory is tricky. The kids rarely remember the same version of events as we do.

Plus, the trip itself unfolded, in large part, because of at least two generations of our own family memories. Our memories aren't individual, but collective. Bill and I dreamed up this trip in part to echo trips taken years and years ago, trips I can only remember through other people's stories.

As we drove up and down the A8, the main highway from Nice to Aix, I thought of my Dad, in a VW beetle, on his legendary post-college trip fifty years ago. I thought of Bill's Uncle Kim and Aunt Maria, who enrolled fifty Junes ago in a program called The Experiment in International Living. They met on a ship bound for Europe, and then told one another that if they were meant to be together, they would meet on September 3 under the *Arc de Triomphe*. Without cellphones or even airmail to sustain their shipboard romance, they met as planned and were married less than a year later. They later lived in France with their young children for two and a half years that became the stuff of family legend.

Bill had wooed me with his memories of his own family's overseas sabbatical almost as soon as we met. I fell for him while he unspooled stories; our family was born out of those early hours of storytelling. I felt safe, warm, and loved when he spoke, hearing the counterpoint to my own happy childhood. Those stories convinced me that Bill was a man with whom I could build a life.

Years later, when we decided to get married, I promised we would live overseas. The trip we planned was built on the model of the stories he remembered. This is the kind of adventure I would never dream up all on my own; it had Bill's happy childhood scrawled all over it from the start.

But now I'm the one who has written it down. Before I started writing our days into this book, I never imagined myself as a storyteller. After all those years of Bill getting to tell all our best stories, I found myself with hundreds of pages of a story. This one you are holding in your hand.

The girls lived it too, and they will decide — either consciously or by chance — what to retell of it all. When they read this book someday, I wonder how much of it will ring true.

Some memories are all our own. We keep them deep inside, all to ourselves. They form our deepest core; each individual's web of memories is no more and no less than her soul. The deepest of these never make it on to any page, into any conversation.

But other memories travel along the lines of generations — through parents to children, then on to the children who may become parents themselves. It's just that we can never truly predict the paths that those memories will take, as they snake themselves forward in time.

Hungry to hold onto these memories as they passed, I wrote another day in my digital diary:

The sun comes up and I wake up without an alarm clock. I open my eyes once more in this remarkable house. It's not mine, but I am so at home here, feeling at peace. During the day, we four are à table together three times, with learning, writing, walking, talking, and looking at the flowers in between. Late in the evening, the sun sets, now off in the northwest rather than straight on from the windows. The garden gets quiet, and the white roses that have spent the day blooming are luminescent in the dusk.

Another day gone, another day truly lived. For this moment, I have everything I need, and I'm trying very hard not to count how many more of these days I have left. I want what I have.

A few years ago I consciously decided to try to adopt this motto for my life: *want what you have.* I coined the phrase as I was writing a toast for my father's 70th birthday party, trying to distill the essence of his wisdom. Dad never said this phrase to me in so many words, but rather enacted it on a daily basis. He never complained about the inevitable challenges of his job, or his family, or the life he had chosen. Instead, he would resolutely look on the bright side, and keep his mouth shut when he couldn't.

During the times in my life since then when I have been able to follow his example, I have been happy. But as with any goal, sometimes I hit the mark and sometimes I fail. "What Would David Do?" Bill often asks me when I've made myself nuts with worry. He reminds me to model myself on my dad's steady positive nature and to want what's right in front of my face. But like any normal, non-David-like human being, I can't always do it. Often I find myself consumed with desire, sometimes bordering on lust, for something distinctly impossible, something I not only do not have now, but could not have ever. Now and again this drives me forward to the next big thing, but mostly it just drives me crazy.

Like when, about a month before we left, we decided to leave earlier than we had planned. I was full of distress and regret (or as full of regret as one can be when one is also full of baguettes and life-altering cheeses). Part of me felt that we had failed — failed the kids and ourselves. We had tired of cheering them onward to a place they didn't want to go.

So we rebooked our tickets, and told Abigail that we were going to stop asking her to speak French at home. The forced-march aspects of the adventure ended.

It was a regretful, deflated little yes. Feeling defeated and not a little loserish, we said yes to our tired, cranky children (rather than the *NO* we use more frequently and reflexively). It wasn't a particularly loving yes. It was not a particularly patient yes, but it did the trick.

Because suddenly, everybody relaxed.

Without some faraway finish line to cross (we will all speak perfect French, we will all love France all the time, we will all embrace this place and one another in joyful kum-ba-ya harmony) our sense of being on an impossible mission evaporated. Or, to put it in a more positive way, we realized that our mission had already been accomplished. We wanted what we had.

And suddenly, in our last month, a whole bunch of tiny victories started to unfold.

One day the sun came out on a Wednesday Market Day, and some of the little girls in the town rounded up our kids and convinced them to go play. The girls may have asked before, but our kids had always been too shy. This time, much to our surprise, they both said yes. Bill and I sat at one of the little tables and drank our breakfast beers with Dermot and Anna-Maria, and the girls went off with some kids to play. It was lovely. We had friends. They had friends. They were off on their own in the market square on a sunny midweek morning, using their allowance to buy cheese. Family victory number one.

Then one day Grace came to me and asked me, quite out of the blue, how she might get Abigail to respect her. She had real concern on her face, and actually listened to my answer, which was that she might first try to actually *like* her sister. We talked about it awhile, and she seemed to understand that there were things that she could do herself to improve their relationship, rather than waiting for her little sister to magically be less annoying.

The biggest fight between the girls was about who got to talk, when. Grace had a hard time waiting for Abigail to finish a thought, and Abigail had a hard time getting her words out fast enough to finish her sentences and stories. When Grace asked me what specific things she could try, I suggested that she work on trying to be patient with her sister while the words formed in her sweet little brain. And then suddenly, after eight and a half years of unabated poisonous sibling rivalry, Grace was taking actual steps to listen to her sister and show her a little love. She said yes. Family victory number two.

And in response? Well, a few days later, Abigail told a long and involved story. For once, nobody interrupted. The story got longer and more detailed, and then slowly drew to an end. She finished up, looked right at Grace, and said, "Would you like to speak now? I'd like to hear what you have to say." Abigail finally had gotten her thought out completely, then politely asked whether her big sister would like to contribute. We all stared at one another in astonishment and surprise: one of us had actually finished a complete thought, then ceded the floor voluntarily. Family victory number three.

And then, one day, with fewer than ten school days to endure, Abigail just woke herself up in the morning, put on her backpack without any fuss at all, and skipped all the way to school. That afternoon, she came home from school, made her own snack, and immediately sat down at the kitchen table to do her own homework. The homework consisted of conjugating *partir* and *danser* in the *futur*, and multiplying big numbers by little numbers, so it wasn't baby stuff like coloring in a worksheet. And when Bill came into the kitchen to ask her a question, she answered, without any effort at all, "*Bah, oui, Papa.*" She didn't even hear herself speaking a foreign language as she said yes.

Another yes. When we stopped forcing things, she wanted what she had.

Once Abigail was relieved of the fear of losing America, once she was certain we'd be going home, she let the words that had piled up inside of her come spilling out with somebody other than her American Girl dolls. I'd say that this was family victory number four, but that achievement was all hers.

To celebrate all these victories, and to put his own quirky stamp on the ending of our voyage, Bill devised a super-hokey candlelit ceremony.

As the sun set, Bill and I began preparing the dining room for the girls' initiation into the Hearty Family Travelers' society, which Bill and I may or may not have invented. We closed the shutters tight, lit candles along the center of the table, and set out little bowls of delicious smelling and tasting things from the Var. There was a bowl of crushed lavender, and one of rosemary, and a slice of salty *saucisson*. We had a bowl of Gerard's mountain-flower honey with two tiny silver spoons, and another bowl of salt taken from the Mediterranean Sea.

We brought them into the room, and gave each of them a tiny taste or smell from each bowl, chanting some mumbled-up version of a faux-French incantation. Earlier, the Elders of the Secret Society, which may or may not have been Bill and me, had written up official certificates in antiquey-looking fonts for each of the girls. Once they had passed the tests of naming each of the Var's most pungent tastes and smells, we awarded them their citations.

Grace received special commendation for several of her more remarkable achievements, including

A trip to the Emergency Medical Department in a Foreign Land
Learning French from a demented professor who never left her house,
And mastering the Art of French Cooking, Jr.

For her part, our little über-patriotic American Abigail was duly recognized for

Nine months of attending school in a Foreign and Often Hostile Land
Learning French in Dread Secret with an enviable Accent Provençal, and
Eating lapin, âne, sangliers, grenouilles, and escargots
(special citation for sheer amount of Tome de Pyrénées consumed)

Abigail couldn't decide whether or not to be mortified by this funny mumbo-jumbo. Part of her wanted to be flattered as we recognized her bravery and flexibility, but mostly she was just hoping to get some bling or at least a cookie out of the event. She was happiest when I hung a little heart charm around her neck. I told her it was the amulet of compassion, which would protect her from all harm.

The poor kid. She hates weird things, and kept rolling her eyes during our little secret handshakes and talking about her achievements like she were becoming a Jedi Knight.

Stuck in this oddball family, a round peg surrounded by squares, Abigail often seems to be wishing we'd just settle down in suburbia, buy all our clothes at J.C. Penney, and get respectable jobs. If any totally normal parents out there have a weird child and would like to swap kids for a weekend, I'm sure that she would be totally grateful.

By the end of the year, American Abigail had spent more time immersed in the French language than the rest of us put together. French school wasn't easy for our sweet-and-sour little girl, and she never let us forget it for a minute. But watching her flinty stubbornness hone itself on the challenges of this year made me so very proud. Through sheer stoic persistence, she grew more than any of us.

As recompense, I ended the ceremony by promising Abigail that as soon as we arrived back home, the next trip to the American Girl store would be on me. I would turn off my usual rant about girly-girl commercialism, and let her revel in the totally familiar and totally normal. I promised to drink tea and buy overpriced plastic things and wave wildly the American Girl flag.

Grace needed no bribes to get right in on the fun of our ceremony, and immediately adopted a faux-serious British accent to give a Hogwartsian dignity to the proceedings. As we read her certificate, she laughed in all the right places and fairly glowed with pride. I awarded her with the amulet of understanding, telling her that as long as she continues to search for the truth, her life will be rich with feeling and experience. But by then, she had learned that lesson on her own.

We planned to roast marshmallows to conclude the celebration. Bill had prepared by stacking firewood in the outdoor barbeque pit that we had never used, due to all the unusually crappy weather.

However, in the way of all things Bill, the brush pile was much more ambitious than it needed to be for the size of the fire pit. He lit the stack with another incantation *à la française,* and the sticks burst into a whoosh of flame.

As the flames leapt into the air towards the little plastic roof that covers part of the terrace, the girls cheered, but seeing disaster, I got more and more nervous. Eventually I ran into the house to get a bucket. By the time I was back, even Bill was scared, and we each threw a gallon of pool water on his raging inferno. The girls stood there, marshmallows on their sticks, looking at us in dismay.

The water wrecked the fire, soaked the hearth, and ruined the mood. Our fire failure also made Bill really sad, so we said yes to a snuggle around the warm hearth of the Disney Channel.

Our bags were packed. Lessons were finished, and the more thrilling European adventures of the Hearty Family Travelers' Society all in the past.

But we were finally saying yes, wanting what we had. Yes. Yes. And *Bah, oui, Papa.*

Learning the delicate dance of making friends in a new place was one of the more dizzying experiences of our time in a tiny French town. At first I blamed all my troubles on the place. But now with my special 20/20 hindsight glasses, certain things are crystal clear.

When we first arrived, I was continually taken aback that nobody greeted my massive people-pleasing American smiles with anything but a glazed, distant hauteur. I tried to be friendly at *le portail,* the big green gate dividing school from home, but I couldn't find anyone there who would meet my gaze. I didn't register; I didn't exist.

Making the classic rookie error of interpreting another culture through my own assumptions, I assumed that I had done something shun-worthy, or that nearly everyone we met was massively stuck up. I assumed I was walking around with spinach in my teeth.

Had we stayed for ten days or so, I would have left with the typical Anglo-American complaint. They were stand-offish. Pretentious. You know, French.

But then I figured out that strangers are treated differently in different places, so it's not a great idea to confuse the friendliness of strangers for real intimacy. I was so down on the whole place for being so unfriendly, when in reality, it was just that I had chosen to surround myself with strangers. They were behaving the way one behaves towards strangers in France, which is to keep one's polite and respectful distance.

But once I did make friends there, I had plenty of people to kiss on both cheeks and invite over for dinner. So what if the good people of Aups walk around looking as though all of their cats just died? If that's how they choose to do things in Eden, who was I to judge?

When you live somewhere long enough, the weird world starts to make sense, and you realize that it's you who is not fitting in. It was not their blank stares that were odd. It was my big American grin. Once I had lived in Aups long enough, I began to see American tourists a little bit as the natives might. Once the weather turned summer-lovely, they appeared more frequently, wearing oddly bland clothing and buying Coca-Cola at the *Supermarché*. They had safe, symmetrical haircuts and good teeth, which I could see because they were smiling like total idiots. They were the old me — the me I would become again as soon as I arrived safely back on American soil.

Bill was right in so many ways. In particular, he was right that I really should, would, and could have learned French. The language barrier and my own lack of preparation only made things worse where friendships were concerned. Even if some French someone did turn up with a friendly, engaging face, I would usually respond with something like "I verily am appreciative of your kindly foodstuffs," or "Weather good now in town think I hope." I missed my own ability to articulate anything other than a pleasantry or a poorly-conjugated literal translation of a banal observation. Back home, I kept wanting to tell people, folks thought I was smart. And funny. Only I didn't know the words for any of that. Who knows who I could have met had my French been less awful.

I also learned something from watching the contrast of Bill and Abigail: once you can speak another language, it's best to do so as freely and un-self-consciously as you possibly can. Bill may have made some mistakes, but they were never, ever begrudged. Abigail's dolls benefitted from her tutoring, but her caution didn't help her to get the real flesh-and-blood kind of friends.

Once I thought about it from this perspective, I realized that I had never taken the time back home to befriend someone whose English wasn't already serviceable.

To have a friend, you have to be a friend, particularly in a second language.

It's also important to look in the right places for friendships. When I first arrived in France, I stood there at *le portail* and smiled, assuming that would be the place to make friends. But I felt only icky vibes there. Instead, our friendships developed around café and dining room tables, not around "play dates," weekend soccer games and children's birthday parties. They grew in private family moments rather than at public occasions.

A lot of things changed as we got to know Jessica and Gerard. Although Jessica grew up in France, deep down she's English, with an extra dose of devil-may-care spontaneity and pretty exceptional hospitality skills. We went over to her house for dinner every two weeks or so for a whole year and were never fed the same thing twice, even though everything was so good I wouldn't have minded a repeat. She was kind right away, and quickly welcomed us in to her life. Her fiancé Gerard, so open-hearted, welcoming and deeply human, became our first real French friend, and through them, we made many more.

Over the course of the year, they welcomed not just us, but also our visiting friends and family to their farmhouse. Jess thought nothing of whipping up several dishes to serve over the course of hours to her happy, comfortable guests. We ate lamb sausage, chocolate mousse, stewed rabbit, perfectly cooked duck, and that ain't the half of it. She gave me endless translations, multiple assists on school quandaries, and many, many glasses of red wine.

Twice in our last week in France, Jess and Gerard invited us up to their beautiful farm, perched right on the ridge between the rolling hills to the south and the craggier bigger peaks of the Alpes-de-Haut-Provence. First they had a *méchoui,* a goat barbeque, with three goat kids roasted all afternoon long on spits. Gerard had made an herbal broom out of branches of rosemary, thyme, and other herbs he plucked out of the field, and swabbed at the little beasties all afternoon as they turned slowly via a contraption run by a windshield wiper motor. It was attached to a tractor battery, and he had adjusted it precisely so that the spits would turn slowly, but not too slowly. Gerard is MacGyver for food.

We ate goat ribs, goat legs, goat cheeks, and even the goat head. We ate our American friend Paula's guacamole and boiled quail eggs, some lovely anchovy paste, as well as cauliflower and spicy sausages (yes, even the children ate all that) and finished up with brownies and Grace's choux-crèmes. The only thing better than the food was the warm and friendly conversation.

The *méchoui,* like the *bouillabaisse* party we had attended a few weeks before at Laurent and Mathilde's house, was mostly Francophones, but really smart engineering sort of ones who can speak plenty of English when they choose. A passel of exceptionally adorable children vacillated between joyfully frolicking about and ruthlessly smacking one another in the head, but none of the parents paid all that much attention *(pas des* helicopter parents in France). The kids would be kids, the grownups stuck close to the table, and everyone had a perfectly lovely time.

And, perhaps because our kids knew that leaving was safely on the horizon, they played too. Generally, at the social events we attended during the year, Abigail circled the periphery and waited for somebody to put on a movie, while Grace chose the place furthest away from all the other kids, and either knit or read a book.

But that day, they jumped right into the fray and onto a real-life trampoline. They spent the whole day with all the other kids, and then at the end of the day, asked us if we all could stay even longer.

Then, a few nights later, Jess and Gerard invited us over again, with just the littler crowd of closer friends that congealed during our year. We had somehow formed a loose group of five British, American, and French families. Once again we sat outside at a long wooden table for hours. Gerard made everybody pizza after pizza after delicious wood-fired gorgonzola-pesto-sausage-olive-mozzarella pizza. The ashtrays gradually filled up with cigarette butts and olive pits, as we laughed and talked and ate Gerard's incredible food.

After a while, I looked up the hill, and there they were — 11 of them — a passel of happy kids bouncing around inside the netted trampoline. There were Spike and Toby, Elise and Clement, Zach, and Cameron and Louise. And then, holding Lajla's two hands, on either side of her, were Grace and Abigail. Seamus was too little, so he just stood clinging on to the net.

I watched them all hold hands and jump in a charmed circle. They all — each one of them — spoke some sort of combination of two languages, and understood one another perfectly well.

I swear it was just the setting sun in my eyes that made me tear up just then.

Perhaps as a result of nearly a full year of being around me 24/7, Bill was attuned to my moods. Seeing me looking at the happily playing kids, he came over and hugged my shoulder as we watched the kids jump and laugh. "Now they have European cousins."

As I walked back to the table, Mathilde and Laurent presented us with a bottle of magic gold elixir. It was marked with the name of their home and the succulent words, "*huile d'olive*": olive oil pressed from the fruit of their very own trees. Don't tell the customs authorities, but of course I packed it with exceptional care to bring it home for the moments when we needed a little golden drop of Provence.

Then Dermot — the charismatic one of our mini-clique — stood up. "Before anybody has to go, we have something to give Bill and Launa." He pulled out a framed photo that everybody had signed, even the under-five set. He had photo-shopped pictures of the four families to look as though they were grinning at us from inside the fountain in the center of town.

Just then, Gerard's daughter Louise wandered by and suddenly grabbed me around my midsection, in an American-style hug rather than the usual French *bisous*. Perhaps it had taken a lot longer than I had suspected initially, but once somebody's kid hugs you for no apparent reason, you no longer have to wonder if you've really become friends.

Then of course, I was standing with my back to the sunset, so I had nothing but joy to blame for my pesky tears.

Au revoir, mes amis: until we return.

CHAPTER ELEVEN

Bonheur

I ALWAYS ASSUMED THAT I WOULD DRAG my bagful of likes, dislikes, quirks, hopes, and disappointments wherever I went. Bill could take us three girls out of Brooklyn, but we would be defiantly the same wherever we went.

This belief accords with the set-point theory of happiness, which is that each of us has a happiness thermostat. As individuals, we tend to hover around the same degree of happiness, despite even radical changes in the circumstances of our lives, like illness or winning the lottery. As Daniel Goleman put it, writing in *The New York Times,* in July 1996,

"There is... scientists contend, a set point for happiness, a genetically determined mood level that the vagaries of life may nudge upward or downward, but only for a while. With time, the grouchy tend to become as cranky as before, and the light-hearted cheery again."

When we left Brooklyn to find a home away, I assumed that this would be true — that despite embracing a life centered around my family, away from the stresses of work, and in a totally idyllic location, I would swing between ebullient and cranky just as I have my whole life. My glass is half-empty or half-full from day to day, but rarely overflows and never ever runs totally dry.

But our year was different in more fundamental ways than any of us could have imagined. Even the precise quality of the happiness I found in France was different. It felt steadier, somehow. More daily and rhythmic.

It's not for nothing that people love France, as the French have preserved and cherished a landscape and a lifestyle to which the rest of the world likes to escape, on the order of 85 million tourists per year.

The people whose ancestors have lived in the French countryside for all of human history have a different way of being happy from the way Americans define the word. While the U.S. Constitution reminds us of our right to pursue our own innovative forms of happiness, the French are dead serious about insuring the preservation of a shared vision they call *bonheur*.

American-style happiness is individually defined: mine may look like yours, but it might not. Our happiness is also fleeting and elusive, characterized by enormous smiles, fulfillment in one's career, and good times rolling on the weekend. Americans are often surprised — shocked even, positively shocked — when the forms of happiness we promised ourselves we'd pursue are shattered, or turn out to be hollow. But, hopeful as ever, we get up the next day and pursue happiness again. There is always something more amazing on the horizon to consume or achieve. And we're just the ones to discover or invent it.

In contrast, the *bonheur* of the French is the sum of a long series of carefully thought-out shared cultural decisions about how to eat, what to drink, when to work, and how to love. It is less about smiles, about individual choices, or the pursuit of the next amazing thing. Instead, it's a comfortably shared sense of how the moments, seasons, and years of life should unfold. It does not need to be invented, but rather preserved and carefully reconstructed.

In its true form *à la provençale, bonheur* is maintained in a series of careful steps from one pleasant, comfortable moment to the next. In the morning, the church bells chimed and we all opened our shutters in the same way. We took our coffee and croissant in the café, sitting down, chewing and gazing out languidly into space. The stores opened and we all got big straw baskets to collect the day's worth of whatever was freshest. Fruits and vegetables in France are bred for their taste rather than for their shelf life: ripe and perfect one day, they were mush the next.

School and work happened for a few hours in the morning, but then lunch was long, and relatively leisurely. It was taken at a real table, often followed by a nap. *(A nap! I'm not kidding!)* In the Var, stores closed for a few hours in the middle of the day, after which everybody learned or worked again in the afternoon. Later, there were *les apéritifs*, dinner, salad, and cheese. As a last step, everyone pulled the shutters closed to mark the end of the day.

Bonheur is sustained as these milestones of daily life are reached and savored fully and in turn. A true French person moves deliberately from shutters to coffee to shuteye after lunch, recognizing that this order of life — so carefully developed over generations of habit and cultural agreement — is the cornerstone of his or her share of life's joy. Happiness is not located in novelty, and it isn't individual. Rather, happiness is found in a carefully choreographed series of pleasant and predictable tried-and-true experiences: *la vie quotidienne*. Daily life.

This choreography is exacting and specific. The French are committed to their *bonheur*, but they aren't exactly likely to be cheerful, friendly, and fun about it. To an American, this rigidity may have a touch of the boring. How could happiness be so predictable? Someone French might answer: this is the way things are done. Fewer promised peaks, perhaps — but also fewer perilous tumbles into the depths.

When French president Nicholas Sarkozy suggested that nations measure themselves (and one another) not just on the basis of gross domestic product, but also by the degree of *bonheur* of their citizens, he got lots of press in France. To the degree that any Americans even paid attention to Sarkozy, they rightly saw this as a shot of socialism across our capitalist bow — and just as quickly dismissed his serious philosophical argument as typically French *fol-de-rol.*

But he meant something a lot deeper than most Americans would care to seriously entertain — for example, how might the quality of life change for typical Americans if we had the kind of security provided by universal health care and low-cost university education? How many leisurely lunches could we enjoy in our lives if we weren't struggling to hold onto our health insurance or pay off supersized mortgages and enormous college loans for ourselves and then for our children?

In Brooklyn, before France, our little family took our happiness where we could find it. Since we were then wholly occupied by the process of being a two-career, two-kid family, running ourselves ragged during the weekdays, we generally took up the pursuit in little bursts. A kitchen dance party each evening after dinner, a Coney Island trip on the weekend, or a vacation with our families. In between to get us through, there would be the fleeting joys of on-line shopping for the grownups, or Poptropica for the kids. We saw happiness as an escape from the routine, or the routine's successful completion. In France, *bonheur* was the routine in itself.

Sometimes we found the happiness we pursued in our escapes or our achievements, and sometimes we were thwarted. We were reminded to find happiness in the little things, for sure (and we certainly did). But we were also routinely encouraged to covet other people's happiness, and then purchase our own, in supersized quantities. If we believed the ads, this happiness would take the form of an ever-improving panoply of amusements, objects, and rarefied experiences.

America holds out the promise that there is always a bigger happiness in store. This is especially true in New York City. Don't get me wrong — I love New York, and precisely 51% of me could not wait to get back. I love New York even when I hate it, and I'm convinced that life there is its own version of perfect. American happiness is unpredictable. It's magical. It is best pursued with vigor to the heights and to the depths.

Before we left for France, I wished on every evening star I could find. "Let me fall in love once more with my family," I murmured at the dark. France granted my wish in ways I never could have anticipated.

During our last days in Eden, I changed my wish once more. Maybe, just maybe, when we all returned, I would find a way to infuse the routine of our lives with the balance of *bonheur*.

Emerging from our year away entailed a series of physical and emotional dislocations. I still sometimes have terror-stricken flashbacks to the moment when the TGV pulled into the train station in Paris as we were heading back to the U.S. At that moment, we had two children, four regular bags, five elephant-sized ones, and two cranky, middle-aged bad backs between us. We had three minutes — four at best — to use those bad backs to get everything off the train.

You don't mess around with the TGV. It arrives on time, and leaves a few minutes later, no matter what group of American idiots is still fussing with heavy baggage. Very unfortunately, our seats were up on the top level of a very full train, which meant that we had been required to haul our enormous bags up a flight of stairs and then back down. We had thought that we would move some of our bags to the downstairs part of the train as we approached Paris, but by the time we got up to do so, the smarter Parisians had already clotted up the space between our bags and the doors.

As soon as the train doors opened and the line of French people ahead of us spilled out onto the platform, we began dragging several of the larger bags down the stairs with us. We shooed the girls out onto the crowded platform, forbade them to move from the bags, and then Bill went back inside to rescue the rest of the luggage. I stood blocking open the door of the train, something I never do in normal circumstances.

I know that I've maligned the French seven ways to *dimanche*, but I have to credit the two incredibly sweet fellow passengers who realized what a pickle we were in: two Frenchmen on the train — they themselves with luggage — got moving to evacuate our bags, fireman-style.

At the same time that these nice French guys helped us out, two older-lady American tourists stood yelling at us. I'm serious: *yelling* at us that they were worried about our kids standing there.

"Hey! Your kids! You can't abandon those children here!" they called out to chastise us, while we tried desperately to move all those insanely huge bags and end up with all four of us on the same side of the closing doors. They assumed, with all the assurance of American tourists, that we also spoke English.

I should have ignored them, or shouted back something rude in French, but I've always had a chink in my armor for the censure of a self-righteous biddy. Once I realized that they were offering criticism rather than help, I added to the chaos by yelling back at them while throwing bags and using my body as a doorstop.

"We're doing the best we can!" I shouted, which is probably the only sensible response any of us can make to a criticism of our parenting.

We made quite a picture: the Americans yelling, Abigail and Grace frozen in their spaces on my command, and a bucket brigade of smartly dressed Continentals chucking our duffels onto the platform. Bill and his human-being-sized backpack came spilling out last, just as the doors slid shut and the train sped towards Belgium.

For ten months we were explorers, pushing again and again into new places and languages and cultures, adding place after place to our list of conquered territories. We were 42 weeks away, mid-August till the end of May, which is the same number of weeks I counted and waited until each of my children was born.

Once the plane touched down in New York, we dove back down into the lives we left, learning what had changed and what still remained. Thomas Wolfe (*You Can't Go Home Again*) and Bon Jovi ("Who Says You Can't Go Home?") disagree, and I wasn't sure what to think.

Complicating things was the fact that we were back, but we were not actually *home*. We had rented out our house in Brooklyn and had movers put our furniture into storage. It would be a few months before we could get back there, and so we planned to spend a second summer staying with friends and our parents in New Hampshire and upstate New York.

It was totally practical in terms of timing and cost. But psychologically, for two little girls weary of being dragged from place to place, returning without a place to land was perhaps another one of our big ideas that wouldn't pan out in the real world.

Our first week back in the U.S., we circled around that desired-for feeling of home like little bugs around a light, relying on the places and the people we loved to keep us warm, fed, and safe.

My friends and family gave so generously to me, which meant I had more to give to the girls. As we travelled, the girls stuck close to my side. They actually held my hands when we walked, pulling a little on my arms. They kept finding ways to lean their heads on my shoulder, and when it was time to go to bed, they wanted to snuggle up close to my body. "I love you so much, Mom," Abigail would breathe into my hair. I know she meant it with all of her heart, but she was also saying, "So much is changing. This is unfamiliar. Please keep telling me that I'm going to be OK."

I became an oxygen tank for them, full of the air of home. I learned to distill its essence to fit it in the tiny vessel of myself. When they needed me, I knew how to charm a small circle to give them that feeling of place, even when things were rocky, or uncertain, or strange. They needed me when France was too French, and then again, differently, when America was not French enough.

It took me so very long to recognize that I could do this for them. But that summer I felt it in their little hands grabbing onto mine. Whenever we made a change from one place to the next, the girls suddenly needed my undivided attention, my care and watching. I opened up the regulator on the tank, and gave them as much of myself as I could. They breathed in home, they breathed in confidence, they breathed in the feeling that *they themselves* could make their way.

Because comforting them was not the whole point. It was lovely, really, to have such sweet girls holding my hands and breathing into my ear how much I was loved. But my aim was to give them what they needed so that they could do whatever they were up to more independently. This extra air built them up so that they could strike out on their own. Gradually they adjusted to each new atmosphere, and started to stay away for longer stretches. Wherever we went, home traveled in me, and then suffused into them. They breathed the air of home, and then they went back out again — strengthened, older, stronger — into a big world that has so much in store.

I should have known the day of reckoning would come to me while I was shopping. Jetlag piled on alienation until one day I discovered that, like The Clash, *I'm all lost in the supermarket. I can no longer shop happily.* After a year in the storehouse of France, shopping like Julia, I somehow forgot how to navigate a box store on autopilot, which is a skill that is the birthright of all Americans. What's worse, I gave it away in exchange for a hunk of cheese, and thus had nobody but myself to blame.

Flash back to July 2009. Bill and I had extracted our family from Brooklyn, where the only grocery options are Bleak, Bleaker, and the Byzantine systems of the Park Slope Food Coop. There are terrific greenmarkets, and the Fairway over in Red Hook, but those both demand a major commitment of time and planning. At the greenmarket, you can only buy what you can carry on the subway, and they don't sell Cheer, or Joy, or All. At Fairway, you have to drive, park, negotiate the chaos of other crazed shoppers, shuttle your grocery bags up multiple flights of stairs, and then re-park the damn car somewhere in the neighborhood. Hardly something you can do every day when you just need a few pork chops and some peaches.

So when we spent the early part of the summer before France in New Hampshire's Upper Valley, home of the Hanover Food Co-op, we thought we had died and gone to homemaker heaven. They had everything you can buy in America, and lots of it. They had little specialty sections, a bulk food aisle, fancy artisanal dairy products and real beef. Unlike the Key Food on 7th Avenue in Brooklyn, the store didn't smell like a long-abandoned port-a-san.

We spent weeks in happy shopping bliss, grazing the snow peas, the clover honey, the organic soda spritzers, the freeze-dried edamame pods, and the polenta chips that taste like Bugles with a Ph.D.

But then came France. I stumbled there as a shopper, hard. Nothing in the supermarket looked familiar, and nothing came in an extra-large. All the words for things were different, so that it took me forever to find horseradish (*raifort*), and sour cream (*crème fraîche*, but only sort of), and toilet bowl cleaner (bleach is, I think, *javel*, although I left the country without ever being sure).

I thought I had readjusted to the U.S. unscathed, but as it turns out, I was only pretending. Whenever I got hungry, I missed the road up from the Bastide, where I would pick thyme and rosemary to put in our dinner. I missed the *marché*, source of fresh apricots, beets, carrots, *dinde* and food all the way through the vegetable alphabet. I missed the *boulangerie*, the spice store, the place that sold only things made of olives and grapes.

And Laurent and Mathilde's Intermarché, which I eventually memorized: all that *rosé* and chocolate and cheese. Whenever I felt like it, I waved my *carte de fidélité* and picked up a little wine and candy, maybe a mushy round of hyper-local *Banon* cheese, runny and wrapped in oak leaves.

I spent nearly every moment outside of the house that year procuring some particularly delicious sort of food from some specific place. I thought I was going to France, when really I was only going grocery shopping.

So when we arrived in the U.S., there remained the business of adjusting back to shopping reality. The Hanover Food Co-op was just as wonderful as it ever was. It was me who had changed.

All the vegetables were stacked up in their hopeful way, but cold and sterile, as though none of them had ever seen a real farm. All that fruit could sit in my fridge for a week and move straight from unripe to pointless without ever acquiring flavor. Industrial-strength cucumbers. There was a bounty of choice, but no straw panniers to put things in. I started to get a little disoriented.

I sought sanctuary in the wine section. I said to Bill, "I'll just go pick up a nice Côte de Provence *rosé.*"

He warned me in the gentle, coaxing voice one uses to talk to crazy people. He had already tried this, and failed. "There won't be any *rosé*, sweetheart."

"Of course there is *rosé,*" I insisted, as though saying would make it so.

I kept pacing back and forth in front of the ports, shirazes and merlots, certain that if I scanned hard enough, that nice bottle of *rosé* would float off the shelf and into my waiting arms.

In the wine section I came up short, but in just about any other aisle I could hardly breathe. There were way too many options among packaged foods. I used to be a person who cherished super-sizing and rampant variety. But that day when I looked at all the chips and cans and dish soaps, it made my head hurt. All that Cheer. All that Joy. All that All.

I wanted a little clarity. A little less process. As William James told us, and Randall Jarrell quoted in his poem about the supermarket, "Wisdom is learning what to overlook." I wanted the edicts of a thousand years of French culture to swoop in and organize the foodstuffs in a particular and specific way, and help me to wisely overlook. I wanted fewer, better options.

I'm all lost.

It's a phase, I told myself with one soothing, reassuring, talk-to-the-lunatic voice. Corn syrup and I had a vibrant, thriving relationship before, and we could rebuild that again. Jarred salsa is my friend. Olives are not the only fruit. *I'm all lost.*

"Food Snob!!!" some other awful voice shouted at me from within my own head. "You're full of *pommes de terre* and foolishness juice! Snap out of it, and pick up some of this nice premade guacamole for dinner!! Get yourself down to the store and buy some of America's favorite tropical fruit: Guar." (This voice was very bossy.)

I'm all lost.

The sanest, quietest voice within told me this: "Get a grip, and make a little spaghetti with red sauce. There is no ill on this earth that cannot be addressed with a nice plate of pasta."

I was back, but my tummy may never return.

I wish I could have put reflexive French verbs in my suitcase to bring home. In France, I didn't "get bored," but rather "bored myself." I did not "get angry," but angered myself. I sat myself down, bathed myself, shaved myself, and even took myself for walks. I didn't just remember something, but reminded myself of it. Reflexive verbs required me to take a whole lot more responsibility for myself. My life and my emotions didn't just happen to me, but rather were experiences I was creating.

France was a grownup place, indeed.

If I learned anything from this experience to take me into midlife, I hope that I have turned "to live" into a reflexive verb. I live myself. My marriage, my children, my house, my life, my ideas, and the way I use my time are not just things that happen to me when I'm not at work. It's no longer that I need to work my life around my job. This life *is* my job.

"*Se marier (avec)*" became my very favorite reflexive verb. In English you "get married," as though your marriage is something you receive. "I married him," we also say, and "he married me," as though these are actions we do to another and have done to us. In English, parents sometimes speak of "marrying their children off" to some lucky (or unlucky) spouse, as though those children were a burden to pass along.

Saying your vows in French, however, means that you *marry yourself with your beloved*. I love the way that this phrase turns things around, ever so slightly, so that it's clear who is responsible. It is you, plural. It is us. We marry ourselves with one another.

The summer we returned was bookended with big anniversaries. Bill and I had our 15th in June, and Bill's parents celebrated their 50th in September. Those big numbers had me reflecting on what happens when we marry ourselves to one another, and what is still ahead.

About a month after returning, Bill and I spent our 15th anniversary with the girls, at New Hampshire's Storyland, the world's cleanest, friendliest, most adorable and un-scary amusement park. After my total freakout at the grocery store, this place revived all my faith in America. It was wholesomeness incarnate. You would think all that wholesomeness and all those Red Sox hats would make us cranky New Yorkers even crankier. But try as we might, grouchy old Bill and I, we couldn't come up with a single legitimate complaint about the place. The whole park was simply adorable, as were the girls, all day long.

The park was all kiddie rides, but all four of us rode them anyway. For once, nobody got scared or overwhelmed. Bill took a picture of me when I took the girls on the raft ride, and when I looked at it later, I immediately recognized the look of joy on my face: the same face I wore the day we got married.

How did our 15 years pass so quickly? Grace's 11? And Abigail's 8? My 40?

I asked myself these questions a lot; but that day a new one occurred to me in all that happiness. It was a scary one: how many more years like this one will I have? A sign on a clock at Storyland sternly warned everyone who would read it: "Enjoy yourself, it is later than you think."

The sign was not properly punctuated, and was, in its pretentious calligraphy, hopelessly cheesy and sentimental. But I read it that day as though it had been painted just for me. It was true beyond true. Having taken an entire year away, just the four of us together, I saw one moment in time having really, truly passed. The first ten years of parenthood all blur into more or less pleasant phases. But the year away was distinct, and irretrievable, marking the clearest of boundaries.

We will never have that year again, the year our children passed from the then of childhood into the now of their very early adolescence.

I tell myself we are halfway between the birth of our first child to the high school graduation of our last. We tell ourselves that this is "midlife," halfway on the greatest journey. But those things are only true if we continue to be very, very lucky. It is later than we think.

But then there is also that first part of the sentence, one of the English language's rare reflexive formations: "Enjoy yourself." One of our promises, upon deciding to marry ourselves with one another, was that we would spend this year together overseas. But another promise we made, more clearly and consciously, and perhaps even impossibly, was to choose to be married to one another, every day of our lives. We were trying to tell ourselves to remember not to let it get old. Not to take it for granted.

I hadn't realized how much that first promise would reinforce the second. Taking this year required us to shake up everything, to shake off the complacency that had grown up around our life together. We shed jobs, homes, friends, possessions, places, languages. We kept only ourselves, our children, clutching our few little bags and boxes. We threw aside just about everything else, and in doing so reminded ourselves of the crucial nature of what was left. Us, marrying ourselves day by day by day.

The bigger anniversary of the summer took a whole week to celebrate. We all got together for a week at the beach, celebrating my in-laws' 50th wedding anniversary — Gus and Linda, with their kids and grandkids, in a rented house on Martha's Vineyard. We cooked big meals and ate on the wide wooden deck overlooking Rhoda's Pond. We canoed around the brackish lake, bought sunflowers and eggrolls at the farmers' market, and swam at as many different beaches as we could. During the only rainy day of the week, we headed into town to go window-shopping and buy bags of gumdrops and licorice. I watched Abigail ride the carousel in Oak Bluffs. She looked so focused, studiously grabbing at the rings each time she passed; clearly, she's just as susceptible as I am to the habit of turning life into a project rather than a game. "I got one every time," she told me, proudly. "It was easy. I got a whole big stack."

One night we drove to Menemsha, a little fishing town that faces each night's sunset. We ate lobster, steamers, and fish tacos together on the porch of a restaurant, surrounded by other families on vacation in their Wellfleet t-shirts and summer tans. It wasn't simply hot, but so stickily warm that we were sweating as we sat still, so the grownups drank Var *rosé* on ice and the kids downed cups of fresh lemonade.

As the days of that memorable week unfolded, I wanted to write down every detail: the taste of the sweet clams in the butter, the rosy shade of the setting sun on our faces, the graying shingles of the houses, the weather-beaten American flag down at the end of the pier. We were celebrating something that can never happen again. I'm pretty sure I irritated everybody with all the pictures that I took, but I couldn't let a moment pass unnoticed.

Perhaps I was so eager to snap photos because my memory had begun to feel like it was fraying a bit at its far edges, for reasons I could only pretend to understand. Whereas once I never lost anything — a name, a place, an idea and its origins — I sometimes felt that summer like the past was a soap bubble, popping just as I reached for it. I told myself that the details were dissolving for some reason or another: like the dislocation of all the travel. Like the impossible fullness of a life's experience. Like I was suddenly 40, my brain was old, and there was just too much to recall.

Or perhaps the new warm swelling of my heart was crowding out the old, cold sharpness of my mind.

In Menemsha, we walked down to the end of the pier and looked over the fishing boats, across an uninhabited green spit of sand, and towards the setting sun. It was almost impossibly perfect — not an amusement park fake version of a fishing village, but the thing itself. It was messy in places and worn in others, yet still so beautiful it might have been composed by an artist. I looked through one window of a blue-gray shack, entirely hung with fishing lures, through the window on the other side, and onwards toward the water beyond. At the end of the pier, some awful destroyed hunk of an old building was slowly rusting into the salt water. We ate soft ice-cream cones, which dripped faster than the kids could keep up. The hot wind blew their hair around and spattered drops of melting ice cream on their shirts and onto the dusty ground.

I wanted to burn every moment into my memory. That evening on the pier was three hours of one day among the hundreds we shared together during the week's vacation, the thousands over the years, the tens of thousands our family can only hope to have if we're as steadfastly lucky and wise as our parents have been. That day on the dock, we had each other in a way that felt perfect. A summer evening can feel like forever, but as I have started to learn, the best of our days fly away against our will. The sun keeps setting. The kids grow up. We ourselves grow older, and the warm wash of our summer memories together will slosh and dilute and slowly fade away.

And that's only if things go well. Fifty years' worth of sunsets is almost too much for anyone to hope for.

After we returned from France, I set up my computer so that every five minutes a new photograph from my hard-drive shows up as the screensaver behind whatever I was doing. There, behind my word processing or pointless internet search emerged one random shot. A blue sky and soft blonde grass from a hillside in France. My friends' children, eating hotdogs on a porch years ago. A sea of a hundred freezing people at Obama's inauguration. My Dad's 70th birthday. Paris. Full moon. Christmas morning. Each image brought forth an instant memory, but also the shock of the unfamiliar: How could I ever have forgotten that?

And the new memories kept coming. On our drive home from Menemsha, we wound slowly around the twisting North Road through Tisbury, back towards Lambert's Cove. We put on music that made us all American-style happy, bouncing around to Hawaii 5-O and Coldplay and Abigail's other favorite, the Black Eyed Peas. As we pulled into the driveway, the previous summer's inescapable hit was playing. We turned it way up and got out of the car to dance on the lawn under a crabapple tree. When Gus, Linda, Laura and Finn drove up, they danced with us, too.

The loud music echoed into the quiet woods. *I got a feelin'... that tonight's gonna be a good, good night...*

That song has played in a whole lot of places, on a whole lot of nights, almost certainly too many. But for that one night it was just ours, as we jumped around on the fallen fruit, all three generations dancing together. It was not the sort of thing we had ever done before — a bunch of closely-related white people grooving to hip-hop on a dance floor of grass and crabapples. I'm almost certain we'll never do it again, but as I discovered while walking on those ripe figs during our first weeks in France, I never know how much fruit will fall at my feet. How lucky I will continue to be.

We all went inside, and the kids got cleaned up and ready for bed. I hadn't been sleeping all that well the previous nights, but wind had finally started to cool the house, and as the cold air came in from below and the warm air drifted out the window of our sleeping loft, I fell in. Deep.

Maybe it was an hour. Or two. Or only 15 minutes, but suddenly I saw Grace standing there, right next to the bed. She was smiling at me, just on the edge of speech. I started to sit up, started to ask her what she needed, and just as the words started to form between us, she dissolved into thin air. A ghost. A trick of sleep. I knew then she was down in her little twin bed, not there in the loft next to mine, but her presence had felt palpable. She was there, and just as quickly she was gone.

Someday this will happen for real. The children I love more than my life itself will be gone. I will wake up one night, and they will be living in other houses, far away. If Bill and I continue to be lucky, do our best to be wise, we will grow old together. I can't even imagine life without him, but I can already see the girls walking out the door, all too soon. If we do our jobs right, each of our girls will find her happy ending somewhere else, in her own time and her own way. Maybe even in rural France.

They will disappear by growing up, and I will have to find them in dreams. They will return of their own accord, like the memories I never wrote down. Like all those summer nights. Like all the photographs I never thought to take. Like all of the moments and days and years.

CHAPTER TWELVE

Bill Gets the Last Word

O UR YEAR AWAY WAS A LOVE letter to our life as a family. Of course,
every good letter has its p.s., and Bill unearthed ours while we were
unpacking our old things to move our Brooklyn life out of storage
and back into place.

I unpack fast, maniacally focused on what I imagine to be the big picture, while
Bill moves slowly, looking carefully at all the letters and photographs he finds
along the way. Sometimes this makes me impatient. But other times, he unearths

rare gems that I would have missed, or ever-so-efficiently chucked in the trash. As he was unpacking one of his very last boxes, he came across a magical talisman.

It was a postcard he sent me in the spring of 1992. He was then in the midst of his epic European tour with Alain, and I was in my first year as a teacher. He broke up with me before he left, yet nearly every day during the ten weeks he was away, a beautiful postcard with his chicken-scratch affection on the back would float into my mailbox. Without e-mail, Internet cafés, texting, or Skype, I had only slips of paper to remind me of his existence.

Nearly every one of the postcards featured paintings or sculptures of beautiful women from the museums of Western Europe. On the back of each one, he would tell me the ways in which that image reminded him of me before describing his day's wild adventures. The particular one he found in that last box was Toulouse-Lautrec's laundress, "*La Blanchisseuse.*"

When he mailed that card, I had not yet started to do anybody's laundry but my own, so I imagine that it was the set of her jaw and the intensity of her gaze that drew him in, reminding him of me. The way she looks out the window, towards something that we cannot see and she cannot stop seeing.

Seeing the card again, I swooned. But Bill quickly reminded me that at the time, I found his postcards irritating. He said that I told him that I wanted him to stop looking at art, and look instead at me. That I wanted him to stop tormenting me with news of his wild times seven thousand miles away. One of the postcards featured the broad marble female back of a Rodin sculpture, and Bill wrote to me about how much he missed my shoulders. When we managed to talk to each other on the phone, I lit into him. "If you love my shoulders so much," I told him, in distress, "then why did you break up with me, and then leave for the whole spring and summer? You're not doing anything over there; why don't you just get on a plane, and come back!"

It's strange, really, that while he broke up with me before he left, his postcards described all the ways in which he did seem to be pining away for me. I suppose on some level I was glad for him that he was having all these wild adventures. And I wasn't precisely unhappy about the wildness of my own. But mostly our breakup felt complicated, and messy, and pointless. I just wanted him to come home. I knew that there was something bigger in our future together, and I was impatient for that to begin.

In retrospect, I realize that this series of cards constitutes one of the most romantic gestures that has ever passed between us. They were written at a rare moment of high drama, at least in part out of guilt. They were received less than graciously, and may have exaggerated the similarities between me and the subjects of the great paintings of Europe. But now it seems fairly astonishing that he took the time, nearly every day, to write to me.

We were young then, and breakup or no breakup, we were seriously in love. Each card landing in my mailbox was a telegram from forever. Back then I read his letters with profoundly mixed feelings. But now, whenever I come across one of them, and I read the rawness of his feeling on the page, the words and the images never fail to melt me.

Enough messy backstory: I should return to the card he found, and why it gives him the last word.

The actual painting of *La Blanchisseuse* hangs in Paris, but this card he sent from the Piazza San Spirito in Florence, a beautiful square surrounding a spare, gorgeous church. In contrast to the wild rococo of the rest of the city, the church there looks downright modern, New-Mexico pueblo plain in its clean lines and freedom from crenellated detail. It is on a much smaller scale than the Duomo, but still it leaves you breathless. It was the first place Bill dragged the three of us when we visited Florence, and reading his postcard, I could see why: it had been there, in that square, that he had seen and predicted our future. The past and the present telescoped together as I read his familiar scrawl:

I love this painting. Please let me have this card back. She's smart, hard-working, yet very sensual and enigmatic, a lot like you. I am sitting in Piazza San Spirito in Florence, having finally broken away from what seemed like a ubiquitous throng of other tourists. You would like San Spirito. It's simple and graceful. I took some photos for you. I also photographed a meat market because it was packed in so beautifully. The counter-people thought I was a major loon but were also flattered, I think. 22 days left. This trip has been too short. We are going to live in a foreign country for at least 6 months. I'm sliding away from allowing CAREER to run my life. I've even thought about bagging my summer job so we could live in Paris.

Maybe next summer....

Here on this card was the outline of our entire magical year, a tarot card from 18 years in the past. He would see the best in me, and love me unceasingly, even when I least deserved it. While the romantic postcards would stop when he returned, the prosaic, daily act of creation that is our marriage would begin. (I would also start, *à La Blanchisseuse*, doing a whole lot more laundry than I ever had before, but that's a different story...)

We would travel, always seeking ways to break away from the throngs of other tourists, and he would find us great places to visit. We would become obsessed with the way that European markets arrange the food in ways both beautiful and appetizing; and yes, the people we met on our travels would find our ardent admiration of their foodstuffs both loony and flattering.

But I most love the flat-out statement he makes here: "We are going to live in a foreign country for at least 6 months." He put it out there, so long ago, as clear fact. And as it turns out, he also predicted the reason why we would leave. We waited until we both felt we needed to slide away, at least for a little while, from allowing some bully all-caps CAREER to run our lives.

His wistful "Maybe next summer..." turned into a wait of nearly two decades, but no matter. We got there. We were there in the Piazza San Spirito, drinking *rosé* while the girls sipped Orangina. The past became the future he had predicted. And, like a lot of Bill's crazy ideas turn out to be, it was good. Really good. Life-alteringly so.

I like to imagine that I am the big picture gal of this family — getting us to places on time, and making sure things get organized and accomplished. We all pretend that Bill's role is to make it all interesting and fun, adding the icing on the cake of my rule-bound approach to things.

But this postcard reveals the picture that has come into focus behind all my deliberate plans and his insatiable appetite for adventure. It proves that so many of our very best moments are — and have always been — when Bill and I together steer the ship. Wait long enough, and the truth wins out. In the glacial pace of decades in a relationship, Bill's powerful desires often trump my insistences. "We will live overseas for at least 6 months," he writes, from the fog of the past. And then, so many years later, we do. We escape the throngs. We walk away from that all-caps imperative. We stare into the eyes of our children for long stretches of time. We take pictures of the churches, the snails, the sunsets, our friends, and the beautiful stacks of meat. Just for a moment, we put down the laundry; we stare, intent on the beauty glowing right in front of our eyes.

Glossary

Avec toute la famille: with your entire family.

Bastide: a grand manor house overlooking a town in Provence.

Bien-être: well-being.

Bisous: ritual kisses given to both sides of the face. In Paris, you give two, one on each side. In southern France, sometimes three or four, so let the more native person lead. Be sure to make kissing noises rather than actually touching your lips to the person's cheek.

Bonheur: French-style happiness, which is not exactly the same as American happiness.

Chemin: a little road or path. If the little road is in the town, it's called a *ruelle.*

CNED *Centre National d'Education à Distance:* The National Center for Distance Education provides a terrifically organized and effective curriculum to students who wish to study the French national curriculum somewhere other than school. When you (or your Dad) finish these booklets and send them in, a real teacher spends a lot of time grading them and sending them back with detailed comments.

Croque-monsieur: grilled cheese with ham. A safe bet if you can't read the rest of the menu and are trying to avoid mistakenly ordering snails (*escargot*), calf's head (*tête de veau*), or pig-bottom sausage (*andouillette.*)

Déjeuner: lunch. Go ahead, have some wine.

Fermé: closed. Which is what things are likely to be from 13:00-16:00 in Provence. Take a nap.

Ne t'inquiète pas: don't worry. Which is easy for anyone but me to say.

Le portail: the gate. In our case, the enormous green gate to the schoolyard past which parents were not invited.

La Rentrée: that awful return to school and work after French people take the entire month of August off for vacation. You'd think the world was coming to an end.

Tarte Tatin: is not apple pie, but you should order it anyway. It's delicious.

Tartines: are baguettes cut lengthwise, usually for breakfast, served with butter and jam.

La vie quotidienne: daily life, raised to the level of an artform.

Thanks

I am proud to say that every single person who helped me to create this book is a friend, which makes me one lucky writer.

My first thanks go to everyone who read the blog I wrote while we were away (whereverlaunagoes.blogspot.com) and then encouraged me to turn its 500 pages of text and photographs into this book. Fellow bloggers jumped on the bandwagon with enthusiasm, and Gaela Schweizer, Gail Henderson Belsito, Mary Michelfelder, Yasmine Zeisler, Lindsey Mead Russell, Katie and Sean Mosher-Smith, Debbie Phipps, Mary Clark, Zaro Weil, Rory Evans, Erin Ash Sullivan, and Susan Banki were my literary cheerleading squad. Mom and Dad were my first publishers, collecting a printout of each new post into a big binder, and pestering me when I neglected to post. For every agent or publisher who said no, or simply didn't write back, I had a friend who answered back, *yes*.

Thanks also to the lovingly critical readers who helped me prune and shape extremely overlong blog posts into an only sort of overlong book: my fellow writers at Joan Wickersham's workshop at the Providence Fine Arts Work Center, Elizabeth Bogner, and Khoi Luu. Hilary Mead and David Englander dedicated extravagant measures of time, wisdom, good judgment, and energy to the text. Anything good here is because they told me to leave it in, and anything bad is a result of my ignoring their good counsel. Thanks also to Kathryn Beaumont, my agent at Kneerim, Williams, and Bloom, a tireless champion who convinced me over *rosé* at lunch in Brooklyn to give the book its current structure and tone.

Scott Sullivan and Stephanie Kaye Turner did a bang-up job with the copyediting, and Greg Simpson with the design.

Thanks to those of you who shared France with us: Jim and Celeste, Hillary Goidell, Jessica Greif and Nick Gorevick, Zaro Weil and Gareth Jenkins, our fellow ex-patriates who explained things we didn't understand, like Michelin stars and how to make right turns while driving. Endless thanks to Michael, Lucia, Milena, Stephanie, Jason, Nicholas, Sydney, Mary, Alain, Alexander, Miranda, Buck, Jackie, Loni, Mom, Dad, Gus, Linda, Laura, Finn, Maria, Bud, Toni, Zeke and Sam, who all made the trip to hang with us, Euro-style.

Thanks to those we met in France who became trusted friends: Jessica and

Gerard, Laurent and Mathilde, Dermot and Anna-Maria, Jay and Meg, Lynn and David, Paula, Ruth and Jean-Claude, and all of their friendly, generous children.

But the biggest, life-size thanks go to the three people at the center of my world, the reasons I wrote every word: Grace, Abigail and Bill, my always and forever. My home address is wherever you are.

Made in the USA
Lexington, KY
12 August 2013